PRESIDENTIAL POWER AND ACCOUNTABILITY

Many analysts now believe that the growth of presidential war power relative to Congress is irreversible. This book was written to contest that view. Its purpose is to identify what would be required to restore presidential war power to constitutional specifications while leaving the president powerful enough to do what is truly necessary in the face of any emergency. Buchanan focuses mainly on diagnosing the origins of the problem and devising practical ways to work toward restoration of the constitutional balance of power between Congress and the president.

The work begins by showing the lack of clear, widely shared standards whose enforcement is needed to sustain the balance of power and draws on the thinking of the founders and political theorists to crystallize such standards. Next it details how, in the absence of standards, agents such as Congress and the Supreme Court with formal influence on presidents and informal agents such as media and public opinion have unwittingly enabled unnecessary power expansion, such as the presidential "wars of choice."

Of course, change of this magnitude cannot be expected to happen quickly. Remedies necessarily involve a reform architecture intended to unfold gradually, with the first step being simply to start a focused conversation (another purpose of this book). Buchanan moves toward specific remedies by identifying the structure and strategy for a new think tank designed to nudge the political system toward the kind of change the book recommends. Lastly, the book shows how a fictional policy trial could take a practical step toward rebalancing the war power.

This is a crucial examination of presidential power and the U.S. separation of powers system, with a focused effort on making a course correction toward the kind of power sharing envisioned in the Constitution.

Bruce Buchanan is a professor in the Department of Government at The University of Texas at Austin. He is a scholar of the presidency and a political analyst whose commentary on the presidency and American politics appears in national and international print and broadcast news media. He is the author of numerous books on the presidency concerning how to make the institution both more effective and more democratic.

PRESIDENTIAL POWER AND ACCOUNTABILITY

Toward a Presidential Accountability System

Bruce Buchanan

Routledge
Taylor & Francis Group

NEW YORK AND LONDON

First published 2013
by Routledge
711 Third Avenue, New York, NY 10017

Simultaneously published in the UK
by Routledge
2 Park Square, Milton Park, Abingdon, Oxon OX14 4RN

Routledge is an imprint of the Taylor & Francis Group, an informa business

Library of Congress Cataloging-in-Publication Data
Buchanan, Bruce, 1945–
Presidential power and accountability : toward a presidential accountability
system / Bruce Buchanan.
p. cm.
Includes bibliographical references.
1. Presidents--United States. 2. Executive power--United States. 3. Separation
of powers--United States. 4. War and emergency powers--United States.
5. Government accountability--United States. I. Title.
JK516.B77 2012
352.23′50973--dc23
2012006003

ISBN: 978-0-415-53654-7 (hbk)
ISBN: 978-0-415-53655-4 (pbk)
ISBN: 978-0-203-11135-2 (ebk)

Typeset in Bembo
by Taylor & Francis Books

Printed and bound in the United States of America by
Walsworth Publishing Company, Marceline, MO.

CONTENTS

LIST OF TABLES AND FIGURE

Tables

Figure

1

INTRODUCTION

Rethinking Presidential Power

Although the Constitution is mentioned often, this book is not intended as a treatise in constitutional law. Instead, it offers new ways to think about an increasingly pressing problem: the erosion of presidential accountability for the use of power. In the process it re-evaluates the workings of the separation of powers and of checks and balances and proposes concrete remedial action. "How to fix it" is not the usual focus of books in the broad subject area of presidential power, but it is the focus here. Given this fact, the book is addressed not just to political scientists and constitutional scholars but to any citizen—whether expert or novice—seriously concerned with the growing imbalance in the separation of powers.

Many now believe that the enlargement of the presidency relative to Congress is irreversible, particularly on matters touching the main concern in this book, which is the war power (Deering, 2005). That pessimistic view is contested here. Without question, new proposals like those introduced below and described in detail in Chapters 5 and 6 are always politically difficult and must overcome other forms of inertia as well. But the specific changes proposed here require no constitutional adjustments. Although they are departures from the familiar they are modest in comparison to the scale of the problem they address. It would be challenging but not impossible to bring them about. They flow directly and logically from the problem diagnosis that generated them. Suggestions for change can be useful thought experiments even if they are not implemented, and that is certainly true of the proposals offered here. But these changes have the potential to do more than just bring intellectual closure to an academic problem diagnosis. Effectively implemented, they can create movement toward rebalancing the war poser.[1]

Political thinkers as diverse as John Locke and Abraham Lincoln usefully remind us of what has been missed due to lack of reflection on the corrective potentials of our separation of powers design. Unfortunately, these still useful reminders are overlooked by the very people who have power to hold presidents accountable: those who "staff" a group of governmental and nongovernmental institutions I call the *presidential accountability system*, or PAS (defined and discussed below, again in Chapter 2 and in still greater detail in the third chapter). As a result, we have failed to keep the presidency in check at key moments—particularly before the initiation by presidents of major wars that were *optional* rather than *necessary*.

The problem has its origins in the nature of presidential responsibility. Because events have forced presidents since George Washington to manage crises and solve unexpected problems, presidential power has grown beyond the intent of the framers. The reason is that new assertions of power have been treated as permanently enlarging precedents. This practice has driven executive power, ratchet-like, in but one direction: upward—to a point where presidents now feel entitled to decide for themselves whether and when to use military power. To be sure, the presidency must be "sufficient unto any need," if it is to meet its unique responsibility for protecting the American political system. But presidential power has expanded beyond mere sufficiency to a point that requires rethinking with the intent to calibrate. That is the purpose of this book.

Calibration

To "calibrate" something is to "gauge its deviation from a standard in order to ascertain the proper correction factors." This may seem unrealistically precise, too "scientific" as an approach to regulating something as emotionally and politically charged as the use of presidential power in real or imagined crises. Yet clear guidance is both needed and available. The standard used here for pinpointing the proper scope of presidential power was suggested by President Lincoln. It involves a dynamic relationship between the idea of "necessity" for presidential action in the face of threat and the constraints of the Constitution. The constitutional limits on presidential discretion may be set aside when emergencies make it necessary. But power so expanded should not be allowed to become permanent through precedent. It must instead "snap back," like a stretched rubber band, to its original constitutional shape once the crisis has passed. This, in Lincoln's view, is the essential correction factor because it preserves the constitutional order. It is the standard that underlies the argument to follow.

The Plan of the Book

The first step toward calibration is to identify and describe the two main sources of the current power imbalance. They are:

- incoherent standards and practices for holding presidents to account (Chapter 2)
- an unconscious, uncoordinated presidential accountability system (Chapter 3).

Incoherent standards are the inevitable result of an unconscious, unthinking, uncoordinated PAS. They join to impose great costs on the American political system.

The most important of these costs are unnecessary wars. Chapter 4 offers detailed examples of three such wars—each a presidential war of choice. As remedies, I first propose a new "think tank" designed to bring the PAS to conscious self-awareness (Chapter 5) and then a new congressional procedure modeled on the impeachment process; the policy trial, aimed at making sure that elective wars are in the national interest before Congress lets them happen (Chapter 6). Brief previews of Chapters 2 through 6 follow.

Chapter 2: Incoherent Presidential Accountability

Presidential accountability standards and practices are currently incoherent because the constraints on presidential power are subject to dramatic change by precedent-setting presidential action, as illustrated in this chapter. This makes such standards "crisis-and-president" driven rather than "Constitution" driven. That in turn makes them unsteady and haphazard rather than intentional and stable—the definition of "incoherent" used here. Coherence, on the other hand, requires a way to deal with emergencies that does not create precedent. This can only be achieved through deliberately orchestrated enforcement of the Lincoln standard and related precepts described here. Enforcement is the responsibility of the PAS which includes three official (Congress, Court, and presidential elections) and four unofficial (media, political opposition, public opinion outside elections, and the anticipated judgment of history) "agents of accountability." These agents already comprise a "system" because each may influence presidential incentives and behavior at any given time, either individually or collectively and whether knowingly or not. They do so by creating a mix of positive and negative incentives for presidents. President Truman's decision to deploy troops to Korea without congressional assent—the most significant war powers expansion in American history—shows why unconscious, unintentional PAS influence is dangerous. To make such influence conscious and intentional is the only way to achieve coherent performance guidelines. The chapter suggests necessary steps and identifies the American people, sovereign democratic overseers of presidents, as both the linchpin and the weakest link of the PAS. Remedying this weakness is among the most pressing reasons for the proposal to bring the now unconscious PAS to a state of self-awareness. But as the next chapter shows, it is not the only reason.

Chapter 3: The Unconscious Presidential Accountability System

Here we examine, in "agent-by-agent" detail, the unique accountability contributions as well as the dysfunctions and limitations of each (for example the Congress, most powerful of the agents, has largely abandoned vigorous war power oversight). The chapter shows that the various agents collectively possess the tools required for effective oversight but that the uneven and unsynchronized oversight typical of an unconscious and unevenly motivated PAS sharply curtails effectiveness. There are two problems in particular. First, the PAS does not now think of itself as a "system." Instead each agent is primarily driven by its own unique incentives and priorities. Second (as shown by the Truman example in Chapter 2) the agents are not always aware of the signals they send presidents; and when they are aware they rarely try to orchestrate the impact on the president. In the absence of cooperative interaction accountability lacunae inevitably emerge.

Chapter 4: Presidential Wars of Choice

Chapter 4 uses case studies of Korea, Vietnam, and Iraq to show the detailed consequences of the most damaging byproduct of the unconscious PAS: congressional abdication of the war power to the president. Due to the elimination of serious president–Congress consultation stemming from the Korean War precedent, Congress now routinely defers to presidents who insist on the need for military action. What is more, the presidents in the cases reviewed in this chapter initiated wars despite lack of clear provocation (e.g., an attack on the United States) and without a vision of the objective backed by well-specified operational plans. In each of these cases, there was a notable absence of a rigorous vetting process before the choice for war was approved by the president. Congress offered little serious oversight until long after the wars were initiated. It was stirred to do so by shifts in public opinion brought on by mounting costs in American blood and treasure made intolerable by the lack of military success. This has become a tradition of failure, in part attributable to the fact that presidents are left unsupervised at the moment of choice. This is the main reason for the policy trial proposal.

Chapter 5: Bringing the PAS to Life: The Presidential Accountability Project

Presidential wars of choice show that the constitutional and political systems as they currently operate do not effectively hold presidents to account. That is why there is need for a conscious PAS in which both its formal and informal components are sensitive to the need for selective and timely coordination to prevent unnecessary power expansions. To make this possible, an organization must be established first to "market" the PAS concept to PAS members and then to create the necessary coordination mechanisms and oversight expertise.

This is a far-reaching proposal. The aim is to create a new "consultancy" think tank in Washington, DC designed to help PAS members achieve something not previously sought: a level of integrated presidential oversight equal to the demands of calibrating presidential power. Full specification of how this think tank would operate is essential to the actual implementation plan. Many (though not all) of these details appear in Chapter 5—enough to clearly illuminate what real change would require at the level of agent practice. The proposed organization's major divisions will be a *Policy Board* and a *Research Group*. The *Policy Board* will work to create agent acceptance of the PAS idea and promote communication and coordination among agents. It will bring the products of the research staff to multi-agent discussions of foreseeable accountability issues. And it will maintain ongoing discussion and refinement of the PAS mission and objectives (e.g., balancing presidential encouragement and restraint, promoting the no-precedent "necessity" doctrine) in light of new circumstances. The mission of the *Research Group* is to apply specialized expertise to various projects identified by the Board. For example, it will assess historically important (e.g., Korea) and more recent accountability cases like the 1990 Gulf War, President Clinton's 1999 Kosovo air strikes, and President Obama's use of drones (unmanned strike aircraft) in search of lessons and strategies for improved oversight. It will also address current issues as they unfold (e.g., President Obama's recent Libyan venture).

Chapter 6: Prospective Accountability for Wars of Choice: Policy Trials

Policy trials illustrate the kind of proposal the Research Group might develop. Such trials would use an established constitutional procedure—impeachment—to put a proposed initiation or escalation of a war (not the president) on trial in Congress before that body approved or disapproved of discretionary military action. The purpose of policy trials is to reduce the likelihood of future poorly conceived military ventures like the Korean, Vietnam, and Iraq wars. They would accomplish this purpose in part by replacing provocative presidential rhetoric aimed at inflaming public opinion with an orderly televised debate on the merits of the president's war proposal. After exposure to such a debate the mass public audience would be focused and well-briefed enough to give members of Congress something they now lack: the political cover needed to take the risk (when merited) of opposing a president bent on war. Finally policy trials are designed to allow the president to make his/her very best case while requiring that it be done in a disciplined way in give-and-take with equally disciplined critics. To illustrate how policy trials would work, President Obama's decision to escalate the war in Afghanistan is revisited and subjected to a fictional policy trial.

2

INCOHERENT PRESIDENTIAL ACCOUNTABILITY

We begin with a look at the workings of a disparate collection of actors that share an important distinction: they all contribute in one way or another to how effectively presidents can be held accountable for their performance in office.

I refer to them as the presidential accountability system (PAS). The PAS comprises familiar constitutional and nongovernmental entities, which include *presidential elections, Congress,* and the *Supreme Court* within the constitutional structure; and *public opinion, news media,* the *political opposition,* and the *anticipated judgment of history* outside it. What do these varied and dissimilar "agents of accountability" have in common? This: whether consciously or deliberately or not, each can influence presidential incentives and behavior.[1]

To my knowledge, no one else has suggested that the institutions and entities that make up the PAS might usefully be conceived of as a group whose members jointly create a mix of incentives for presidents. Yet thinking of them as an "assembly" that constitutes a "system" for holding presidents to account is useful because it brings to mind possibilities not usually considered for addressing presidential accountability problems, particularly the unnecessary expansion of presidential power. Because I want to make clear in the first few pages exactly why this topic is important, we start with a brief look at one classic case: President Harry S. Truman's unilateral 1950 decision to send U.S. troops to Korea.

Truman's Decision

The details of U.S. involvement in the Korean War are presented in Chapter 4. In focus here is a much narrower look at *why* Harry Truman, a president who was blindsided by the surprise North Korean invasion of the South, so quickly came to believe it was acceptable to respond by sending U.S. troops to repel the invasion without the formal approval of Congress. Truman's is a cautionary tale because his decision was in large part a consequence of incentives unwittingly created for him by the expectations of human actors within the various agents that make up the PAS. These actors were themselves blindsided by the invasion, and were simply not thinking about how their own reactions might be interpreted by the president or of the net effect on Truman and through him the constitutional balance of power that their unpremeditated reactions might have.

Three of the most influential signals came from the political opposition in and outside Congress, from public opinion, and from the news media. Truman considered involving the Congress. But he soon concluded that it would be better to do what he thought was right quickly and on his own. Why? The first reason was because he knew that neither public opinion nor the news media would oppose bold presidential action. The view was widespread at the time that the invasion of South Korea was a Cold War Soviet ploy to test the United States, and that the United States had to respond immediately (it would later become clear that neither assumption was accurate). The second reason Truman avoided Congress was because he knew a congressional forum to discuss Korea, even though it would surely approve U.S. military action in Korea, was also sure to feature Republican attacks blaming the president for the recent Soviet development of the A-Bomb and the fall of China to the communists. A bold presidential move in Korea, on the other hand, would at least temporarily silence Truman's partisan critics. Third, avoiding Congress was easy because, initially at least, being ignored was acceptable to a majority in that body. Members of the House of Representatives actually stood and cheered when the word reached them that Truman had sent in the troops. Finally, Truman, like many presidents an avid reader of presidential history, was influenced by his sense of what history would expect of a strong president in his situation: decisive action in support of U.S. interests. And he was influenced by his Secretary of State, Dean Acheson, who advised him to protect presidential discretion by acting on his own (Hamby, 1995: 538–39; Cumings, 2010: 12–13).

So, encouraged by green lights from the people and the media, by his own desire to avoid partisan attacks on himself, by his identification with assertive past presidents, and particularly by the absence of a red light from Congress, Truman deployed the military without authorization from that body. In the end, this would have the effect—not explicitly intended by Truman or anyone else, so far as I can discover—of establishing a precedent that effectively shifted the war power from the Congress to the president (Savage, March 22, 2011a: A12).

The Reality of the Unconscious PAS

The PAS conjured here is quite real, in the sense that its component parts, whether knowingly or not, obviously do create a mix of what presidents will perceive as incentives, as the Truman example shows. But unlike social systems consciously designed and continuously refined to sharpen their influence on the behavior of particular human "targets" (e.g., schools and students; political parties and voters; corporations and customers), the *members of the PAS are not primed to be cognizant of themselves as participants in a shared enterprise with specific goals.* They should be because without shared goals they *cannot* be attuned to the implications for effectiveness of the incentives they now jointly but often unconsciously create for presidents. Effectiveness has no meaning without a goal. Few anywhere within the PAS were giving much thought even to *whether* they were sending signals to the president, let alone to how any signals they might be sending were being interpreted by Truman; or whether those signals were having some intended effect. There was no PAS concept to encourage such thinking; therefore these considerations simply did not arise. They cannot be expected to arise without some prior commitment on the part of the actors to begin thinking in these terms.

Why a Self-Aware PAS is Necessary

The Truman case serves as our introduction to the PAS because it underscores the importance of the influence that its component agents wield. Truman's decision to invade Korea without congressional approval led to the most significant expansion of presidential war power in American history. The factors that encouraged Truman to bypass Congress show why it is important to strive for a *conscious* PAS. There are multiple sources of influence on presidents, the most significant of which are the agents in the now-unconscious PAS. (See endnote 1.) If the effects of these influences are not to be unwitting and unintentional, ways must be found to integrate them into consistency with one another when necessary and possible, with the intent to send deliberate signals and to avoid unintentional ones.

But again, shared intentions among a group of influential agents require prior agreement on the ends and means of presidential oversight, deeply informed by the record of oversight experience (both part of the mission of the proposed PAP; see Chapter 5). Only this can sensitize agents to the need for vigilance against repetition of past mistakes. Agents also require mechanisms of communication and coordination to facilitate timely signaling when it is called for. *Lacking such things, the unconscious PAS is not equipped to manage events like Korea in a way that allows the president to do what is required without setting precedents that unnecessarily alter the balance of constitutional power.*

Precedents Undermine Accountability

Precedents make coherent accountability impossible. They do so by usurping the power to define what acceptable standards of presidential performance are. The power shifts from the constitutional actors charged with the task—people, Congress, and Court—to the president acting in the name of crisis. For example, Truman's action overturned the war power standard explicitly stated in the Constitution. "(T)en years after Roosevelt told France that that only Congress could make military commitments, President Harry S. Truman, confronted by the North Korean invasion of South Korea, sent American forces to war on his own" (Schlesinger, 2004: 53). A presidential act that prior to the Korean crisis was deemed unconstitutional by Truman's predecessor, and potentially grounds for impeachment, came to be viewed instead as an established presidential entitlement. As a result of an unexpected invasion, a power once thought to be the permanent province of the Congress can now be claimed by any post-Truman president contemplating the need for military action.

The issue seems largely, if not completely, resolved. For example, the debate was briefly rekindled by President Barack Obama's March 2011 decision to send U.S. fighter jets to Libya to join allies in a military effort to force an end to Libyan government killing of antigovernment rebels. A bipartisan group of U.S. lawmakers argued that the president had exceeded his constitutional authority by ordering American forces to take military action without congressional permission. President Obama and his legal advisors immediately disputed this interpretation. One news account of the dispute notes that since the Korean War presidents of both parties have ordered military action without congressional approval. But it also notes that "(m)ost legal scholars agree that the nation's founders intended to separate the power to decide to initiate a war from the power to carry it out" and that scholars also say "(t)he divergence between presidential practice for the past 60 years and the text and history of the Constitution make it hard to say whether such action is lawful … ." Despite President Truman's assertion that the U.N. Security Council's permission to act was enough, that claim was disputed at the time. Nevertheless, Truman's claim "became a precedent. Subsequent presidents added more such precedents" and they continue to do so (Savage, March 22, 2011a: A12). Some experts continue to dispute the constitutionality of such action (e.g., McConnell, January 10, 2012: A13). But those who have occupied or recently sought the presidency consider the question settled. For example, in response to a media request that they express their views, only one of five candidates for the 2012 Republican Party presidential nomination said that a president "should not order a military attack without Congressional permission unless there was an immediate threat … the other four candidates agreed that a president could do so if he decided it was necessary" (Savage, December 30, 2011b: A1).

Incoherence Defined

Standards set and changed in the way illustrated by the Truman case are not just inconsistent with the Constitution; they are also incoherent. By this I mean that they emerge haphazardly rather than intentionally, disrupting continuity and signaling instability. They reshape the political order of which the presidency is part, sometimes unwisely sacrificing things worth keeping (for example, the constitutional separation of the power to declare war from the power to execute war once declared). And because they emerge, willy-nilly, in haphazard and spontaneous ways, from unexpected events rather than from deliberate plans they have encouraged an *indiscriminate* escalation of presidential crisis power.

The Origins of Incoherence

What causes incoherence? Four overlapping and interactive sources can be identified. *First* are crisis-driven power expansions that get interpreted as precedents. *Second* are illimitable doctrines of presidential power, espoused and defended by presidents and their associates, which assert that the emergency actions of presidents either cannot be challenged or can be justified outside the Constitution. *Third* is the emergence of a political alliance of the presidency and the people (sometimes called the "demo-cratization" of the presidency) which pits longstanding public receptivity to strong presidential leadership against efforts to curb unnecessary power expansion. *Fourth* is the tendency of Congresses and Courts to follow the lead of the public in tolerating the claims of assertive presidents, with the effect of weakening other PAS agents.

Crisis-Driven Power Expansions

Power expansion didn't start with Truman. Presidential crisis actions have estab-lished precedents dating from the Washington Administration. They have been widely chronicled (see, for example, Small, 1932; Binkley, 1937; Hofstadter, 1948; Rossiter, 1960; Tugwell, 1960; Burns, 1973; Schlesinger, 1973; Goldsmith, 1980; Graff, 1984; McDonald, 1994; Riccards, 1995; and Milkis and Nelson, 2008). Presidents since Truman have picked up his claim to vast inherent powers (Savage, 2007: 20) secure in the knowledge that presidents before Truman had acted with similar boldness and been rewarded for it.

Early Examples

Presidents before Lincoln asserted power in order to address potential threats to the nation (e.g., Washington's Neutrality Proclamation, aimed at keeping the United States from being swallowed by entanglements in European wars) or to respond to extraordinary opportunity (Jefferson's reaction to Napoleon's offer to sell the Louisiana Territory to the United States). Lincoln acted aggressively to repel threats to the survival of the political system posed by the Civil War. What do presidents before and after Lincoln, such as FDR, George Washington, Thomas Jefferson, Theodore Roosevelt, and Woodrow Wilson, have in common with Lincoln himself? They were all seen in their times as controversial figures and by opponents as despoilers of the Constitution while in office. Now, however, they are ranked first through sixth, with Lincoln at the top, in a recent compilation of historian and political scientists surveys conducted between 1948 and 2005 (Ragsdale, 2009: 30). As these "greatness" rankings suggest, what those presidents did has stood the test of time in the judgment of history.

The National Security Presidency

The unconscious PAS does not stop presidents from finding ways to address pressing national concerns. But neither does it try to make sure that necessary crisis action stops short of undermining the constitutional balance of power. Lincoln's failure to entrench his concept of emergency power (once the emergency is over, power should "snap back, like a stretched rubber band," to its original state) is nowhere better illustrated than by the growth of the "national security" presidency in the modern era (FDR to Obama). This crisis-expanded "national security" presidency has some distant roots in the Civil War and gathered momentum from the 1917 U.S. engagement in World War I, which placed the United States and its president on a world stage. The sense of danger intensified significantly after the 1941 U.S. entry into World War II. It began to seem dominant during the Cold War-driven Korean and Vietnam conflicts. As a consequence of 9/11, Afghanistan, Iraq, and the terror war, the sense of danger now seems unending and presidential ascendancy, permanent (Deering, 2005; Bacevich, 2010a; Wills, 2010).

The two world wars and the Cold War with the Soviet Union prompted congressional authorization of such things as the development of an unprecedentedly large and sophisticated military capability, a power-centralizing National Security Council within the White House, and a vast defense/foreign policy/intelligence establishment (the "Military–Industrial Complex" that President Eisenhower warned against in his 1961 Farewell Address). Such institutional entrenchment in the face of perceived threat further encouraged presidential assertiveness, and acceptance of it from all corners of the PAS, including the Supreme Court. The Court's controversial 1936 declaration, in *U.S. v. Curtiss-Wright Export Corp.*, that the president is the nation's "sole organ" in the field of international relations, foreign policy, and national security made sense to many in the context of world tension and war, as did later Court decisions at least obliquely supportive of presidential crisis powers. In the 1952 decision, *Youngstown Sheet and Tube v. Sawyer*, for example, President Truman lost the case, but a majority of the justices, to one degree or another, accepted Truman's claim that the president has an inherent, unstated constitutional power to act in times of national emergency. And in *United States v. Nixon* (1974) President Nixon also lost when he was ordered to turn over his Watergate tapes. Still, for the first time the Court conceded the existence of a limited executive privilege under the Constitution. Though the decision held that executive privilege was overridden by the explicit constitutional right that defendants have to a fair trial and due process, it could prevail when a president claimed the need to protect military, diplomatic, or sensitive national security secrets.

Though Presidents Madison and Polk had each initiated discretionary wars—the War of 1812 with Great Britain and the 1846 Mexican War, respectively—it was not until Truman's 1950 action in Korea that the precedent of clearly discretionary presidential use of the power to initiate war was set in motion. Truman acted without a traditional *casus belli* such as a direct attack on the United States, and without prior congressional approval. Later presidents claiming the same right acted in ways that would lead to a firmly established presidential "entitlement" accepted by Congress and the people and unchallenged by the Court. Presidents Johnson (in 1965) and the second President Bush (in 2003) would cite Truman's Korean action as precedent when initiating optional wars in Vietnam and Iraq. In effect, Truman's action had "persuaded several successors that presidents possess the inherent power to go to war whenever they choose" (Schlesinger, 2004: 14).

Illimitable Doctrines of Presidential Power

Even if a conscious PAS can be coaxed into existence, to be effective it will require guidance from parameters of executive power like those suggested later in this chapter. As of now there is no agreement on such parameters—another reason why presidents often feel free to define their own standards to fit their circumstances. Modern presidents not only feel entitled to take actions justified by precedents. Like George W. Bush, they may also see reason to expand their claims in ways that further distort the constitutional order. Vindicating their power assertions has been of great concern to presidents who took action that drew significant criticism. Most problematic for present purposes are exculpatory doctrines that do not respect the constitutional balance of power. Two such doctrines can serve as illustrations: inherent powers, and extra-constitutional prerogative.

Inherent Powers: Hamilton, Nixon, Bush

Alexander Hamilton, anticipating presidential power claims later to be made by Presidents Harry Truman, Richard Nixon, and George W. Bush, was dismissive of constitutional checks on the executive. Hamilton argued that the Constitution should be understood as empowering government to take all necessary action without limitations. In other words, the Constitution *implies* whatever presidential power is necessary to address any threat or need. Hamilton asserted the need for enough executive power to address any contingency. To a degree his critics found astonishing, Hamilton as treasury secretary encouraged President Washington to act as the prime mover of national government. Thus, he was instrumental in designing and (in President Washington's name) obtaining legislation to create the Bank of the United States to put the new nation on a firm economic foundation. In his 1793 essay debate with Madison (Helvidius), Hamilton (as Pacificus) asserted the president's right to set the foreign policy of the United States by declaring its neutrality in the war between France and Great Britain. He noted that unlike Congress, whose constitutional powers were limited by Article I to those "herein granted," there was no such qualification in Article II's grant of executive power. And when the Whiskey Rebellion emerged as a defiant challenge to a tax imposed by Congress, Hamilton persuaded Washington that such a challenge to federal law required a forceful military response (though a show of force proved to be sufficient to quell the rebellion).

Because he sees the executive power to take action deemed necessary as inherently constitutional, Hamilton acknowledges no need to seek retrospective approval. The issue of precedent does not arise for him because precedent is not needed to justify presidential action. Hamilton acknowledges impeachment as the tool of choice for bringing a president to heel. But since power is inherently unbounded, impeachment cannot rest on excessive power claims. This effectively deprives impeachment of any practical significance. If a president may do whatever seems required without any need to justify such actions to Congress and the people in light of constitutional limits, there is little left to serve as a basis for impeachment (Kleinerman, 2009: 112). For Hamilton, the most meaningful remedy for displeasure with executive performance was the next election.

For his part, President Richard Nixon fits himself into the inherent power camp by asserting, flatly and famously, that in matters touching national security, "When the president does it, it is not illegal" (Black, 2007: 1012). He plainly believes that a president's judgment in this area cannot be questioned. Though he cites Lincoln as his authority (Kleinerman, 2009: 168) he does so inaccurately. Nixon does not acknowledge (as Lincoln does) the president's responsibility, implied by the structure of the Constitution and its impeachment provision, to explain and defend his actions to the Congress and the people.

President George W. Bush took his claims to extraordinary powers even further. He not only asserted the right to all the expanded powers established by past presidents during wartime (Kleinerman, 2009: 2). But at the urging of Vice President Cheney, he also drew on the alarm and distress sparked by the 9/11 attack on the United States and the alleged permanence of the post-9/11 war on terror to assert unique new claims (Savage, 2007). His advisors argued, for example, that because the war had no foreseeable end, the presidential strength necessary to prosecute it should not be seen as temporary. Because terrorism threatened both domestic and international security, crisis powers could no longer be understood as restricted to the international arena. And for reasons less clearly explained, it came to seem essential to the Bush Administration that the president's actions not be subject to challenge or question by Congress, insisting instead that "an expanded presidential power capable of overriding the laws of Congress is constitutionally guaranteed" (Kleinerman, 2009: 4). The Bush Administration insistence on the inherent legality and constitutionality of executive discretion meant that it felt no obligation to offer a political defense of its position (Goldsmith, 2007: 210, 212). By claiming an inherent power to do what he deems necessary that cannot be challenged even by Congress, Bush, like Hamilton, Truman, and Nixon, asserts that inherent power is beyond question.

Illimitable power doctrines undermine coherent accountability by violating the accountability principle imbedded in the separation of powers design. Lincoln arguably went even further than Bush and others in the inherent power camp in claiming emergency executive powers independent of Congress. But unlike Bush, Lincoln signaled respect for the constitutional order by seeking "legislative ratification of his actions" (Matheson, 2009: 89). Ratification ensured congressional agreement with Lincoln's view that his extraordinary executive measures were necessary to preserve the constitutional order. For Lincoln, undeniable *necessity*, which must be explained and defended anew each time such a claim is made, is the *only* justification for using such measures. In letters and speeches he made plain his view that the executive may set aside the Constitution *if and only if doing so is truly necessary to save it* (as Lincoln believed it to be during the Civil War). But if the Constitution were to actually be reinstated once the crisis had passed, then executive power would have to revert to its pre-crisis state. Otherwise, a new and different order would be set atop the original order after every emergency, the very definition of incoherence. Furthermore, if a crisis has passed, extraordinary executive powers are no longer necessary. Because their preservation would needlessly undermine the original Constitution, Lincoln insisted that crisis powers should not be regularized or institutionalized (i.e., established as precedent; see Kleinerman, 2009: 165–217). By arguing against the power of precedent to permanently efface the limits that presidents must respect, and by showing how necessary power may be deployed without evading accountability, Lincoln embodies the constitutional alternative to illimitable presidential power.

Extra-Constitutional Prerogative: Jefferson

When Thomas Jefferson was presented with a stunning opportunity to purchase the Louisiana Territory from France, he knew such an act would be unconstitutional because the document made no provision for the acquisition of territory. He explicitly sought to avoid the "implied powers" rationalization that Hamilton endorsed. But after deciding there was not time to pass a constitutional amendment authorizing the purchase (fearing Napoleon might change his mind) Jefferson concluded that he must violate the Constitution, then "throw himself on the people" to vindicate his action, and ask the Congress to do the same, in order to justify a territorial acquisition he believed to be in the highest national interest (Koch and Peden, 1972: 573–74).

Napoleon's offer was indeed tempting, and Jefferson would be praised for the good he brought the nation by succumbing to the temptation. In an October 1803 letter to Jefferson, for example, David Campbell of Tennessee captured the grounds of general gratitude to Jefferson: "You have secured to us the free navigation of the Mississippi ... You have procured an immense and fertile country: and all these great blessings are obtained without war and bloodshed" (quoted in Malone, 1970: 325).

But one critique of Jefferson implies that benefits justified in this way undermine the Constitution by not taking it seriously. In this case as in many others Jefferson embraces extra-constitutional, publicly approved *prerogative* "for reasons that are merely expedient to the good of society rather than necessary for the survival of the constitutional order." When it is set to the side, the Constitution is undermined (Kleinerman, 2009: 155).

This interpretation of Jefferson's *modus operandi* is based on the "heretofore misunderstood" centrality of a powerful and democratic executive in Jefferson's political thought that may, in the name of the public interest (as ratified by Congress and the people at the president's urging), actually dismiss the Constitution by winning agreement to set it aside whenever circumstances tempt such action (Kleinerman, 2009: 148–64). Jefferson made it known in various letters to associates that he thought constitutions should not be viewed as permanent, and that members of Congress and the people themselves should, like the president, have the prerogative of violating the law when the public good required it. These views underlie Jefferson's "striking willingness not only to exercise prerogative as president but also to call on his generals, members of Congress, and even the average citizen, to ignore the laws" (Kleinerman, 2009: 151). Jefferson explains his attitude most famously in his letter of September 20, 1810 to John Colvin:

> A strict observance of the written laws is doubtless *one* of the high duties of a good citizen, but it is not the *highest*. The laws of necessity, of self-preservation, of saving our country when in danger, are of higher obligation. To lose our country by a scrupulous adherence to written law, would be to lose the law itself, with life, liberty, property, and all those who are enjoying them with us; thus absurdly sacrificing the end to the means.
>
> *(Malone, 1970: 320)*

In Kleinerman's view, Jefferson's concept of prerogative has a "permanently extra-constitutional quality" (Kleinerman, 2009: 166). All executive prerogative action is by definition outside normal constitutional bounds. The question is how it is to be justified. The political philosopher John Locke and Lincoln argue that prerogative actions can be justified only if they are *constitutionalized*; that is, shown to be necessary to preserve the Constitution itself. But for Jefferson all that is necessary is that the prerogative act is *popular*; that the people and Congress be persuaded by the president to agree that it is an expedient move that advances the nation's interests. Jefferson's practice undermines the Constitution because, instead of being deployed within that compact, presidential prerogative is approved *outside* it. Kleinerman continues:

> Rather than limiting the range of executive prerogative, Jefferson's standard invites its extension to limits that only the boundaries of popular judgment establish. These boundaries are neither well-guarded by the people without a constitution to guide them nor well-respected by presidents who believe they enjoy a popular mandate to reflect the peoples' will. Thus, in turning to Jefferson as an alternative to the seemingly limitless nature of Hamiltonian prerogative, we have encountered a version of prerogative at least as limitless and perhaps more so.
>
> *(Kleinerman 2009: 158–59)*

The Presidency–Public Alliance

Interestingly, the word "accountability" was rarely used in the ratification debates over the Constitution (Borowiak, 2007: 999). Even so, the concept was central to the framers' deliberations, and the role of the people in holding presidents accountable arose in the debate over a single versus a plural executive. The plural form was preferred by those restive at the prospect of an executive too reminiscent of a British king. But in his Federalist 70 defense of the single executive Alexander Hamilton pointed to the greater ease it afforded of spotting and punishing misbehavior. A single president would be *conspicuous* enough to be held to account, because his solitary status would highlight his agency and his responsibility. It would ensure that incompetence or misbehavior would be readily discovered, and responsibility swiftly and accurately attributed. Moreover, the increased threat of punishment faced by a lone execute implied a profile high enough that the "restraint of public opinion" could be a factor in keeping him in check.

Democratization of the Presidency

Hamilton mentioned public opinion in order to signal his respect for the people, as the task of "selling" the Constitution by means of the persuasion campaign embodied in the *Federalist* publication project required (Elkins and McKitrick, 1993). He well knew, however, that as the founding document was actually written, the impact of public opinion on the president was designed to be limited. That is how things worked during the presidencies of George Washington and John Adams. But contrary to the wishes of Hamilton and other founders that the people be kept at a safe distance from the executive an extra-constitutional bond would begin to form between them as early as the election of 1800. That was when Thomas Jefferson, the third president, became the first to claim a popular mandate. Bruce Ackerman explains:

> Despite the intentions of the Framers the presidency had become the focus of an intense partisan struggle over the country's future; and *despite the mechanics of the electoral college,* Jefferson was on firm ground in insisting that his party had won the election and had thereby gained a mandate from the People.
> *(Ackerman 2005: 94–95, emphasis added)*

In 1829 Andrew Jackson took this unintended relationship with the American people to the next level. He would be the first president to not only appeal to the people over the heads of their representatives in Congress, but also to famously assert that as the only nationally elected official (other than the vice president) *he, as president, was the truest representative of the American people,* and, indeed, actually "embodied" the people (Corwin, 1957: 21). As Godfrey Hodgson (2009) notes, the American Revolution and the political developments that it inspired not only created the world's first large republic but also had "replaced divine right, and hereditary right, and customary legitimacy, with the supreme authority of the people."

The People's Representative

This set in motion the gradual emergence of what today is *the signature accountability relationship in American representative democracy: that of the presidency and the people.* The democratization of the presidency permanently elevated the political importance of the mass American voting public as a singular national constituency within the American political system. "The people" alone were able to bestow democratic legitimacy on those they elected to high office because they were by definition "the source of all sovereignty" (as Andrew Jackson put it). Because such sovereignty is vested more or less exclusively through the popular vote rather than the Electoral College vote (as Ackerman contends in the quotation above), it is the people who generally control access to the presidency. Winning the presidency has required the active support of the American people from the beginning, but particularly since 1800.

As a result of these events (and their reinforcement by the strong connections with the people established by many subsequent presidents) the popular link has taken root to such an extent that in 2008 political scientist Michael Nelson could write that "(i)n the long term the attitude that the *president is the peoples' main representative in government* took hold widely and deeply in the American political system" (Nelson, 2008: 92, emphasis added). The corollary, that as their principal representative the *president was accountable primarily to "the people,"* would soon follow. Borowiak (2007: 1006) puts the general democratic principle this way: "In a republican government where citizens are considered the highest authority, they are the ones to whom officials should ultimately be accountable."

Critiques

The elaboration of the popular connection, from the post–1824 expansion of the electorate to the early 20th–century presidencies of Theodore Roosevelt and Woodrow Wilson, presaged what contemporary scholars have variously (and unhappily) termed the "plebiscitary" (Ceaser, 1979), "personal" (Lowi, 1985), and "rhetorical" (Tulis, 1987) presidency. For Ceaser, the evils of the plebiscitary presidency are many, but center around authority derived from an informal relationship with the people rather than the Constitution, which leads to an overreliance on the art of a popular leadership that inevitably fosters unrealistic expectations (Ceaser, 1979: 258). Lowi also criticizes the bypassing of mediating institutions such as parties and Congress and the emergence of unrealistic expectations, but notes that "built–in barriers" to meeting such expectations set up a dangerous cycle in which presidential failure is followed by frantic White House efforts to create false images of success, followed by adventurism abroad, followed by further public disenchantment, which pushes the succession of presidents to ever greater rhetorical deception (Lowi, 1985: 134–75). For his part, Tulis (1987, 2003) premises his critique of popular leadership on the inconsistency of its most cogent theoretical justification (offered by Woodrow Wilson, who based his defense of popular leadership on its *necessity*, given that the founder's presidency was too weak) with the founding perspective's greater fear of demagoguery and strong preference for constitutional rather than popular power. Tulis allows that the popular president is better equipped to reconstitute the political agenda when some crisis makes it necessary. But he argues that the very qualities of personal and/or rhetorical presidential leadership that make this possible also "tend to subvert the deliberative process, which makes unwise legislation or incoherent policy more likely" (Tulis, 2003: 102).

The entrenchment of this unintended presidency–public linkage extends all the way to the present where "the task of shaping presidential speech to influence and manipulate public opinion—when necessary by appealing over the heads of Congress in order to induce Congress to support the president's policies—has become a central element in the art and science of presidential conduct." Robert Dahl captures the irony from the framers' point-of-view: "(T)he presidency has developed into an office that is the very embodiment of the kind of executive that the framers, so far as we can discern their intentions, strove to avoid" (Dahl, 1990: 152).

Some have challenged the idea that the consequences of this development are uniformly undesirable. Brandice Canes-Wrone (2006), for example, offers evidence to suggest that the interactions of presidents and people do not routinely lead either to improper presidential responsiveness to public demands (pandering) or to public shifts of opinion in response to demagogic presidential appeals, the sorts of things the framers most feared. She finds that presidents increase their prospects for legislative success by publicizing already popular initiatives Congress is not initially disposed toward enacting, which is the incentive for "going public." But whether for good or ill "going public" has become standard presidential procedure. As one of the public presidency's closest students recently concluded, "presidents will not soon abandon public strategies" (Kernell, 2007: 235). This is true even though presidential appeals often fall "on deaf ears" (Edwards, 2003).

PAS Deference to Public

The emergence of a special link between the president and the mass public had another important consequence for presidential accountability—deserving of separate billing as the fourth and final source of incoherence considered here. It *altered the president's relationship to other "checking and balancing" institutions—the Congress, the Court, and the rest—in ways that reduce their willingness and ability to influence let alone discipline the president.* A popular president is less likely to be challenged by Congress because its members are themselves reliant on popular support for their positions. Voters in states and districts favorably disposed to the White House often use their representative's support for the president to determine their level of support for the representative. That gives the latter more incentive to support than to "check and balance" the executive (Hickey, 2011).

Similarly, popular presidential actions or policies are infrequently challenged by the Supreme Court. The Justices understand that their own otherwise unenforceable power of judicial review would endure only so long as the Court's interpretation of the Constitution does not "stray too far from what a majority of the people believed it should be" (Friedman, 2009: 4). These things show why the accountability relationship of the people to the president is different from that to be found between citizens and executives or legislators at any other level in the American system of representative democracy.

The Citizenry: PAS Linchpin by Default

For good or ill, then, the public's stature as the source of all sovereignty, its historic strengthening of the president and the consequent reluctance of other PAS agents to risk defying popular presidents make the people the most important of all presidential accountability agents; indeed the linchpin of the PAS. It is they who put the president in power and they who can remove him or her. This alone makes them the decisive accountability agents in American representative democracy. But it is also the people who give presidents a vital source of leverage not envisioned in the Constitution. Andrew Jackson showed that by virtue of winning a national election, *a president can successfully claim that he alone acts in the people's name and on their behalf, empowered both to fight for their policy preferences and to protect their interests in crises*. This in effect *weakens* all the other agents in a position to influence presidents. It does so because all the other accountability agents—unofficial as well as official— cannot match a president's ability to influence the public. They more often must respond to rather than shape public opinion. And they know that in their own interests they cannot ignore a clearly expressed public will. When the will of the people is clear, united and stable, all other accountability agents must reckon with it.

Even though most accountability agents have the means and opportunities to exert some measure of independent influence over the executive, they are rarely willing to use it in the face of public disapproval because *in one way or another they too wield their various powers at the pleasure of the people*. They are either themselves electorally accountable to the people (again, Congress) or needful of popular support for their own access to power (the political opposition) or dependent on the people's reaction to their products for political influence and economic survival (e.g., the news media) or (like the Court) reliant on public respect and tolerance to ensure continued acceptance of their own legitimacy.

The people's special status means that other accountability agents are not only deferential to and influenced by public opinion but also that *they themselves* need the people's support to be effective in their own roles. They often cannot do their best work in their own spheres without the support or the political cover of public opinion. This is particularly true of the Congress.

The Problem

This kind of reliance of other agents upon them is yet another reason why the people are the de facto linchpin of the presidential accountability system. But now we come to the problem: the people as a whole are not well-schooled to this work, not politically socialized in classrooms and/or families to realize their enormous political significance and to accept the responsibilities that accompany it.[2] What is more, they are not naturally drawn to politics unless mobilized by emotionally compelling issues or events or by televised spectacles such as congressional hearings (e.g., the Army McCarthy hearings, Watergate hearings, and Clinton impeachment hearings). This means *they are not routinely able to apply their special influence potential to important political work involving presidential accountability.* The frequent inaccessibility of an informed and focused public when it is needed means that special arrangements—coordination mechanisms additional to elections—will sometimes be required if the people's unparalleled moral and political authority is to be deployed effectively when necessary. This fact underlies the policy trial proposal set forth in Chapter 6.

Unreliability

When it is authoritatively marshaled (i.e., mobilized, unified, clear, stable, and focused) and brought to bear with surgical precision on specific choices, public opinion will prevail. It does not often achieve this pinpoint state because there are so few authoritative mechanisms for educating, coordinating, and targeting public influence in decisive ways outside elections and spontaneous crystallizations of the popular will (e.g., in response to an economic crisis). Nevertheless, the people's electoral monopoly over access to power, the unparalleled significance of their poll-tested political opinions, and their sovereign constitutional status (Amar, 2005: 5) make their will and their expectations for presidential performance, always at least potentially, by far *the most important* sources of guidance for presidents among accountability agents and, as noted, the default linchpin of the PAS itself. By "linchpin" I mean a potentially unifying source of influence on other PAS members as well as an authoritative source of guidance for presidents. The people are the default linchpin because no other accountability agent can match their constitutional legitimacy.

But this linchpin PAS status exists by default, and the people do not always deliver. They are not always ready when needed. As just implied, their readiness ebbs and flows with the (often unpredictable) extent to which they are actively engaged in particular questions, or presidential oversight more generally, and the extent to which their will is (to repeat) *clear, unified, and stable* on any consequential matter. When public opinion has these attributes on a matter touching executive activities, presidents know there will be rewards for compliance and risks of punishment for defiance. When public opinion is not coherently mobilized (a not uncommon occurrence) the popular impact on the situational incentives confronting presidents and other elites can vary from uncertain to negligible. Elites may then compete to shape public opinion and establish the leading interpretation of it, and claim popular support; either as a consequence of official signals like general and midterm elections, or the unofficial and often ephemeral drift of poll-tested opinion (see Chapter 2).

As the people became an extra-constitutional source of power for presidents, and as presidents themselves became representatives and tribunes of the people, the potential for the kind of strict oversight of presidents envisioned by Alexander Hamilton in Federalist 70 began to wane. It was further diminished as the number of forceful presidents later deemed "great" increased. The people's energizing of the presidency and that institution's emergence as what Clinton Rossiter called a "breeding ground of indestructible myth," a place where strong leaders go to do great things, helped crystallize a different public view of the presidency than had existed at the time of the founding (presumed to be wary and skeptical by the authors of *The Federalist*).

This perspective shift was made easier by the earlier failure of leading founders to establish a national citizen development program (please revisit endnote 2). It meant that there would be no sustained critical citizen vigilance or wariness of the sort envisioned by Thomas Jefferson and other early national leaders (again, see endnote 2 and Buchanan, 2008c). After democratization, when public unhappiness with particular presidents emerged it was as or more likely to stem from failure to meet great expectations than from exceeding constitutional bounds.

The lack of a citizen development program did not rule out the emergence of popular displeasure with presidential handling of 20th-century episodes like Vietnam and Watergate, both examples of spontaneous citizen agreement. Nor has it slowed the emergence, after the Great Depression of the 1930s and 40s, of a public tendency to blame presidents, and vote them out of office, for unsatisfactory economic conditions. The 2008 economic crisis that inspired both fear and blame for the president (the latter adroitly intensified by opposition politicians) is just the most recent example. It is also the case that spotty political socialization has not prevented the near-spontaneous emergence of popular support for other major shifts in national policy direction. Ackerman (2010: 4), for example, has argued that citizens achieved enough clarity and unity on their own to "give their government marching orders" at four key "constitutional moments" (the Founding, Reconstruction, the New Deal, and the Civil Rights revolution) without need for any special civics training. In 1991 Ackerman described such moments as times when "deep changes in popular opinion gained authoritative constitutional recognition" (Ackerman, 1991: 41).

In Table 2.1's terms, these unscripted negative and positive public expressions can be classified as examples of *negative* and *positive sanctions*: withdrawing or bestowing approval that had the effect of punishing or rewarding leaders according to how the public saw their performances in context. But they were spontaneous reactions, not

TABLE 2.1   The Presidential Incentive System

	Sanctions	Incentives
Negative (punishment)	• Loss of election • Impeachment and conviction • Loss of poll support • Loss of Supreme Court Decision	• Avoid unacceptable behavior • Avoid poor performance • Spin bad news
Positive (reward)	• Re-election • Popular support • Historical acclaim	• Keep promises • Solve problems • Seek great achievements

planful applications of sanctions by a population knowingly playing a role for which it had been prepared, like jurists, legislators, journalists, and historians are formally prepared for their respective roles. In some cases the attentive public may be well-prepared to apply its considerable weight to good effect; often it is not. For the most part, especially during crises, the president's citizen-supervisors have most often been enablers (e.g., the early stages of wars of choice) and only infrequently a source of informed restraint. Their ability to punish presidents is real, but not often used. Except when it comes to economic conditions, or failed wars, the people are generally tolerant presidential taskmasters.

Unfulfilled Potential

Public influence within the PAS is simply too great not to question the wisdom of leaving citizens so largely at the mercy of their own instincts, without either more comprehensive civic education or substantial nonpartisan briefings on questions before them, official decisions about which are likely to be influenced by their poll-tested reactions. As the "source of all sovereignty," the arbiters of access to the presidency and the linchpin of the PAS, the people effectively *embody* American democratic accountability. Are they sufficiently prepared to wield their influence to best effect despite these reservations? Most political theorists and social scientists do not think so.

Political theorists have long doubted the commitment of the people to vigilance against improper uses of executive power and social scientists have questioned their civic competence more generally. For example, political theorist Benjamin Kleinerman, citing the British political philosopher John Locke's similar argument, contends that people "do not naturally care" whether or not discretionary presidential power exertions are arbitrary rather than necessary. Kleinerman also points out that "there was no overwhelming outcry against the claims advanced by the Bush administration of a rightful and inherent authority to set aside and even defy the laws" (Kleinerman, 2009: 52). He suggests that oppositional elite "cuing" is required to make citizens aware of violations and their constitutional importance (Kleinerman,

2009: 10). And in the introduction to their recent edited collection of recent social science research on democratic citizenship, Eugene Borgida and his co-editors note that:

> when social scientists rely on their empirical work to address the concerns of democratic theorists, the core question of civic competence arises. Ideal characteristics of ideal citizens are posited with regard to qualities such as political knowledge and expertise, understanding and internalization of democratic norms and values, political interest and involvement, rational deliberation and emotional passions, and so on. Accordingly, social scientists have concluded, based on several decades of empirical research, that American citizens, despite participating in a longstanding and reasonably robust democracy, fall far short on almost every normative criterion.
>
> *(Borgida et al., 2009: 2–3)*

Thus the people seem unaware of the significance of their place in the political system and largely indifferent to the considerable responsibility that it entails, let alone of their role in empowering presidents while simultaneously (and unintentionally) loosening the other accountability chains that restrain them. Better prepared and more effectively deployed citizens would almost certainly tighten the chains loosed by democratization. That is what it will take to put the PAS in charge of setting and enforcing coherent limits on presidential power.

Prerequisites of Coherent Accountability

Below I discuss two of the prerequisites of coherent accountability: clear guidelines for presidential performance, and more effective use of existing presidential incentives to encourage compliance with the guidelines. Of course a conscious PAS that works to build acceptance for a coherent accountability policy built around these two features is also a prerequisite. A plan for bringing that consciousness about is discussed in Chapter 5.

Clear Guidelines

The presidency, successful though it has been at solving national problems, has deviated with unnecessary regularity from the constitutional balance established for the war power, to the detriment of the separation of powers. A president who acts outside or in violation of the Constitution would, under the dicta of Locke and Lincoln, be impeached and removed unless the Congress and the people agreed that the president's act had been *essential to preserving the constitutional order itself.* Lincoln's famous words describing his Civil War actions capture exactly this requirement: "I felt that measures otherwise unconstitutional might become lawful by becoming indispensable to the preservation of the Constitution through the preservation of the nation" (Nelson, 2008: 98). Deviations from this standard have involved assertions of prerogative that were not shown to be necessary to preserve the Constitution. Prime examples of such assertions include Jefferson's purchase of Louisiana and Truman's dispatch of troops to Korea.

The correction factors for such circumstances include the four guidelines that follow. Observing them would not weaken a president's capacity to respond as needed to authentic emergencies. Neither do they in any way prevent presidents from continuing the presidency's record of effective service to the nation. They merely correct for unnecessary power claims and expansions.

The War Power Guideline

Except in extraordinary, time-sensitive emergencies (when the kind of congressional and national discussion that should precede a declaration or an authorization of war is not possible) Congress must authorize the deployment of military force. The reason is that the Constitution vests the initiation power in the Congress. "Most legal scholars agree that the nation's founders intended to separate the power to initiate a war from the power to carry it out" (Savage, 2011a: A12). Truman's move was arguably the most constitutionally destructive act in American history because subsequent presidents have won general acceptance for the idea that Truman's action established a precedent.

Consider the following view of *why* the framers separated war initiation from implementation. In his February 15, 1848 letter to his friend William Herndon, then Congressman Abraham Lincoln observes:

> The provision of the Constitution giving the war making power to Congress, was dictated, as I understand it, by the following reasons. Kings had always been involving and impoverishing their peoples in wars, pretending generally, if not always, that the good of the people was the object. This, our convention understood to be the most oppressive of all kingly oppressions; and they resolved to so frame the Constitution that *no one man* should hold the power of bringing this oppression upon us.
>
> *(Basler, 1990: 220–21, emphasis in original)*

Restoration of adherence to this constitutional provision is the intent of the first guideline. The threats of impeachment, potential conviction, and removal from office are the ultimate measures for ensuring such respect.

The Prior Approval Guideline

The second guideline is a corollary of the first, tailored in response to the elective presidential wars seen frequently in the last half century. It covers military options potentially worthy of U.S. involvement but clearly not essential to the survival of the republic. In such cases, which typically afford sufficient time, the Congress must approve *before* military power is used by the president. Two scenarios—one small, the other large—are envisioned.

When a president's proposed military action is small in scale and portrayed as limited in size and duration, as in the March 2011 Libya operation, the congressional leadership should convene a special joint meeting of four congressional committees to review and make a recommendation to the Congress to approve or disapprove the president's plan. The relevant committees are the House and Senate Foreign Relations Committees and the House and Senate Intelligence Committees (the Select Permanent Committee on Intelligence in the House, the Select Committee on Intelligence in the Senate).

When a president contemplates optional military action on a large scale and of uncertain duration (e.g., Korea, Vietnam, Iraq) a more extended proceeding—a policy trial—is indicated. A policy trial is a congressional proceeding that puts the president's proposal for military action on trial on the merits. The proposal must be approved formally by Congress and informally by the American people before the war policy can be implemented. (See Chapter 6 for an extended description and hypothetical illustration of such a proceeding.) This will give presidents the opportunity to build congressional and public support before acting, while preventing optional military action if public and congressional majorities deem the president's proposal to be unnecessary or ill-advised. Formal prospective accountability for a war policy proposal allows disagreements to be addressed rationally without need for peremptory action potentially unsettling enough to Congress and public to result in impeachment and conviction of the president under item 1 above (the war power guideline).

Sufficiency Guideline

No presidential power should be used—whether extra-legal or constitutional—that is not needed to achieve the desired result. This guideline is intended to increase the sensitivity of all caught up in alarming circumstances (which may invite impulsive overreaction) to the importance of keeping in mind this important principle: the president should go far enough but no further—even in the midst of provocative events like the 1950 North Korean invasion of South Korea or the humanitarian temptation of Libya. In the fearful climate of Korea (without benefit of a sufficiency guideline) Truman arrogated more power than was necessary to meet the need he and others saw in Korea. There was no need to move on his own authority, given the virtual certainty of timely prior congressional approval if he had sought it. If Truman had sought and received congressional approval before acting (thereby respecting the constitutional standard, acknowledged by Franklin D. Roosevelt, Lincoln, and the legal scholars referenced above) Americans' unhappiness with the experience and outcome of the Korean War might have provoked a more robust congressional vetting of Vietnam and Iraq. (Instead, there was only perfunctory debate, due to resignation in the face of the Truman precedent that the president could not be stopped.)

When presidents seek and receive thoughtfully grounded authorization (as opposed to pressured, largely unreflective resolutions like those featured in the cases of Vietnam and Iraq; see Chapter 4) *"ownership" of the war is shared with Congress.* Given the exclusively presidential ownership that goes with peremptory wars and Americans' eventual disenchantment with the Korean, Vietnam, and Iraq Wars and the presidents who initiated them, sharing the original decision with Congress and the people would seem to make better political sense for presidents as well as good constitutional sense.

The Necessity/No Precedent Guideline

This guideline is the most deeply rooted of the four in the primacy of the constitutional order. Its essence can be stated simply. When necessity precludes prior approval and forces prerogative presidential action, the no precedent standard is automatic. A president may violate the Constitution in order to save it. But because the absolute necessity of each violation must be established in its own right, entirely independently of what has gone before, the very concept of precedent is irrelevant. What matters is the ability of the incumbent to justify, to the satisfaction of Congress and the people, in a deliberative setting, a claim that presidential handling of each specific crisis was necessary to save the Constitution. What does *not* matter is the existence of similar actions of previous presidents (i.e., precedents). They cannot determine the acceptability (or lack thereof) of otherwise unconstitutional prerogative action. It is "the explicit claim in Locke and the implicit claim in Lincoln that the exercise of prerogative establishes no precedent for the future exercise of prerogative" (Kleinerman, 2009: 181).

If the judges of presidential prerogative are Congress and the people, what is to be the basis of their judgment? As also noted earlier, Locke and Lincoln argue that extra-constitutional (prerogative) executive action can be justified only if it is *constitutionalized*; that is, shown to be necessary to preserve the Constitution. Why must every unconstitutional act be justified in such fundamental terms? It must be done because any departure from the Constitution, even if for a very tempting opportunity (e.g., the chance to acquire the Louisiana Territory), is against the law. Jefferson himself initially respected the importance of this principle by seriously contemplating, and writing, several constitutional amendments to sanction his act before succumbing to the temptation to ignore the Constitution and act on readily available congressional approval (Malone, 1970: 314, 328).

The rationale for such a strict rule is clear: A constitution that can be set aside for reasons other than its own preservation is a constitution whose force is perpetually contingent; always potentially less important than the latest tempting expedient. If it is subordinated once for reasons short of its own preservation, there is nothing to prevent it from being marginalized again and again. It becomes perpetually vulnerable to the lure of convenience. It is hard to reverse such a practice once the polity has moved down this slippery slope. Korea and the subsequent wars of choice it justified are clear demonstrations of this fact.

Executive prerogative, the idea that the executive must be able to do what is necessary to protect the nation and its constitution, was intended by those who conceived and refined the concept (Locke, the founders, and particularly Lincoln) to enable such discretion without establishing a permanent executive dictatorship. To avoid tyranny justified in the name of safety, it is necessary to have a compact that provides constitutional liberties for citizens and establishes limits on executive prerogative. Such a constitution must be respected enough to entrench a rigid expectation that the constraints it imposes on the executive intended to preserve liberty, civil rights, and the separation of powers are restored, are respected, and enforced once the crisis has passed. There can be no such restoration (and no coherent accountability) if precedent is allowed to permanently expand the power entitlements of executives.

Effective Use of Existing Incentives

Despite the existence of constitutional and various less formal incentives to guide presidents in these and other circumstances (most are summarized in Table 2.1) there has never been a well-considered and detailed plan for deploying incentives to encourage either constitutional respect or outstanding performance. In Federalist 57, for example, James Madison identified just two prerequisites for good presidential conduct: incumbents of wisdom and virtue, and institutional checks. He made no mention of other supplemental possibilities, or of the potential utility of coordination among incentives. To be sure, Madison, Jefferson, Adams, and Washington, among others, had earlier tried to establish a national system of public education that might have equipped citizens to be vigilant monitors of presidents, functioning as a kind of third line of defense after virtue and institutional checks. But the idea generated little political support and was "off the table" by the time of the 1787 constitutional convention (Brown, 1996; Buchanan, 2008c). (See previously introduced endnote 2.)

How are enforcement of guidelines and encouragement of effective performance to be accomplished? Primarily through adroit, well-coordinated deployment of the familiar formal and informal sanctions depicted in Table 2.1. As the table shows, these sanctions create both positive and negative incentives for the president. They represent the carrots and the sticks available to the PAS to give presidents reason to toe the lines that accountability agents draw. Chapter 3 will show more comprehensively what the Truman vignette illustrated: that these tools have not often been effectively used as a coordinated incentive system. But if better-orchestrated (by voluntary PAS adherence to a coherent strategy, as suggested in Chapter 5) they can be sufficient to "incentivize" compliance.

The formal and informal sanctions and the negative and positive incentives associated with each were either constitutionally defined or have emerged in practice since the founding. The matrix contains two rows, one for punishments, which is labeled "negative," and the other for rewards, labeled "positive." Brief assessments of each follow.

Negative Sanctions

While the list in Table 2.1 of negative sanctions could be extended (critical media coverage, for example, is treated as implicit), what is listed would be daunting to any president who knew it would be used to maximum effect. In practice their application has been uneven. Most visible is the regularly scheduled potential for *loss of election*, which is the major retribution available to an American electorate that is unhappy with a president's performance. In practice, however, most presidents who have sought re-election since FDR (eight of 11) have achieved it (five of eight), suggesting that it is an accessible rather than a particularly hard-to-achieve goal. Potential drops in poll-tested public support outside elections can motivate presidential efforts to meet expectations when they are able to. But they often cannot, as when the business cycle pushes unemployment up despite a president's best efforts to prevent it. It is also the case that factors unrelated to performance (illustrated in the next chapter) may affect election outcomes, which blurs the performance-related meaning of electoral defeat.

What, then, of impeachment and conviction? Impeachment is rarely used and no impeached president has ever been convicted and removed from office (although President Nixon was driven to resign in the face of near-certain impeachment and conviction). Its most recent use in the case of President Clinton was highly politicized, and as the partisan divide in Congress increases, the likelihood that impeachment could be converted to an unbiased disciplinary procedure is severely compromised. Still, impeachment remains Congress's ultimate constitutional weapon for disciplining presidents. Though it now seems improbable, if circumstances led to its being used more frequently and fairly it might yet become a potent incentive.

Presidents are also accountable to the Supreme Court (whose chief justice presides at Senate impeachment trials of presidents, and whose members may, if a relevant lawsuit is filed and lower court decisions are appealed to them, grant a writ of certiorari and review the constitutional propriety of a presidential assertion of power). But we see elsewhere in these pages that Supreme Court decisions have more often empowered than disciplined presidents.

Unofficial accountability agents able to influence incentives include the political opposition, the media, and historians (not depicted in Table 2.1). Note, however, that excepting future historians looking back at a past presidency (whose influence works through the real-time anticipations of particular incumbents, as in the Truman example above) citizens are able to wield electoral or market influence over these sources of reckoning for presidents, which can in turn affect their influence on presidents.

In sum, the negative sanctions, intended or presumed to give the president reason to avoid behaviors likely to result in loss of support and/or power, are not always deployed with maximum effectiveness when they are deployed at all. What is more, presidents have the resources to fight back. They and their allies often "spin" bad news by disputing critics and otherwise using the bully pulpit and supportive media to argue for the most favorable possible interpretations of performance episodes under attack. The net effect is to limit the potency of negative sanctions.

Positive Sanctions

It is not surprising, then, that when it comes to influencing presidents the incentives created by the positive sanctions significantly outweigh those spawned by the checks and balances. It is harder work to restrain or discipline presidents than it is to encourage them. For reasons detailed in Chapter 3 official accountability agents have either been reluctant (e.g., Congress) or unable (e.g., the Court, voters in elections) to emphasize either strict supervision or swift and sure performance-related punishment. Because it is unconscious the PAS has not devised integrated strategies for holding presidents to strict account: the implicit recommendation of the scholarly literature on political accountability.[3]

The will to succeed (the more impressively the better) has been the driver of the stellar historical record of presidential achievement and of the extraordinary growth of presidential power. The positive row of Table 2.1 depicts the payoffs for good performance: from the general, such as keeping campaign promises, to the significant, such as passing important legislation, to the epochal, such as resolving system-threatening crises like the Civil War. Good performance is "incentivized" by the prospect of the formal re-election reward, by the unofficial but still prized chances for contemporary popular support, and of course by the ultimate prize: a transformational legacy and historical acclaim. As noted, many assertions of presidential power, hotly controversial at the time (usually on constitutional grounds), yielded results that have in retrospect been viewed very favorably in the eyes of history. Washington's Neutrality Proclamation, Jefferson's purchase of the Louisiana Territory, and both Lincoln's and FDR's wartime measures are all cases in point. It is to make possible achievements that require extraordinary means that doctrines like "necessity" and "prerogative" were advanced to justify departures from constitutional limits.

The most powerful of the immediate positive rewards is bestowed by citizens who vote to re-elect an incumbent president. Just as with electoral defeat various nonperformance considerations may affect the outcome. But despite the potential complexities of such voting decisions, re-election to a second term bestows a prized validation on those who achieve it. Every president who wins re-election interprets it as definitive approval of his performance in office, and most historians see it as necessary if not sufficient for greatness (presidents who did not win re-election do not enjoy high rankings in most polls of historians assessing presidential greatness).

When President George W. Bush spoke of the 2004 presidential election as an "accountability moment," he made it clear that he interpreted his re-election victory as evidence of public endorsement of his policies and as a reward for good performance. Many of his political opponents and other critics would have disagreed. But it was an understandable view given the traditions of American politics. The prospect of such rewards as re-election, enhanced public prestige, a good professional reputation, and the esteem of history together lead most presidents to strive mightily to perform as impressively as possible. They do so because they sense the truth of Niccolo Machiavelli's insight: "Nothing makes a prince more highly esteemed than the assumption of great undertakings and giving rare examples of himself" (Machiavelli, 1997: 81). But as the foregoing shows, the major problem for the PAS comes not from the insufficiency of positive sanctions, but from the ineffective deployment of constraints.

Assessment

The model in Table 2.1 is a straightforward incentive system sufficient in design and formal authority to serve its implicit purpose: striking a healthy balance between the encouragement and restraint of presidents. This system could elicit acceptable presidential performance if it were applied in a consistently effective way (i.e., its elements selectively deployed and coordinated as needed by situationally relevant PAS agents) to enforce clear standards. Why, then, have the rewards incited more ambition, achievement, and power expansion than the punishments have evoked restraint? Because the four sources of incoherent standards discussed earlier—crisis-driven power expansions, illimitable power doctrines, democratization of the presidency, and the tendency of other PAS agents to take their cues from a too tolerant public—have "loosed presidents from their shackles" by preventing the most effective use of the incentive system.

Conclusion

Effectively deployed, the separation of powers can encourage a responsible presidency. Yet since the founding, presidential power has grown willy-nilly, on the fly, in response to events, more by accident than by design, with no sustained follow-up efforts to temper such growth with efforts to keep constitutional checks and balances relevant as a source of meaningful influence on presidential practice. Limiting doctrines like calibration, necessity, sufficiency, constitutional balance, and resistance to precedent have all been suggested, here and elsewhere, as ways to reconcile the need for crisis action with the ideal of constitutional restraint. And even if authentic threats and crises made substantial growth of military capability and commander-in-chief power inevitable, the acquiescence of Congress in the latest critical step—the de facto cession to the president during the Korean crisis of the power to initiate unprovoked hostilities—was not inevitable. That, by any reasonable measure, was a step too far. It is the principal reason why proposals for remedial action remain essential. This is true even though each new unprovoked military action (Korea, Vietnam, Iraq, and now Libya), once accepted, makes redressing the imbalance that much more of an uphill struggle.

Presidential accountability that can sustain a meaningful link to constitutional limits presupposes a clear goal, sought and achieved through consistent enforcement by agents of accountability of explicit performance standards. But the dissimilar actors that mete out the rewards and punishments in Table 2.1 are currently animated by varying expectations and disagreements that limit their ability to signal clear performance guidelines for presidents or to make and enforce them consistently by orchestrating incentives.

If PAS actors are ever to wield the positive and negative sanctions to best effect they must first come to think of themselves as an influence network which occasionally has interests in common. To deal with such moments they must develop ways to avoid sending the president ambiguous or conflicting signals. Only then will we have a truly *contemporary* separation of powers system. In that system the agents will continue to contest their disagreements when that is called for, as separation of powers implies. But they will also have developed ways to speak with one voice when they see a need to send consistent signals in an effort to influence presidential responses to specific performance challenges like Korea.

Might the current unself-aware PAS ever be equipped to rise to such a challenge? The answer requires that we conduct an inventory of existing strengths and weaknesses of the agents themselves, as preparation for assessing the overall performance of the PAS and identifying, later in this book, a strategy for bringing the PAS to life.

3

THE UNCONSCIOUS PRESIDENTIAL ACCOUNTABILITY SYSTEM

The first step on the path toward a self-aware PAS community is to understand the presidential accountability system as it is, agent by agent. Our review begins with the three official agents, arrayed across the columns of the matrix in Table 3.1. The top row juxtaposes the *formal accountability powers* of each official agent. Row two compares recent but potentially correctable *dysfunctions*. Row three features the *intrinsic limitations* that more fundamentally undermine the accountability potential and impact of each agent.

For the four unofficial agents (see Table 3.2 below) row one identifies potential influences rather than formal powers. But as in Table 3.1 the row two dysfunctions are also potentially correctable. And for both official and unofficial agents intrinsic limitations are either theoretically or practically beyond redress, creating lacunae that must either be compensated for by other agents, or be tolerated or changed through fundamental reform.

Official Agents of Accountability

National Elections

The symbolic centerpiece of the PAS, as of American representative democracy itself, is the national electoral process, which (given that electors have so faithfully reflected the popular vote) vests the registered voters that "staff" it with the pivotal decisions of who shall become and/or remain president. Presidential elections establish the electorate as the *source* of presidential power and legitimacy. Presidents are, in the first instance, accountable to those who give them power to "act in certain ways expected" by the power granters (Pitkin, 1967: 55–57) and re-election is, in the theory of democratic accountability, the core incentive to do so.

TABLE 3.1 Official Agents of Accountability

	Elections	Congress	Court
Power	• Re-elect or remove president	• Hearings • Prior restraint of presidents through legislation, power of the purse • Impeachment and conviction	• Judicial review may approve or disallow assertions of presidential power
Dysfunctions	• Voters not always well-informed or focused on accountability • Proximity bias of fixed term	• Re-election incentive • Partisan loyalty trumps institutional loyalty, subverting use of accountability powers	• Perceived or actual partisanship weakens Court's legitimacy

Limitations	• Re-election not an incentive for second-term presidents
	• Election outcome not always driven by performance or results
	• Results not always visible
		• Supermajorities nearly unattainable, making unlikely:
		  – Impeachment convictions
		  – Cloture motions
		  – Veto overrides
			• No prior restraint

TABLE 3.2 Unofficial Agents of Accountability

	Public opinion	Media	Opposition	History
Influences	• Break president's hold on congressional party • Flip control of Congress	• Enable accountability agents with information • Discourage presidential misbehavior	• Offer voters alternative presidents and policies • Encourage compromise • Discourage misbehavior	• Legacy inspires presidents to aim high against long odds
Dysfunctions	• Often too unfocused to use elections to punish or reward president	• May get story wrong • May overlook story	• Defeating president may become more important than solving problems	• May invite ill-fated identification with defiant past presidents
Limitations	• Poor socialization • Authoritative only through electoral connection	• Can't discover all-important presidential transgressions	• Standing threat to cooperation, which is needed for problem-solving	• Standing invitation to discount critics in favor of expected historical approval

As noted, the status bestowed by the franchise also makes majority opinion a source of leverage on presidents and other PAS members *outside* as well as *within* the electoral context. Anointing a source of *portable high-status leverage* for use in implicating other agents (particularly Congress) in accountability projects like vetting potential wars of choice may be the greatest contribution that the electoral process can make to the rejuvenated PAS envisioned in Chapter 5. By themselves, however, elections are often imprecise accountability instruments.

Dysfunctions

The looming re-election test is a consideration in virtually all first-term presidential decision making. The voters have the power to re-elect or remove a first-term incumbent based on performance or any other reason they deem relevant. This ensures that citizen expectations will be taken into account by candidates for re-election. Yet as noted in Table 3.1's "dysfunction" row it is clear that election outcomes are not always performance related, and that when they are, there is often proximity bias.

As for the relation of the vote to performance, V. O. Key famously observed that voters "are not fools," but neither are they close students of politics. As noted, the political system has never adopted a systematic method for instilling any particular sense of responsibility in its citizens for choosing and supervising presidents or other public officials with care. This means that voters lack a socialized incentive to become well informed for these tasks and most do not. This makes it more likely that voters will fall back on heuristics (low-information short-cuts) such as party loyalty or feelings of discomfort with the challenger (often reinforced by negative campaign advertising). Thus, their Election Day choices are often influenced less by detailed incumbent performance assessments (or new candidate qualification assessments) than by other concerns. In 2004 this seemingly led a narrow majority to re-elect George W. Bush despite the fact that on the biggest performance test facing the president at the time, 52 percent told exit pollsters that things were going badly for the United States in Iraq and an identical 52 percent said that the Iraq War had not made the United States more secure (CNN, 2004). The "other concerns" in this case seem to have been reservations about the challenger John Kerry, and fear of changing presidents in the midst of a war.

Proximity bias is created by the fixed four-year presidential term. It discourages a balanced overall assessment of the presidential record. The reason is that early-term events are less vivid in the public memory and therefore less significant than proximate events as determinants of votes. For example, Jimmy Carter was defeated in 1980 because of bad news near Election Day: double-digit inflation, the unresolved Iranian hostage crisis, gasoline shortages, the failed hostage rescue attempt, and his flawed performance in the debates against Ronald Reagan. But had his signal achievement—the September 1978 Camp David Accords that secured peace between Egypt and Israel—occurred in late October 1980, the election outcome might have been different.[1]

These things are, at least in principle, subject to improvement. Significant numbers of citizens might, in time, be socialized to pay more attention to substantive presidential performance, and to weight early and late-term achievements more equally. If this happened, presidents would have greater incentive to focus on performance. Even so, less tractable barriers to the link between performance and electoral reward would remain.

Limitations

Among the intrinsic limitations on presidential elections as instruments of accountability is the fact that meaningful results are often not yet visible to electorates by Election Day, and the fact that the 22nd Amendment removes the electoral incentive for second-term presidents. Both of these limitations are beyond conceivable repair.

Even if voters were not distracted by nonperformance considerations the electoral calendar could force them to evaluate an incumbent before meaningful performance results were visible. Policy success and failure, which research shows to influence the mass public when either is clear (Brody, 1991; Buchanan, 2010), and which also shape historians' rankings of presidential greatness (Ragsdale, 2009: 30) may not yet be clear and therefore remain controversial. That was true of President Obama's health care reform measure in 2012 and was also true of President George W. Bush's highest profile initiative, the Iraq War, in 2004. In such cases (and to the extent votes turn on perceived performance rather than other criteria) the focus is necessarily on whatever sense particular groups of voters decide to make of whatever outcome evidence they deem valid enough to affect their votes. Many voters, particularly those associated with the politically conservative Tea Party movement, but also more orthodox Republicans and Independents, believed they knew all they needed to know about the actual and probable impact of the Health Care Act by 2010, let alone 2012. By late March 2012, just 36 percent supported Obamacare with nearly half opposed (Newsmax, 2012).

That raises another problem. Some visible conditions may be *invalid* indicators of performance (e.g., bad economic news blamed, with limited justification, on such presidents as Obama in the run-up to 2012, on the first President Bush in 1992 and on Carter in 1980). Obama's 2012 electoral prospects were uncertain at this writing. Neither Bush nor Carter was re-elected. Other "visible" indicators are at best *incomplete* (e.g., acts that signal boldness, such as invading Afghanistan, as the younger Bush did after 9/11; or increasing troop strength in Afghanistan, as President Obama did in 2009. Such acts might or might not yield clear results in time for voting decisions).

Incomplete information is almost always a dilemma for voters, who must decide anyway. But the point to notice here is this: election victories are not always rewards for keeping promises or solving problems (Table 3.1) because they are not necessarily performance based. Re-election may be treated by historians and presidents themselves as a core test of the presidential mettle. But it will often be debatable whether a particular election outcome should be interpreted as a reward or a punishment for a job well or poorly done, or even for meeting (or failing to meet) the expectations of voters, as the presidential incentive system and the theory of accountability posit.

Since the 1951 ratification of the 22nd Amendment restricting the president to two terms, only first-term incumbent presidents who seek re-election experience the re-election incentive. For second-term presidents there is no such incentive and thus no purely electoral accountability for performance other than the potential of gaining or losing party seats in Congress (sometimes affected by mid-term votes cast to reward or punish the president, as discussed below). After his own 2004 re-election and the loss of control of Congress to the Democrats in 2006, for example, President Bush had no further personal electoral concerns. His willingness to disregard strong majority public (and narrower majority congressional) opposition to increasing troop deployments to Iraq in 2007 suggested that either he no longer had (or, given his individual proclivities, might never have had) the incentive to respond to voter preferences.

How Elections Serve the PAS

In sum, elections are imperfect instruments of accountability. The uncertain link to performance or results, the proximity bias, the frequent invisibility of results and the disincentives introduced by the 22nd Amendment explain why. Elections contribute importantly to the PAS, however, by enshrining the principle of accountability and by bestowing a moral authority on the people that can be deployed flexibly and selectively outside presidential election seasons in response to accountability problems like wars of choice. But use of that resource requires alliance with other accountability agents, most particularly the Congress.

Congress

The U.S. Congress is often described as the most powerful and independent legislature in the world (e.g., Kernell and Jacobson, 2006: 256). The potentially decisive formal instruments of accountability at Congress's disposal, instruments that make a Congress with the will and the supermajority votes needed to exert them an overmatch for any president, go to the heart of Congress's unique role in the PAS. That role is to facilitate the leadership of the presidents it supports (e.g., by approving and financing their legislative agendas or uses of the war power), but also to disapprove, guide, restrain, or even disable through investigative hearings, legislation, the power of the purse, impeachment, and conviction any president whose actions provoke the extraordinary levels of consensus in both House and Senate required to take such decisive steps. The key point, however, is this: among the agents of accountability, *only Congress is constitutionally able to impose prior restraint on the use of power by a president.* But as we see next, its dysfunctions and limitation severely constrain the will of Congress to check the president.

Dysfunctions

An unfortunate consequence of the re-election incentive in an age of terrorism (in contrast to the post-Watergate era) has been to reduce the willingness of legislators to risk the electoral consequences of working to check the initiatives of presidents pressing the limits of their powers. It is easier and safer to do nothing. If things go well members can claim credit for not standing in the president's way. If things go poorly, members can blame the president (Rudalevige, 2006: 276). The dysfunctional effect is to sap the will to exercise oversight of those best positioned to check the president.

Another dysfunction is the adulteration of accountability that occurs when partisan loyalty trumps institutional loyalty (Table 3.1). Since the mid-1970s Congress has lost its moderates and split into two polarized ideological camps: conservative Republicans and liberal Democrats (McCarty et al., 2006: 3). Adulteration accompanies polarization, and comes in the form of a variable accountability standard. Congresses organized by the party in opposition to the incumbent president are likely to oversee and restrain with vigor (e.g., the 110th Congress), whereas congresses controlled by the president's party are likely to overlook presidential mistakes and transgressions (e.g., the 109th Congress) (Levinson 2006).

109th Congress

The 109th Congress took an uncritical stance toward Bush policies and mistakes. When in 2003 Republicans found themselves in control of both houses of Congress with a Republican in the White House for the first time since 1954, "(t)he majority saw itself more as a group of foot soldiers in the president's army than as members of an independent branch of government." There was little serious oversight of the executive, and long-standing norms of conduct in both houses were put aside in the name of service to the president's program. "A very aggressive assertion of executive power was met with institutional indifference in Congress" (Mann and Ornstein, 2006: xi). Congress's institutional responsibility to hold President Bush accountable for his use of the war power in Iraq, his management of Hurricane Katrina, and of the Walter Reed Hospital problem, were among the "accountability moments" neglected by the 109th Congress during the second Bush term.

110th Congress

The Democratic 110th Congress, on the other hand, attempted vigorous oversight of President Bush when it assumed control of both houses in January 2007. The zeal with which Democrats set about "restoring accountability" as House Speaker Nancy Pelosi put it was palpable. "In a vivid display of their new power Democrats across Capitol Hill … approved a flurry of subpoenas to fuel a series of investigations of the Bush administration." In response to Republican charges that Democrats were using their new majority to support "fishing expeditions" and "witch hunts" solely to embarrass the president, House Oversight Committee Chair Henry A. Waxman retorted that when Republicans controlled the oversight committee during Bill Clinton's presidency, "more than 1,000 subpoenas were issued to the executive branch" (Lewis and Lipton, April 26, 2007: A17).

"Report cards" on the Democratic Congress suggested that "after years of inattention Congressional oversight of the executive has intensified, most sharply regarding the war in Iraq. And hearings have appropriately focused more on policy and administration than personal scandal." But the Democrats were criticized for continuing certain Republican departures from "regular order"; departures that improperly limited the minority party's participation in the deliberative process (Mann et al., April 28, 2007: A27; Mann et al., January 19, 2008: A31). Would the Democrats rise above partisanship by keeping their promise to return to regular order? Not entirely, because they continued the practice of avoiding conference committees to settle final bills in order to exclude Republicans (called "ping-ponging"; see Carnerale, October 12, 2007: A8; Hulse, September 26, 2007: A1). But on the issues that swept them to power—promises to end the Iraq War, restore fiscal discipline, and check President Bush's powers—the Democrats were unsuccessful (Weisman and Kane, December 20, 2007: A1).

Limitation

The reason Democrats were unsuccessful is a vivid example of Congress's limitation as an accountability agent: *Full access to Congress's plenary accountability powers requires supermajorities*, which have been historically hard to muster on any controversial vote regardless of partisan balance (Burns, 1973: 46). The task approaches impossibility when partisan margins of control are narrow, and remains extraordinarily difficult even when, as in 2009, one party has only nominal rather than secure access to the 60 votes needed to impose cloture on filibusters, which are delaying measures that stem from Senate rules, not the Constitution. The need to muster 60 votes to impose "cloture" on (i.e., to end) the filibuster and proceed to a vote on the merits of legislation introduces yet another potentially narrow margin that invites both between-party and within-party political bargaining. When the opposition party is united the nominally dominant party must do what it takes (including "buying" votes with special "compromise" concessions) to defeat the filibuster. That describes the situation in 2009 and 2010, when Republican filibuster unity forced the Democrats to make concessions to holdouts within their own coalition. The Democrats barely managed to exploit their access to 60 cloture votes to ram through a historic health care measure that, due to the realities just described, fell well short of what policy analysts free of political responsibility regarded as ideal. Early in 2011 another in a long series of efforts to reform the filibuster emerged, with the usual uncertain prospects (Klein, January 4, 2011: online).

Despite the 2006 Democratic Party takeover of the Congress, their majority in the Senate was a tenuous 51–49 (due to two Independents who caucused with the Democrats) and in the House, 233–198. Democrats had captured Congress due to public unhappiness with Iraq and other Bush policies (see "Public Opinion" section below). Their victory and the change in partisan control it brought let the Democrats lay claim to an accountability mandate. Nevertheless, Republican unity in Congress behind the president's nationally unpopular policies meant that Democrats, with such narrow majorities in both houses, were unable to muster the two-thirds majorities needed to override presidential vetoes of Iraq War funding measures that contained timetables for withdrawing troops. Similarly, Republicans in the Senate used cloture-proof filibusters to prevent Democrats from scheduling up-or-down policy votes. By early December of the first year of the 110th Congress there had been no fewer than 72 motions by Democrats to stop Republican filibusters—more than in any previous year in Senate history. Most dealt with the Iraq War (Herszenhorn, December 2, 2007: wk 5). The president's refusal to compromise (Stolberg, December 14, 2007c: A23), the unity of congressional Republicans on filibusters and sustaining vetoes (Hulse and Pear, December 21, 2007: A22), occasional Democratic Party disunity (Rogers, December 13, 2007: A1), and the perceived success of the Iraq troop increase known as the "surge" (Deans, November 11, 2007: G3) all helped to frustrate the Democrats' efforts to "hold the president accountable," especially on the Iraq War. Political scientist Barbara Jordan (referenced in Krugman, December 21, 2009: A29) offers useful historical context. She finds that in the 1960s threatened or actual filibusters affected only 8 percent of major legislation. By the 1980s that had risen to 27 percent and after the Democratic takeover in 2006 it rose to 70 percent.

Public Guidance: The Clinton Impeachment

It will be instructive to look in some depth at the impeachment and acquittal of President William Jefferson Clinton, the first elected president and the only modern president to be impeached by the House and tried by the Senate. The story is flattering to neither the president nor the Congress. But it shows how Congress approached its only modern use of its ultimate accountability weapon in an era of divided government and intense partisanship. Especially important for the argument in this book, it also demonstrates that, when they are well briefed and their preferences are clear, the people can wield decisive influence on Congress's willingness to use its power to discipline the president.

Many congressional Republicans, eager to impeach President Clinton for perjury and obstruction of justice in the Monica Lewinsky affair, expected that the tawdriness of Clinton's "inappropriate" relationship with Lewinsky, a White House intern, would lead the public to agree that the president should be removed from office. Republicans expected that public revulsion would yield a net gain of Republican seats in the mid-term elections of 1998, which would imply approval of a move to impeach. When their party unexpectedly lost five seats to Democrats, Republican leaders in and outside Congress initially saw it as clear evidence that the public did not want the president removed from office. Subsequent opinion polls also showed strong majority opposition to impeachment or resignation, prima facie evidence that the public did not want the president ousted. Confronted with this evidence a number of moderate Republican Congressmen signaled that they would not vote for impeachment articles if they came to a vote in the House of Representatives. Few admitted it plainly, but the subtext was fear of electoral reprisal. As columnist William Safire concluded, "Most will base their vote against impeachment less on the rule of law than on a simple judgment: whether this helps or hurts them in the next election" (Safire, November 30, 1998: A27).

Nevertheless, conservative party leaders were not dissuaded. They increased the pressure on the moderates to support impeachment. Shortly thereafter the House Judiciary Committee voted out impeachment articles, and moderates began to reverse course, with most eventually voting to support impeachment in the House vote. What explains their change of heart? The reasons varied from one representative to the next. Some were irritated by Clinton's continuing refusal to admit that he had perjured himself. Others concluded that their constitutional duty required it. Still others shared the widespread belief that conviction of the president in the Senate remained unlikely due to continued public opposition. Perhaps most telling, however, was an argument slowly gaining currency among Republicans that their initial fear of certain electoral reprisal was probably not justified. For those in "safe" districts, the biggest political threat was from within their own party, in the primary elections (Calmes, December 16, 1998: A1). A great many Republican Congress men and women were from districts where a vote to impeach would be popular. Also reassuring, especially to those from competitive districts that had supported President Clinton in 1996, was the view that any political fallout from the inquiry would diminish to insignificance long before the next national election. After all, public opposition to impeachment, though remarkably stable and widespread, had not shown the kind of passion or intensity needed to keep it in play long enough to influence an election then nearly two years away. People were simply not invested enough in the outcome. Said one prominent Republican, "The attention span of Americans is 'Which movie is coming out next month?' and whether the quarterly report on their stock will change." In all probability, two years would be enough time for voters to be distracted by a succession of newly compelling concerns, including the fight to redefine the Republican Party and to capture its presidential nomination. Said a Republican campaign strategist in touch with House Republicans, "When we have a front-runner and a standard-bearer, the party will be cast in that person's image, not in the Judiciary Committee's image" (Berke, December 14, 1998: A1). That proved to be true. When public opinion came to seem less threatening to their future electoral prospects, congressional Republicans felt increasingly free to disregard it.

But if a vote to impeach was electorally safe for most Republican members of the House, a vote to convict could be dangerous for some Republicans in the Senate. The state of national public opinion was the most important reason why most observers thought the outcome of the Senate trial to be a foregone conclusion from the start. From October, 1998 to the February 12, 1999 Senate vote to acquit, public opinion was remarkably stable: strong majorities consistently opposed convicting Clinton. "Beyond the beltway … opinion polls (showed) that the public overwhelmingly believed Clinton had lied under oath and obstructed justice yet did not want him removed from office for it" (Baker and Dewar, February 13, 1999: A1). Per Article I of the Constitution, a two-thirds majority of those Senators present was required for a conviction on either of the two charges brought by the House. The vote closely followed party lines. For the perjury vote, 10 Republicans joined all 45 Democrats in voting not guilty. On the obstruction of justice charge, five Republicans joined all 45 Democrats in voting not guilty. The net effect of these Republican defections was to prevent even a majority, let alone the necessary two-thirds supermajority in support of removing Clinton from office. Five moderate Republicans from the Northeast voted against both counts. Three of the five—John Chafee of Rhode Island, James Jeffords of Vermont, and Olympia Snowe of Maine—were up for re-election in 2000 in states carried by Clinton in 1996.

In sum, the vote in both houses of Congress closely followed party lines with the numbers of Republicans in the House being sufficient to vote out two articles of impeachment, but the numbers in the Senate nowhere near enough for Republicans to muster the needed two-thirds majority to convict on those articles. The House had enough votes to muster the simple majorities required to impeach (perjury article, 228 to 206, 52 percent in favor; obstruction of justice article, 221 to 212, 51 percent in favor) because enough Republican members felt insulated from majority public sentiment outside their districts to cast favorable votes. But key Senate Republicans voted to acquit primarily because of the electoral incentive created by public opinion in their home states. Even without those partisan defections, Republicans would not have been able to recruit Democratic votes, arguably because congressional Democrats, some of whom were appalled at Clinton's behavior, were as sensitive to public opinion as their colleagues across the aisle.

Reflecting on the significance of these events, the constitutional scholar Richard Pious criticized the impact of public opinion on the Clinton impeachment trial as a move toward "the parliamentary system" of "confidence" or "no confidence" in the executive that we have "rejected throughout our constitutional history" and described this trend as "bad for the presidency and for the American people" (Pious, 2003: 264). But for good or ill, that argument had been trumped by the early 19th century democratization of the presidency described in the first chapter, which opened the door to the occasional display of the kind of public influence we see here. In this particular instance mass public influence arguably served as a healthy counterweight to elite partisanship. Because Congress was closely divided along party lines during the Clinton impeachment, voters (who were then and generally are far less ideologically driven than their representatives—see Fiorina, 2006) were well-positioned to temper what might otherwise have been a more purely partisan exercise.

Pious goes on to argue that "Clinton got off because the polls were with him and the polls were with him because the White House spinmeisters succeeded in winning over public opinion." A more plausible interpretation is that in this case at least, majority public opinion was not an artifact of White House or any other spin. The facts of the case were too widely and well known and too easily understood for public opinion to be so easily up for grabs. The mid-term election results and other polls taken before the debate moved to the Senate suggested that opposition to removal congealed on its own, and had two sources. First was the belief that Clinton's misbehavior, though deplorable, simply did not reach the level of an impeachable offense. Second was a judgment that the zeal displayed by House Republicans during the nationally televised impeachment hearings of the Judiciary Committee was excessive and unseemly, which further undermined the credibility of the case against Clinton.

How Congress Serves the PAS

Congress's unique role in the accountability system is to use its unmatched plenary power to discipline or encourage the president as needed in specific contexts. But it has shown that it cannot do this job as well by itself as it can with outside help—such as it got in the Clinton impeachment case, or could get from special PAS arrangements involving political guidance and cover provided by a similarly well-briefed public (see Chapter 6). The reasons outside help is needed were on display in the 109th and 110th Congresses. The day-to-day complexities of congressional sessions are too great to capture and focus authoritative public attention—the kind members cannot ignore—on any single decision, let alone every action. Without intense public scrutiny to influence how members interpret their partisan and electoral interests such incentives are more likely to push members in more narrowly partisan directions, away from what the public will would be if it were accessible. The examples above suggest that when the people are focused in an informed and sustained way Congress is more likely to be both responsive and effective.

Supreme Court

The Supreme Court is an authoritative and, within its relatively narrow province, a generally effective agent of accountability, with a distinctive approach to its responsibility for empowering and (less often) restraining presidents. Although it is generally regarded as above the political fray, it has never been beyond the reach of public opinion. For example, one recent book posits a virtual "marriage" between Court action and the views of ordinary citizens, suggesting that Court decisions and popular sentiment, while not always in synch, "come into line with one another over time" (Friedman, 2009).

Following the emergence of the doctrine of judicial review (*Marbury v. Madison, 1803*) the Court has held presidents to account by approving or disallowing specific assertions of presidential power on constitutional grounds (Hall, 2005: 536). The criteria behind Court decisions touching presidential power are *constitutional interpretations*, necessitated by (among other things) the brevity and vagueness of the language in Article II. As a body with no coercive power to enforce and no electoral mandate to justify its sometimes bitterly resented decisions the Court has had to evolve a sophisticated strategy for building and sustaining its own legitimacy and influence. The enhanced legitimacy that has resulted from its record of generally deft positioning and performance has enabled the Court to have even its contentious decisions accepted as legitimate for most of American history.

Recent Accountability Cases

Historically, particularly in the national security arena, the Supreme Court has encouraged presidents more than it has restrained them (Matheson, 2009: 79). For example, it has endorsed the controversial idea that the president is the "sole organ" in foreign affairs (Justice Sutherland in the 1936 *Curtiss–Wright* case). And it has at least indirectly validated the idea that the president has "inherent power" to do what is necessary to resolve emergencies (in the 1952 *Youngstown* case the majority disallowed Truman's seizure of the steel mills, but accepted, to varying degrees in different concurring opinions, Truman's claim of inherent unstated constitutional power to act in emergencies).

The mixed signals of *Youngstown* aside, judicial deference to the executive has been the norm in time of war. This makes four recent Supreme Court decisions striking down Bush Administration power assertions a departure from the custom, dating from the 1950s, of using procedural dodges to avoid judgment. According to presidential constitutionalism expert Scott Matheson, it also illustrates how the Court may embolden another accountability agent: the Congress. Matheson argues that for much of the Bush presidency Congress was passive in the face of executive power claims. But the Court set limits and the executive "retreated in the face of judicial review" which helped to encourage the "welcome participation of a coordinate branch" in the form of congressional pushback after the Democrats assumed control in 2006 (Matheson, 2009: 88, 89). These four cases, plus a recent lower court case of similar import, side against the president by tilting toward civil liberties rather than national security.

In *Hamdan v. Rumsfeld* (2006) the Supreme Court, by a 5–3 margin, repudiated the administration's plan to put Guantanamo detainees on trial before military commissions, saying that they were not authorized by federal statute and violated international law (Greenhouse, June 30, 2006: A1). Two other features of the majority decision cut against the administration's understanding of its powers. The Court ruled against the administration's argument that the congressional authorization for the use of military force passed shortly after the September 11, 2001 attacks on the World Trade Center could be interpreted to authorize the military commissions. This ruling put in jeopardy the administration's argument that the same authorization might legitimize its domestic wiretapping program (see below). The Court also ruled that a provision of the Geneva Conventions known as Common Article 3 applies to Guantanamo detainees and is enforceable in federal courts. Article 3 requires humane treatment of captured combatants and prohibits trials except by "a regularly constituted court affording all the judicial guarantees which are recognized as indispensable by civilized people" (quoted in Greenhouse, June 30, 2006: A1).

In response to the ruling that the military commissions were not authorized by federal statute, Congress passed the Military Commissions Act of 2006. Signed into law by President Bush shortly after its passage, the Act established rules for trying detainees before special military tribunals, narrowed the Geneva protections available to detainees, and dismissed several hundred detainee lawsuits from the federal courts, replacing habeas corpus review with a more limited and streamlined process. This law also rejected the high court's view in *Rasul v. Bush* (2004) that Guantanamo detainees may file habeas corpus challenges in U.S. courts. And it tested a proposition set out in *Hamdi v. Rumsfeld* (2004) which held that U.S. citizen-detainees accused of being enemy combatants must be able to examine the factual basis for detention and be given a fair opportunity to rebut the government's allegations before a neutral decision maker. Granting of habeas corpus rights would meet this standard. But the opinion leaves open the possibility that the standard might also be met by an "appropriately authorized and properly constituted military tribunal." The 2006 Military Commissions Act attempted to meet the standard with the "limited and more streamlined process" noted above (Richey, October 17, 2006: 1). But in a 5–4 2008 decision, *Boumediene v. Bush*, the Court held that the 2006 Military Commission Act cannot deny full habeas corpus rights to Guantanamo detainees because the procedures it established were not an adequate substitute (Greenhouse, June 13, 2008: A1).

Another liberty versus security ruling in August 2006, this one by federal district court judge Anna Diggs Taylor in response to a lawsuit filed by the American Civil Liberties Union, deserves mention. Judge Taylor ruled that the National Security Agency's program to wiretap the international communications of some Americans without a court warrant, secretly approved by President Bush shortly after the 9/11 attacks, violated the Fourth Amendment to the Constitution prohibiting unreasonable searches and seizures, and also the 1978 Foreign Intelligence Surveillance Act (FISA) which requires warrants from a secret court for intelligence wiretaps involving people in the United States.

The principled political disagreement over this issue (and the detainee cases) is well illustrated by the contrasting views expressed immediately after the Taylor decision on the leading editorial pages of liberal and conservative America: the *New York Times* and the *Wall Street Journal*. These views well capture the essential differences that have divided both the Supreme Court (split decisions) and opposition elite opinion on the scope of presidential power. Said the *Times*: "The ruling eviscerated the absurd notion that ... the Congress authorized Mr. Bush to do whatever he thinks is necessary when it authorized the invasion of Afghanistan ... [this judge has] reasserted the rule of law over a lawless administration ... " (Ruling for the Law, August 18, 2006: A18). Said the *Journal*:

> In this [terror war] environment monitoring the communications of our enemies is neither a luxury nor some sinister plot to chill domestic dissent. It is a matter of life and death ... The real nub of this dispute is the Constitution's idea of "inherent powers" ... the Constitution vests the bulk of the war-making power with the President. It did so, as the Founders explained in the Federalist Papers, for reasons of energy, dispatch, secrecy and accountability ... Judge Taylor can write her opinion and pose for the cameras—and no one can hold her accountable for any Americans who might die as a result.
>
> *(President Taylor, August 18, 2006: A18)*

Why did the Court abandon its traditional deference to the executive at war in these cases? It did so because the Bush Administration has been among the most aggressive in history in its attempts to expand presidential power at the expense of individual liberties (Matheson, 2009: 6). Even some conservative justices had doubts about Bush arguments in particular cases (Bravin, June 26, 2008: A10). Nevertheless, the fundamental, principled disagreement between liberal judges seeking to protect individual liberties and conservative judges who generally favor granting more deference and flexibility to the president in wartime is likely to continue.

But according to some analysts, this disagreement extends beyond principle and beyond presidential power. If they are right, it points to dysfunctions that, while potentially correctible, constitute a latent threat to Court legitimacy.

Potential Dysfunction

A threat to the Court's legitimacy is posed by decisions perceived as unprincipled. The Court's ever-present need to be wary of tarnishing its hard-won standing is illustrated by the debate over the legitimacy of its 5–4 decision in *Bush v. Gore* (2000) which effectively awarded the presidency to George W. Bush. Critics argued that the conservative Court majority violated *stare decisis* (the doctrine that lower courts should generally let themselves be guided by relevant high court decisions in similar cases) by stipulating in its majority opinion that its ruling was "limited to the present circumstances" and could not be cited as precedent. The substantive holding on the facts before the Court was that "the recount was unacceptable because the standards for vote counting varied from county to county." This made good sense. But by disallowing the application of this sensible principle to similar disputes across the country, where its relevance was patent, the Court majority reinforced the impression that the purpose of its decision was not to promote uniform vote-counting standards in the service of democratic values, but merely to anoint its preferred candidate, George W. Bush as president, which the substantive holding happened to justify (Cohen, August 15, 2006: A22). This controversial decision led many to criticize the Court for a tilt toward partisanship. Evidence of polarization on the Supreme Court bench also comes from studies showing that since 1990, conservative and liberal Justices have tended to appoint ideologically like-minded law clerks, who go on to work for ideologically like-minded law firms, law schools, and presidential administrations (Liptak, December 22, 2009: A16). It may seem unsurprising that like-minded lawyers in all these institutions would use their legal skills to promote their shared ideological priorities. But this practice is inconsistent with the idea that the Supreme Court responds only to concerns grounded in the rule of law rather than to the Justices' political or ideological preferences.

Recent books by two prominent scholars highlight the Court's vulnerability to charges of politicization. Such charges are currently leveled by liberal critics but have frequently been made in the past by conservative critics. The first book interprets the history of the Court to show that with the exception of the Warren era, it has been a "choke-point for progressive reform," its members "unelected and unac-countable politicians in robes" most often protective of the interests of powerful elites (Burns, 2009). Similarly, Lucas Powe (2009) accuses the Court of excessive responsiveness to electoral sentiment (example: Rehnquist Court rejections, driven by the 1994–2006 Republican ascendancy, of "positive, progressive, legislation" aimed at improving society). Such critiques show that the Court's legitimacy, which depends in great measure on sustaining a reputation for impartiality and for standing above the political fray, cannot be taken for granted. The Justices now, for the first time in half a century, display perfect alignment between their partisan affiliations and their ideological predispositions (Liptak, February 6, 2011: wk 3). The 5–4 decisions in cases like *Citizens United* in 2010, which allowed unlimited corporate spending in elections, or a potential 5–4 conservative majority rejection of the Obama health care legislation (unpredictable at this writing) bid to keep questions about the Court's impartiality alive.

Intrinsic Limitations

Finally, the Court's presidential accountability powers are circumscribed, by Con-stitution and tradition, in ways the Congress's powers are not. As a body that does not issue advisory opinions, the Court may not prospectively authorize presidential freedoms or dictate presidential limits. It may only *react* to presidential actions already taken and brought before it by someone with standing to sue in a legal proceeding based on discrete, typically narrow questions. For example, no federal court would be likely to accept a case framed to challenge a broad question like the president's authority to initiate war. The barriers would include separation of powers (wars are the province of Congress and the president), the question of who would have the standing to sue, the justiciability of such a broad question, and the Supreme Court's tradition of avoiding "political" questions.

How the Court Serves the PAS

The Court's decisions are its major accountability "product." It hasn't always been so (see, for example, President Andrew Jackson's dismissive treatment of the Court's 1832 decision in *Worcester v. Georgia*). But contemporary Court decisions can change the behavior of sitting presidents, as with the Bush detainee cases and the 1974 Watergate case, *United States v. Nixon*. And when the majority verdict in a case becomes clear and undisputed judicial precedent, future presidents are constrained or empowered unless and until the decision is overruled.

Justice Robert H. Jackson's concurring opinion in the 1952 *Youngstown* case, which has been described as "the leading Supreme Court guidance on presidential powers" (Matheson, 2009: 80), is of particular importance to the PAS. This opinion asserts that presidential powers are not fixed but fluctuate depending on their disjunction or conjunction with those of Congress. When the president is implementing congressional will, executive power is at its maximum. When the president acts without clear congressional guidance, he is acting on his Article II powers alone. But when the president defies implicit or explicit congressional directives presidential powers are at their lowest ebb. Jackson's formula also invites a durable PAS coalition by effectively aligning the Court with Congress as a guardian of the latter's will.

The Jackson opinion shows that the Court has a pedagogical potential as well as a decision function. The opinion offers a blueprint of use to accountability agents and presidents alike; a constitutional rationale for when presidents are to be encouraged and when restrained. It and Lincoln's doctrine of necessity are building blocks for the nascent PAS lore of guiding principles for the balancing of encouragement and restraint.

Unofficial Agents

Table 3.2 anticipates the analysis of the four unofficial agents of accountability. Identified in successive rows of the matrix are the potential influences, dysfunctions, and the more fundamental limitations of the four major unofficial agents of accountability, identified in the columns (please refer to Chapter 2 endnote 1).

Public Opinion

Public opinion as expressed through votes in congressional elections (and through polls that anticipate the results of such voting) is a force for accountability because it can strengthen or break a president's hold on his congressional party and affirm or change the partisan control of Congress. A president's co-partisans in Congress will consider the implications of supporting or opposing the president's initiatives for their own re-election prospects. A public supportive of the president and his policies encourages a similar congressional stance, which rewards the president. But the reverse is also true. For example, poll-tested public unhappiness with his performance not only cost President Bush policy support in the run-up to the 2006 mid-term elections but control of Congress in their aftermath. Exit polls showed that it was adverse public judgment of the president's performance in Iraq and his handling of the economy that helped make it happen (Zeleny and Thee, November 8, 2006: A8). Some 37 percent of those asked in exit poll interviews said that one reason for their vote was to "express opposition to George W. Bush." Voter dissatisfaction with Iraq (with 57 percent disapproving and 68 percent saying Iraq was important to their vote) and with the economy (fully 98 percent called it important to their vote) was clearly blamed on the president.

The 2010 mid-terms, which yielded an historic 60+ seat loss for Democrats in the House of Representatives, led President Barack Obama to admit ruefully that he and his party had "taken a shellacking." The exit polls reported that 37 percent said one reason for their vote was "to express opposition to Barack Obama" and 55 percent disapproved of his performance as president. Fully 63 percent said the most important problem was the economy, and 52 percent said they thought the president's policies "hurt the country." But while most voters were not enamored of either Obama's policies or his job performance, more blamed Wall Street than the president for the economic downturn (CBS News.com, 2010, Exit Poll for House Race, online).

The year 2010 saw the 39th mid-term election between Democrats versus Republicans since these parties first faced off in the 1850s. Twenty of the 39 featured repudiations of the president and his party (Sabato, November 4, 2010b, online). Since World War II, the House of Representatives has flipped parties on seven occasions: 1946, 1948, 1952, 1954, 1994, 2006, and 2010 (Sabato, September 2, 2010a, online). The mid-term election fortunes of Bill Clinton (1994), George W. Bush (2006), and Barack Obama (2010) are only the most recent demonstrations of the fact that a voting public spontaneously moved by its reaction to a president's performance can use a mid-term election to punish that president and potentially to alter the direction of national policy. Far less often, a mid-term election result may reward the president, as the 2002 elections rewarded President Bush with rare gains in Republican Party seats in Congress.

Dysfunction

About half the time, however, mid-term results are not obvious punishments or rewards, but outcomes whose implications for the president are inconsequential or unclear. Departures from relative apathy require significant levels of voter consensus and mobilization. This highlights a common dysfunction of public opinion from the standpoint of the PAS: it is often not unified or focused enough to use congressional elections, or public opinion polls, to affect the president's incentives. The reason, as noted in Chapter 2, is that most citizens are not well-socialized to the accountability task.

Intrinsic Limitation

The intrinsic limitation is institutional. The people lack established coordination mechanisms with legitimacy comparable to elections for targeting their influence outside of elections. Absent special mechanisms like specially designed opinion surveys or the policy trial proposal described in Chapter 6, this limits application of citizens' extraordinary potential to influence presidents and Congress to instances of spontaneous coordination.

How Public Opinion Could Better Serve the PAS

There are several high-profile examples of spontaneous coordination. For one, pervasive public unhappiness with U.S. experience in World War I pushed Congress to pass the Neutrality Acts of 1935 and 1937, restricting the president's ability to direct military aid to nations engaged in war (Howell and Pevehouse, 2007: 11). For another, widespread public alarm over the 1957 launch of Sputnik by the Soviet Union forced President Eisenhower and the Congress into a variety of new science, technology, and military spending, as well as passage of the National Defense Education Act (Pach and Richardson, 1991: 170–78). Public opinion has also been highly influential in a variety of high-profile congressional proceedings, such as the Army–McCarthy hearings, the McCarthy censure, the Irvin Committee hearings on Watergate, and the Clinton impeachment and Senate trial. Although Richard Nixon blamed his decision to resign on the loss of political support in Congress (Black, 2007: 982), adverse public reaction to Watergate directly affected both Congress and the president. These examples show that public opinion has been spontaneously decisive. But mechanisms for routine authoritative mobilization of opinion other than elections do not yet exist.

There are non-electoral coordination models such as opinion polling and issue referenda, though in their current forms they suffer from flaws that often undermine their credibility as expressions of the public will. Such flaws can be fixed but this alone would not make them authoritative. That vital status is attainable only when public opinion is deployed in a way that keeps its normative significance alive despite a non-electoral application. That would be most likely to develop around recurring issues, like wars of choice. Both citizens and elites would come to know that prospective wars would, whenever the need arose, routinely elicit a deliberative congressional process (i.e., a televised briefing of the public on the pros and cons) followed by poll-tested public judgment that both would view as authoritative. How it can work is described in Chapter 6.

News Media

The unique function of the news media in the PAS is to *enable other accountability agents with information*, without which there can be no accountability. Reporters seek and disclose evidence of presidential misbehavior and achievement so that other agents may use it to punish and discourage the first but also to encourage and reward the second. Particularly since the "blood feud" of investigative reporter Jack Anderson and President Richard Nixon (Feldstein, 2010), followed by the Watergate scandal of the early 1970s, presidents have attracted the attention of aggressive investigative reporters who work more diligently to find and disseminate evidence of presidential incompetence and wrongdoing than of good performance.

The knowledge that they are being watched in ways that can lead to adverse publicity or worse gives most elected officials incentive to avoid disapproved behavior but also creates an incentive to act strategically to avoid unfavorable coverage (Arnold, 2004). Presidents readily use all available tools whether what is protected is merely embarrassing or potentially illegal or unconstitutional. *Secrecy is the ultimate antidote to presidential accountability*. Presidents use it when possible and respond with "spin" (e.g., less damaging reinterpretations of unfavorable news) when it is not (Table 2.1). To penetrate a presidential veil of secrecy is not easy. The success of Woodward and Bernstein has driven all subsequent presidents to tighten their control over information (Woodward, 1999).[2]

The Media Challenge

In response to this clamp-down on access to information, reporters can only try to find knowledgeable inside sources and persuade them to talk. Reporters may also have to persuade editors to let them continue digging before the news payoff is clear, as Woodward and Bornstein did. Then they must assemble and interpret what is often a morass of confusing and conflicting interview testimony and other evidence. If the information is complex, as it was in the Watergate case, it can take time to piece the story together so that the big picture comes into focus in a meaningful way. To learn enough to raise serious questions about the propriety of a president's behavior, then, is rarely an easy task. But by finding and disclosing such information, news organizations make it possible to discipline miscreant presidents like Richard M. Nixon.

Dysfunctions

Even when reporters do get a lead on a story, things can go awry. For example, they may simply get it wrong (e.g., the meaning of the 1968 Tet Offensive during the Vietnam War, which misportrayed as a military failure what was in fact a victory (Woods, 2006: 824)). Sometimes reporters and editors fail to provide enough coverage of an important story. This occurred in connection with the 1989 Savings and Loan Bailout, made necessary by irresponsible federal deregulation of that industry accompanied by increased federal guarantees against financial failure. The result was a multi-billion dollar scandal that cried out for accountability but that received too little media coverage or explanation to convey to the public the magnitude or the importance of what was happening and who in the Reagan Administration was responsible (Greene, 2000: 79–83).

Intrinsic Limitations

If a president succeeds in imposing a veil of secrecy, as many have, reporters will be denied any opportunity to cover a story with potentially far-reaching implications for long-term U.S. interests. An important example was the 1953 overthrow, by the Eisenhower Administration using the CIA, of the democratically elected government of Iranian Prime Minister Mohammad Mossadegh. The reasons included Iranian nationalization of the British-owned oil industry and the alleged communist sympathies of the Mossadegh government. According to Eisenhower biographer Stephen Ambrose: "The methods used were immoral, if not illegal, and a dangerous precedent had been set. The CIA offered the president a quick fix for his foreign problems. It was there to do his bidding; it freed him from having to persuade Congress, or the parties, or the public." The CIA was an asset that greatly extended the President's powers—"at the expense of also greatly extending the risks of his getting into deep trouble" (Ambrose, 1990: 333). As Stephen Kinzer notes, the American press at the time played an important supporting role in the coup (although they were carefully kept from any knowledge that the United States was the source of the coup) by erroneously portraying Mossadegh as a communist pawn (Kinzer, 2006: 124). Since 1953 was near the height of the Cold War, it is not a certainty that press disclosure of the coup at the time would have gotten Eisenhower into trouble. Yet prior disclosure might have prevented an action that has poisoned U.S.–Iranian relations from that day to this.

In the end, the press cannot know and report everything the president does. This keeps an uncertain but probably high percentage of important performance episodes off the accountability docket.

The Political Opposition

All presidents face organized opposition from the rival political party in elections, in Congress, and in the marketplace of ideas. No political system can be authentically democratic without such opposition (Heims, 2004). The PAS relies on it to ensure vigorous policy debates, to flag broken promises, to criticize policy mistakes and their consequences, and to appraise competence across the range of presidential activities. By researching and trumpeting a president's real and perceived missteps, the opposition party makes voters aware of potential accountability issues. This spurs the incumbent to perform well and avoid mistakes because the opposition offers not just criticism but alternative presidents and policies. This is of particular value to voters because it enables them to use the franchise not only to choose presidents but to change the direction of the government when performance is lacking (Schattschneider, 1942; American Political Science Association, 1950).

The Litmus Test

The PAS works best when an opposition party's criticism is credible enough to be taken seriously by both president and citizens. This is most likely to occur when the rival party is known to be willing to bargain with the president to get compromise solutions to national problems. According to Brownstein, oppositions were credible and influential from Franklin D. Roosevelt's second term through the presidencies of Truman, Eisenhower, Kennedy, and Johnson until his 1964 landslide election victory, a period that Brownstein calls "the age of bargaining" (Brownstein, 2007: 58).

Dysfunctions

The willingness to bargain for solutions allays the impression of implacable bias against the president, which opposition parties have before and currently nurture, and which undermines their usefulness as agents of accountability. Dysfunctions arise not only when (as illustrated in the discussion of Congress) partisans elevate "team" loyalty above institutional responsibilities, but also when they elevate political victory above achieving solutions to national problems. Thus, Republicans sabotaged President Clinton's 1993 health care reform proposal rather than bargain to improve it (Buchanan, 2004b: 108) and Democrats returned the favor by refusing to bargain with President Bush on Social Security reform in 2005 (Brownstein, 2007: 344). Similarly, Republicans consistently refused to support any of President Obama's legislative agenda, finding themselves labeled "the party of No." The strategy began in the House of Representatives early in the Obama presidency when House Republican Whip Eric Cantor of Virginia was able to deny President Obama a single vote on his stimulus bill (Nagourney, February 15, 2009: 1). It persisted until the "lame duck" session of Congress following the 2010 mid-term election, during which a compromise tax bill that preserved the Bush tax cuts for high-income earners and an arms control treaty with Russia supported by most Republican foreign policy experts were passed with bipartisan votes. But upon the arrival of the new Republican majority in the House in January of 2011, leaders announced plans to attempt a repeal of the president's signature health care reform bill. Other examples ensued, but these are sufficient to illustrate the hyper-partisan atmosphere that took root early in the Clinton Administration and has grown more intense ever since.

Intrinsic Limitations

The fact that there have been significant periods of bargaining between presidents and opposition parties suggests that destructive partisanship can sometimes be superseded (Fiorina, 2006; Brownstein, 2007). What is intrinsic, however, is the *perennial threat to fair-mindedness that is posed by the opposition's enduring primary incentive, which is to replace the president with one of its own.* This threat is epitomized by the now-famous comment, made by Senate Republican Leader Mitch McConnell of Kentucky in an interview with *National Journal* in October of 2010. McConnell said: "The single most important thing we want to achieve is for President Obama to be a one-term president."

This is the intrinsic limitation of partisanship as the mode of organizing the government. It makes it permanently tempting (if not always feasible) to withhold cooperation and to exaggerate the out-party critique of the incumbent. His conviction that this incentive cannot be permanently transcended is why first President George Washington spoke against the legitimacy of "factions" in the early republic. By their very nature factions undermine the search by virtuous leaders for the common good. Proto-parties emerged in America from intense disagreements between the ruling Federalists and the opposition Democratic-Republicans over the proper scope of the federal government. But they soon morphed into career development vehicles for politicians. By one influential account parties have thrived not because they strengthened accountability or clarified choices for voters but because they help reduce the problems politicians face in their efforts to win and hold office in the face of vigorous competition (Aldrich, 1995: 10–27).

History

If the incentive of first-term presidents is re-election, the concern of most re-elected presidents will be their legacy. Both motives attract people of great ambition to the presidency. As Alexander Hamilton observed in Federalist 72, "The love of fame, the ruling passion of the noblest minds, will prompt a man to plan and undertake extensive and arduous enterprises for the public benefit." Presidents know that they will be judged by history and aspire to be judged favorably. They also know that the basis for the reputations of the most highly ranked presidents— George Washington, Abraham Lincoln, and Franklin D. Roosevelt—is achievements of lasting value gained through bold leadership that solved the major problems of their times. This legacy has inspired many subsequent presidents to aim high: history's most worthy positive incentive. History also offers other models of importance to particular presidents. Richard Nixon, for example, admired Woodrow Wilson as a man of thought and action because that is how he wanted to see himself (Reeves, 2001: 27). Bush the elder is said to have taken heart from Truman's unlikely 1948 election in the face of his own long odds in 1992. These models are harmless. But others, whose reputations were controversial in office but sharply improved thereafter (e.g., Washington, Lincoln, and Truman) invite the dismissal of contemporary criticism in favor of the president trusting his own judgment. Washington, Lincoln, and Truman did exactly that. Each made decidedly unpopular decisions during his presidency that inflamed critics but that ultimately did no lasting damage to their legacies.

Potential Dysfunction

The anticipated judgment of history is a component of the PAS whose impact is especially sensitive to the chief executive's aspirations and reactions to his particular situation. To be sure, the personal characteristics of the people who hold this office affect how they interpret all the PAS incentives they perceive. But individuality can be especially important in this context. For example, to a beleaguered president who wants to believe his own unpopular choices were right, these historical models of resoluteness in the face of criticism can be very reassuring. They offer the additional hope of a reputation for steely resolve in the face of sustained public and congressional disapproval. In an interview on the fifth anniversary of the invasion of Iraq, Vice President Richard Cheney articulated this view.

> Think about what would have happened if Abraham Lincoln had paid attention to polls, if they had had polls during the Civil War. He never would have succeeded if he hadn't had a clear objective, a vision for where he wanted to go, and he was willing to withstand the slings and arrows of the political wars in order to get there. And this President has been very courageous, very consistent, very determined to continue down the course we were on and to achieve our objective.
>
> *(ABC News, March 19, 2008)*

Cheney refers, of course, to President George W. Bush. The circumstances that allowed Bush not only to defy but to trump his Iraq War critics are rare in presidential history: a re-elected president with no further electoral incentive facing a Congress narrowly controlled by the opposition party but a party without sufficient votes to override most vetoes or to find the 60 votes needed to force changes to his policy. Given these advantages, a determined president temperamentally able to endure sustained and strident opposition (LBJ found such criticism hard to bear; Bush seemingly did not) is in a position to hold his ground. As a result, the standoff between President Bush and the Democratic Congress continued through his last day in office, leaving his Iraq policy firmly in place.

The likelihood is that some future presidents will do as Bush did: emulate presidents like George Washington. They will do so precisely because, as President Bush put it, President Washington's "will was unbreakable" (Stolberg, February 20, 2007a: A16) and that is how they want history to see them.

It is possible that such a president will turn out to be right in the eyes of history, and come to be seen as courageous rather than merely stubborn by later generations. This possibility was famously recognized by Abraham Lincoln. But Lincoln also said that without good judgment, an "indomitable will" can be "nothing better than useless obstinacy" (quoted in Miller, 2008: 60). Behavioral research shows that all people, presumably including those more prone to self-correction than Bush (a man whose stated belief is that "as a leader you can never admit a mistake," and who professed to rely on gut instinct rather than policy analysis (Perret, 2007: 340)), are vulnerable to biased thinking (e.g., stereotyping, overconfidence, resistance to correction and confirmation bias; see Nickerson, 1998: 175; Kuklinski and Quirk, 2000: 169). Further, such biases are very likely to be exacerbated by the deferential treatment that is routine for presidents, denying them reliable corrective feedback (Buchanan, 1978). Bush may be an extreme case, but the point remains: the examples of defiant past presidents are standing invitations to any incumbent to discount contemporary critics (who can include his own advisors) in favor of trusting his own judgment (potentially succumbing to his own uncorrected biases) in hope of eventual vindication.

Intrinsic Limitation

A president free to ignore Congress, public opinion, and "the effective use of information and advice" inside the White House (George, 1980) is accountable only to history. The possibility that history may but also may *not* vindicate such a president is why Table 3.2 identifies the chance of an "ill-fated" identification with role models as a potential dysfunction within the accountability system. But whether any particular president succumbs to this temptation or not, the incentive to emulate defiant predecessors is also identified in Table 3.2 as an intrinsic problem because absent drastic system redesign it is not possible to eliminate the chance that when such a choice is made by some future president it will result in damage to the national interest.

Ironically, then, the lure of historical acclaim is at once the most important inspiration for extraordinary presidential achievement yet also the least amenable under current constitutional arrangements to any sort of regulation, even by a conscious PAS. It is potentially a dangerous incentive because it has inspired some incumbents to bend or break rules and defy critics, sometimes destabilizing the constitutional balance of power in the process. It may do so again.

Conclusion

The seven agents as they are now (i.e., before any suggestion that they cooperate) were themselves held to account in this chapter. Their dysfunctions and limitations (Tables 3.1 and 3.2) show clearly why the sanctions in Chapter 2, Table 2.1 are not always applied in ways that motivate acceptable presidential performance. Elections are disturbingly blunt instruments for motivating presidents. The Congress will not use its plenary power without political cover. The Court cannot speak unless spoken to and may be finding it more difficult to resist its own partisan impulses. Public opinion is often unpredictable; not always focused enough to be a consequential presidential incentive in or outside elections. The news media can report only what it knows or notices, and sometimes gets the story wrong. The political opposition often undermines its own credibility by refusing to compromise. And the lure of historical acclaim may elicit mere obstinacy as readily as it evokes great achievement.

Smoothing all these rough edges to bring presidential incentives into a consistently useful pattern in support of the guidelines outlined earlier is, in this light, a daunting project. Nevertheless an approach to doing so is sketched in Chapter 5.

We turn next to case studies of three presidential wars of choice. Together they supply a detailed description of the costs associated with the most important problem now facing the unconscious PAS: the constitutionally destabilizing tradition of uncheckable presidential war making. As we will see, this tradition is in large part a consequence of the dysfunctions and limitations of the agents—particularly their inability in isolation from one another to devise ways to compensate for their weaknesses in order to impose discipline and restraint on presidents.

4

PRESIDENTIAL WARS OF CHOICE[1]

There are many examples of questionable presidential actions made possible by the gaps in the complex American system for holding presidents to account. But here I concentrate on what has emerged since World War II as the most pressing: inadequate prospective vetting of presidential wars of choice by Congress and the American people.

By "wars of choice" I mean conflicts initiated by presidents against nations that had not attacked the United States but conflicts that were portrayed as both necessary and urgent nonetheless. The high costs and unpredictable consequences of any war, the lack of authentic opportunities for Congress or public opinion to influence the decision for war in the three cases discussed below, plus the emergence of majority popular and congressional dissatisfaction with the progress and results of those particular wars (normative democratic judgments made by the American people and their representatives that are neither endorsed nor opposed for purposes of this analysis) are among the reasons why they are reasonably considered the most important problem facing the network of formal and informal checks and balances that make up the presidential accountability system.

There have been many unprovoked presidential military initiatives (Kinzer, 2006). But the Korean, Vietnam, and Iraq Wars—the largest and most important in the modern era—are the examples in focus here.

Each was initiated by a president who justified his action as a response to a pressing threat to the national interest requiring prompt action, giving the impression that there was little time for sober reflection by Congress or the public at these key moments of choice. Each also reflected a departure from the norms observed by the most authoritative war president, other than Abraham Lincoln, in American history: President Franklin D. Roosevelt during World War II. Ten years after Roosevelt told France that only Congress could make military commitments,

President Truman sent troops to Korea without consulting Congress (Schlesinger, 2004: 53). President Johnson and both Presidents Bush, with that precedent in mind, asserted the power to do the same, though each sought (and, in the tense atmosphere each helped to create, readily got) congressional resolutions authorizing them to use force. And with the partial exception of the Gulf War (see Perret, 2007 for a contrary view) each war proved costly in terms of American blood, treasure, and credibility, leading to recriminations against each of these presidents for what, in retrospect, came to seem (to many citizens and analysts) to be ill-considered and ill-advised wars. Contemporary analysts of global affairs often perceive a decline of American influence in the world and attribute it in part to such "misuse" of presidential power (e.g., Brzezinski, 2007).

Why do presidents start major wars? In part because, beginning with James Madison in 1811 and James K. Polk in 1846, they have discovered that they can; and also because they became convinced that in context it served some vital national purpose to do so. There has always been significant principled opposition. For example, in 1847 newly elected congressman Abraham Lincoln (who would later as president go to great lengths to avoid being the initiator of the Civil War) expressed a "clear-cut position against President Polk's presidentially initiated war, and against such a war of choice as an instrument of state policy" saying that it had been "unconstitutionally and unnecessarily" started by the president (Miller, 2008: 108). Nevertheless, Madison and Polk in the 19th century, Truman and Johnson in the 20th, and Bush-II in the 21st each initiated a major war because they were convinced that it was the right thing to do in context.

The cases of Korea, Vietnam, and Iraq, which are reviewed below, display three important commonalities. First, *none was preceded by what experts would regard as sufficiently systematic or rigorous analysis of the policy alternatives before deciding for war.* This was and is possible because presidential discretion in this area is unlimited (Schlesinger, 1973; Schlesinger, March 18, 2005; Yoo, 2009; Wills, 2010). To be sure, disciplined choice procedures cannot guarantee an outcome that will be perceived as successful in the long run by Congress and the American people. But if there is utility in careful analysis, they can improve the odds of such an outcome. As matters stand, decision procedures will be disciplined if and only if the president insists. None of these presidents insisted. Moreover, in all three cases Congress deferred to, or authorized, presidential initiation of military action despite the lack of explicit provocation (e.g., an attack on the United States or some other durably convincing justification) and without a clear presidential vision of the objective backed by well-specified operational plans that could stand the test of time. This is a tradition that leaves presidents unsupervised at a critical stage.

The second commonality, potentially a consequence of the first, is that *all three of these wars came to be perceived as unsuccessful and/or unnecessary and/or not worth the cost by popular and congressional majorities.* Put another way, the mounting costs in blood, treasure, and international credibility did not strike most Americans as justified by the perceived level of success of these initiatives. In retrospect, the record suggests that each president overinterpreted and oversold the provocations, to one degree or another, as many historians and political scientists have subsequently argued about each conflict.

Third, *the loss of majority popular support well before the conclusion to each of these conflicts sparked enduring and bitter partisan and nonpartisan mass and elite recrimination against the decision for war.* The presidencies of Harry S. Truman, Lyndon B. Johnson, and George W. Bush each sustained massive political damage. In the case of Vietnam, which is (to date) the most obvious example, the backlash of revulsion delegitimized not only the president but the office (cf., the influence among political journalists and academic elites of Arthur Schlesinger Jr.'s "Imperial Presidency" argument (Schlesinger, 1973); see also Rudalevige (2006), *The New Imperial Presidency*, written in response to the George W. Bush administration). Another cost to success was exacted at the bargaining table. In his review of Gideon Rose's 2010 book on how wars come to an end, David Sanger (November 7, 2010: br41) observes that "(i)t was in Vietnam that Washington learned a crucial lesson of Korea—namely, that once the American public has abandoned a war effort, winning a good settlement is just about impossible."

The costs to the polity in lives, resources, lost opportunities, international prestige, trust in government, and domestic discord posed by such wars explain why the need for *prospective accountability* deserves more explicit attention than it has yet received. In the Constitution, Article I's stipulation that it is the Congress, not the president, that declares war implies that the national legislature has a constitutional claim on prospective control as well as merely retrospective judgment of how well the president prosecutes wars that Congress authorizes. Prospective accountability for a potential presidential initiation of an unprovoked war is defined here as unprecedentedly authoritative and rigorous pre-invasion "peer-review" for presidents bent on elective war—to be undertaken only when military action can safely be deferred.

I will argue in Chapter 6 that prospective accountability has the potential to yield two important benefits, rooted in shared as against exclusively presidential responsibility for war. It can increase the chance of setting policy (in particular the choice for or against war) that will stand the test of time (i.e., be judged as acceptable to authoritative majorities in retrospect); and it can increase the chance that blame for perceived failure, always possible under the best of circumstances, will be more widely shared, and thus less likely to yield delegitimizing domestic recrimination and discord.

Three Wars of Choice

The case summaries that follow serve two purposes. The first is to illustrate the commonalities noted above. The second is to portray the complexities and challenges that such wars pose for a prospective accountability remedy. The cases show that the national political climate at the time a choice for war is made (and/or the dominant position of the president) can easily disable or prevent the use of "systematic and rigorous review of policy options" advocated by presidential decision-making scholars such as Burke and Greenstein (1991: 3). That is why I argue (here and again later) that measures like the recently proposed "War Powers Consultation Act of 2009" (National War Powers Commission, July 8, 2008), which rely on voluntary presidential compliance, are inadequate. To effectively address this problem will—alas!—require far stronger medicine.

Korea

Korea is the first modern example of a major elective presidential war, made possible because in that highly charged atmosphere neither Congress nor the American people had an opportunity to object (not that they would have objected in this case) at the moment of choice. Nevertheless, the Korean precedent is especially important because it would lead their advisors to tell Presidents Johnson and Bush that they were free to initiate wars without need of formal congressional, let alone public, approval (Schlesinger, 2004: 14).

Policy Context

On June 24, 1950 North Korean forces invaded South Korea in an effort to unify the nation under communist dictator Kim Il Sung. It was he, not the Soviets, who instigated the invasion, although Stalin's approval was required (Kaufman, 1986: 32). The Soviets had contributed armaments to Kim for years, and the Chinese would eventually enter the war when American forces, despite Chinese warnings, approached their border with North Korea. But neither the Soviets nor the Chinese had advance word of the invasion, and neither was eager at that time to provoke a confrontation with the United States, which they knew to be a superior nuclear power (Halberstam, 2007). The U.S. Cold War with the Soviet Union had been underway since 1946, but advancing the Soviet cause in the Cold War was not the motive for the invasion. Kim's incentive was uniquely personal and Korean: to provoke and win a civil war that would settle old scores with the South Korean leadership and unite the country under his rule (Bernstein, 1989: 420; Cumings, 2010: xv–xvii).

The Cold War's emergence had ended the presumption of an eventual peaceful unification of the two zones of occupation established by the victorious allies (the Soviets and the United States) on either side of the 38th parallel at the end of World War II (August, 1945). Soviet and American troops had withdrawn from the Korean peninsula after the establishment of the north and south zones. But civil tensions had mounted between the two Korean factions on either side of the parallel, and international tensions intensified as Western nations responded with alarm to the postwar rhetoric and behavior of the Soviet Union in support of communist insurgencies in Europe and the Middle East. Since George F. Kennan's formulation of the containment doctrine from his Moscow diplomatic post in 1946, the idea of resisting Soviet expansionism had taken firm root in America: first as the Truman Doctrine opposing the subjugation of free peoples everywhere, and then as NSC-68, in April of 1950, which codified an aggressive militaristic brand of containment as official U.S. policy toward the Soviet Union, which was presumed to be the puppet master over all insurgencies with discernible communist links.

U.S. Domestic Political Climate

Recent international setbacks and domestic political developments had spawned a climate of "fear and alarm ... conspiracies and treachery ... hidden enemies and nuclear weapons" (Perret, 2007: 138). Among the setbacks were the recent news (September, 1949) that the Soviet Union had successfully tested an atomic bomb, that Mao and the communists had defeated the nationalists in the Chinese civil war (December, 1949), and the rise of the demagogic U.S. Senator Joe McCarthy (R, WI) and his incendiary, mostly ill-founded charges of communist infiltration of the U.S. government. These events fueled an acrid partisan debate which ended the bipartisan foreign policy consensus that had produced the Marshall Plan. It led to Republican Party castigation of Truman's Far East policy and branding of the president as "soft on communism."

Truman's Leadership Style and Decision Process

Why did the Truman Administration decide on military action in a part of the world that it had just a few months earlier, in a speech by Secretary of State Dean Acheson, seemingly dismissed as having no military or strategic importance to the United States (Kaufman, 1986: 31)? Korean War historian Bruce Cumings contends that Acheson's failure to include Korea among the nations identified as under U.S. protection was deliberate and intentionally misleading (Cumings, 2010: 72). The United States, which knew that the North Koreans had Soviet and Chinese ties (and which assumed that the Soviets intended to use North Korean proxies to continue the expansionist behavior it had already displayed in Eastern Europe on the Korean Peninsula), had long since concluded that it would defend South Korea if it were attacked by the North. But Acheson did not want to say so publicly, both because the American high command wanted to keep the Soviets, the Chinese, and the South Koreans (who might have pressed for armaments if the United States tipped its hand) guessing about U.S. intentions. The United States also wanted the North Koreans (who had been locked in border skirmishes verging on civil war with the South for two years) to move first, so that the United States could take the problem to the United Nations, which it knew would sponsor and legitimize a forceful response to unprovoked aggression (Cumings, 2010: 72).

When the North Koreans attacked the South, it came without warning, and the unexpectedly quick and virtually complete collapse of resistance in the South galvanized the United States into action. Cumings portrays the decision to intervene in force as one made by Acheson and authorized by Truman (Cumings, 2010: 11–12). But the recently published correspondence between the two men makes it clear that this was no "master–puppet" relationship. The two men were fully in accord (Geselbracht and Acheson, 2010). What is more, there were deliberative proceedings during which Truman could have changed any pre-ordained decision, had he so desired.

The consensus among high administration officials as they gathered at Blair House in Washington for a series of meetings to formulate a response in the five days immediately after the North Korean invasion was that the Soviets had clearly chosen to test the United States in Korea. This interpretation quickly gave that small nation a vastly greater public prominence and operational importance than it had previously enjoyed. As would happen later in Vietnam, Truman and his advisors mistook a civil war in which one side enjoyed significant communist support for a Soviet ploy with clear intent that required a decisive response. In fact, the international implications were murkier than that. U.S. decision makers did not realize the extent to which the North Koreans, the Russians, and the Chinese, though bound by a hierarchical alliance with the Soviets clearly on top, had their own disagreements, feuds, and not always synchronized agendas (Halberstam, 2007; Cumings, 2010).

The president, a man of impulsive outbursts ("We've got to stop the sons of bitches no matter what") that he usually disciplined before acting (Greenstein, 2000: 41), was as careful as he thought he could safely be in building the case for his decision to go to war. When he started the discussion with his foreign policy and national security group at Blair House across the street from the White House, he asserted that he had "a completely open mind," although everyone present could sense his inclinations. In fact, it seemed clear to one close student of his decision process that the president made his basic choice during the first 24 hours after learning of the North Korean attack (May, 1973: 70). Still, Truman and his advisers examined the situation deliberately, exploring the options that their presumptions and limited information let them take seriously in their rushed circumstances. They found themselves moving inexorably toward full-scale military mobilization even as the president expressed trepidation: "I don't want to go to war" he said despairingly (Hamby, 1995: 537), but given the mind-set that dominated the U.S. government and the country, the die was cast from the beginning. Group-think revulsion against Munich-like appeasement of aggression and instinctive fears of losing America's international and the president's domestic political credibility had set the stage, quickly leading to air and sea support for the beleaguered ROK (Republic of Korea) forces (Janis, 1972: 50–74). But as the South Korean resistance continued to crumble under the onslaught from the North, General Douglas MacArthur's urgent last-minute request for U.S. troops to prevent the worst pushed the president to make his June 30 decision to send American troops to resist the North Korean invasion and restore the 38th parallel. As he later explained to a group of

Congressmen: "I just had to act as Commander-in-Chief and I did" (Bernstein, 1989: 425).

Congress Excluded

Importantly, no members of Congress had been invited to the decisive meetings of administration officials that led to war (Patterson, 1996: 211). But Truman did have various brief contacts with congressmen between June 25 and June 30. On June 27, for example, he informed congressional leaders that the United States was committed to the defense of South Korea and would defend it with air and naval support (Hamby, 1995: 537). The congressmen offered no serious objections and the meeting lasted less than half an hour (Patterson, 1996: 212). Truman asked Senator Tom Connally, Democratic chair of the Foreign Relations Committee, if he should request a declaration of war. In advising Truman not to do so, Connally undoubtedly knew he was telling the president what he wanted to hear (Patterson, 1996: 213). Truman's closest advisors were split, with Acheson opposed and Averell Harriman strongly in favor of seeking congressional approval (Halberstam, 2007: 99). Relatedly, before his June 30 decision to send in the troops, at least two Republican Senators had asked the president if he would seek a congressional resolution of support before committing U.S. ground troops. Truman told them he would take it under advisement. But in retrospect it seemed clear that he had already rejected the idea. He knew he could get the equivalent of a declaration of war if he asked for it. But he also knew that the ugly political climate would ensure a lengthy airing of Republican criticisms of his Far East policy—something he chose not to endure (Halberstam, 2007: 99). Perhaps most important, the broad view of executive power that Truman had developed from the time Andrew Jackson had been his boyhood hero did not dispose him to seek congressional permission (Hamby, 1995: 539). In short, he thought that the Constitution implicitly gave the president whatever power was necessary to preserve, protect, and defend not only the Constitution but the national interest as the president perceived it.

Results and Appraisals

Initially, both Congress and the public enthusiastically supported the president's peremptory action. When Truman's decision to send in troops was announced, members of Congress stood up and cheered, even though they had not been consulted (Patterson, 1996: 211). All hoped and prayed that this "police action" as Truman styled it, launched under legitimizing U.N. auspices, would be swift and effective. Poll-tested public support for the decision was extremely high, near 77 percent, at the beginning when most people expected a short and successful war. Support persisted at strong majority levels until October 19, when the Chinese entered the war. At that point public support for the war dropped precipitously— some 25 points—as it took on a new and more painful appearance. In two of the three polls that asked relevant questions, support remained below 50 percent for the remaining two and one half years of hostilities. Interestingly, these polls display little further reactivity even to major events (e.g., General MacArthur's successful Inchon landing, mounting casualties that eventually exceeded 30,000, the firing of General MacArthur, or protracted negotiations for a truce; see Mueller, 1973: 51). One likely reason for this was the fact that unlike Vietnam the Korean War was not as extensively or as vividly televised. That meant the "true brutality of the war never really penetrated the American cultural consciousness" (Halberstam, 2007: 4). Another reason may have been the successes of the recently disclosed yet quite extensive public relations effort to garner and sustain support for the war (Casey, 2008). Still, the fact is that Americans gave up on the war. In October, 1951, 56 percent of respondents agreed with the Gallup Poll proposition that Korea was a "useless war." In March, 1952, 51 percent said U.S. involvement was a mistake. After April of 1951, Truman's approval score would never exceed 33 percent (Hamby, 1995: 564).

As the war became more difficult than originally expected the elite political consensus that had spontaneously formed at the hour of the invasion evaporated. Support in Congress weakened and fragmented (Halberstam, 2007: 99). The denial of a formal role to Congress was not a heated constitutional issue at the time of Truman's decision. But that issue would emerge when conservative Republicans who had offered only token resistance in July by October began to complain (due to the accumulation of much bad war news) that Congress had not been consulted. Partisan attacks on the president became increasingly acrimonious. By early 1952, after another year of some war highs but mostly lows and setbacks, a battlefield stalemate had emerged and Republicans were in high dudgeon. Senator Robert Taft, by then a GOP presidential candidate, summarized the emerging consensus about Truman, not only within the Republican Party but beyond it. Citing (among other things) his firing of General MacArthur and Truman's lack of progress toward ending the war, Taft concluded that "the greatest failure of foreign policy is an unnecessary war, and we have been involved in such a war now for more than a year ... As a matter of fact, every purpose of the war has now failed. We are exactly where we were three years ago, and where we could have stayed" (Howell and Pevehouse, 2007: 12).

Given its $361.2 billion price tag (in 2005 U.S. dollars) and the loss of some 36,940 American lives (Cumings, 2010: 35) "Truman's War" would continue to be seen as a costly failure even after the military stalemate ended, on July 27, 1953, in an armistice that achieved Truman's stated objective of restoring the pre-invasion 38th parallel. Decades later this achievement would be credited by such respected historians as Alonzo Hamby (1995: 538) and James Patterson (1996: 236) as having promoted world stability and made the best of an extremely difficult situation. Truman himself would by then also be extolled as a near-great if not great president (McCullough, 1992). But scholars such as Schlesinger (1973, 2004), Bernstein (1989), Perret (2007), and Halberstam (2007) have, for various reasons, disagreed with the most positive assessments, particularly those touching Truman's decision to go to war in Korea.

Five critiques of that decision are worth noting here. Some involve information not available to Truman and his advisors. Versions of others were made at the time during the administration's decision meetings, but to no effect. Still others could have been made but were not. These, and some of those made to little effect within Truman's war council, might have been taken more seriously if Truman's five-day prospective review of U.S. options had included members of Congress and if it had been understood that the deliberations would be followed by a congressional vote on a resolution of support.

First, as most Korean War scholars acknowledge, the administration invited trouble by sending misleading signals to North Korea, Russia, and China concerning its attitude toward Korea. When Secretary of State Acheson's January 12, 1950 speech identifying the strategic perimeter the United States would defend failed to mention Korea, Kim Il Sung and his sponsors were mistakenly encouraged to believe the United States would not seek to repel an invasion. That, in fact, had been one of Stalin's preconditions for approving Kim's attack on the south (Perret, 2007: 142). The time pressure created by an unexpected invasion was, for this reason, a problem of the administration's own making. As noted, this U.S. failure to send clear signals was deliberate, although Truman scholar Alonzo Hamby (November 20, 2010: C8) maintains that neither Truman nor Acheson "ever fully confronted the probability" that the North Korean attack was prompted by Acheson's public exclusion of South Korea from America's Asian defense perimeter. Doing so might have sparked consideration of whether the North Korean invasion could accurately be viewed as a deliberate provocation of the United States. In fact, the Soviets and North Koreans sought what they perceived as low-hanging fruit, not a major confrontation with the United States.

Second, the details of Kim's long effort to persuade a reluctant Stalin to give the green light (Halberstam, 2007: 47–51) refute the core presumption of Truman and his advisors: that they faced a calculated Soviet military challenge which, if not answered quickly and in kind, would undermine the American position in the world. Recently opened Soviet archives show that Stalin was not the perpetrator of the invasion. He was *at most* cautiously willing to support the chance for a low-cost addition to the Soviet bloc, provided that it featured no confrontation with the United States (Halberstam, 2007: 92). To be sure, the Truman team could not know Stalin's mind at the time. But a more accurate understanding of the root of the invasion (as the first bold move in a Korean power struggle) *was* achievable at the time, and had the potential to expand the group's sense of the available American options, perhaps tempering the rush to war.

Third is the militarily untenable situation that would instantly be created by a decision to go to war. It flowed from the need to project a steady supply of well-trained American ground troops onto the Asian mainland in sufficient numbers for as long as it took under what U.S. military leaders knew to be brutal battleground circumstances on the Korean peninsula. Worse, vastly superior numbers of enemy troops would always be close by and available, if not from North Korea then from China, which felt a debt of gratitude to North Korea because of its commitment of troops to the insurgent's side in the Chinese civil war that established the People's Republic of China (Cumings, 2010: 25). Moreover, the North Koreans were always able to avoid being forced to quit by reverting to a guerrilla struggle of the sort later made famous in Vietnam. All this meant that the prospects for a U.S. victory were foreseeably dim to nonexistent from the outset (Perret, 2007: 144). Military leaders expressed reservations along these lines at the early Blair House meetings, but they soon understood that Truman did not want to hear their "wary counsel" so they stopped offering it (Bernstein, 1989: 426). If the deliberations had included Congress, this argument might well have carried more weight.

Fourth, even though most American and pro-Western observers initially wanted a strong U.S. response and felt that Truman did the right thing by sending in the troops, this sentiment did not necessarily force the president's hand. Some scholars have argued that despite this early and widespread emotional reaction, Truman might have been able to avoid committing the United States to war without producing a backlash at home or disrupting the alliance system (e.g., Bernstein, 1989: 443; Hamby, 1995: 538). This option, not seriously discussed in the Truman meetings, had a better chance of being considered in a formal, interbranch deliberative context.

Korea Conclusion

The *fifth* and most important critique of President Truman's decision is that it was not vetted and voted up or down by Congress. That set a precedent which not only encouraged subsequent wars of choice but that put the seeking of a congressional resolution of support entirely at the discretion of the president instead of a constitutional requirement. This seemingly permanent transfer of the war power to the president leaves every future incumbent contemplating the use of the military free of any obligation to rigorously defend his policy. The participation of Congress, the ultimate constitutional authority on matters of policy, settles any question of the legitimacy of policies that otherwise can amount to little more than presidential fiat (Wittes, 2008). It would also reduce opportunities for purely partisan exploitation of success or failure. But because Truman did not seek congressional approval and Congress did not officially object, it has become very difficult since 1950 to force presidents to prospectively and rigorously defend their war policy choices. The status quo from that time forward is that "presidents possess the inherent power to go to war whenever they choose" (Schlesinger, 2004: 14).

As noted, subsequent presidents initiating major military projects (Johnson and the two Bushes) would each assert that the Truman precedent justified unilateral action. But mindful of his political fate and of the political benefits greater deference to Congress obtained for Presidents Eisenhower and Kennedy, each would seek resolutions of congressional support. As we see next, these emotionally inspired resolutions did not protect either Johnson or the second Bush from a backlash against their wars as success proved elusive while the costs continued to mount.

Vietnam

The seeds of U.S. involvement in Vietnam were sown when after World War II the French, former colonists of Indochina, reclaimed their lost colony from the Japanese. That intensified an insurgency, led by Ho Chi Minh and his Vietminh supporters, which France chose to resist for reasons unrelated to the Cold War (Perret, 2007: 71). The United States had provided substantial aid to promote French recovery from the world war. But with the fall of China to the communists the Vietminh— nationalists first but with communist ties—suddenly had a powerful neighboring ally.

Antecedents: Truman, Eisenhower, Kennedy

The 1950 outbreak of the Korean War intensified the Cold War and shifted U.S. Indochina policy from anticolonialism to containment. That led President Truman to send direct U.S. aid to the French military effort in Indochina to prevent their defeat and halt the spread of communism (Burke and Greenstein, 1991: 28–29). In 1952, President Dwight D. Eisenhower inherited the Cold War and reasserted the containment policy. Though leery of another land war in Asia, Eisenhower did not challenge the proposition that the United States had a significant stake in the future of Southeast Asia (Burke and Greenstein, 1991: 60). The president tried but failed to muster the domestic and international support he felt he needed to intervene militarily to save the French, so there was no U.S. intervention. Lack of U.S. support probably helped to ensure a Vietminh victory in their battle for independence from the French at Dien Bien Phu in 1954.

Shortly thereafter, in what Eisenhower and Secretary of State John Foster Dulles saw as a major U.S. setback, Vietnam was divided by treaty into separate nations: the communist north under Ho Chi Minh and the more chaotic anticommunist south, initially under Ngo Dinh Diem. In an effort to reunify the country under communist rule North Vietnam and Viet Cong guerillas in the south began attacking South Vietnamese forces. Eisenhower responded by seeking a triumph to offset the embarrassing loss of North Vietnam to the communists. In a move later described by two biographers as far more significant than his much-praised non-intervention at Dien Bien Phu, Eisenhower "fastened the prestige" of the United States to a very unstable South Vietnam—effectively making America its guarantor in the eyes of the world—by sending weapons and economic aid to South Vietnam (Pach and Richardson, 1991: 98). His successor, President John F. Kennedy, upped the ante by deploying 16,500 U.S. military advisers to assist the South Vietnamese forces by seeking to instill in them the will and the skill to defend themselves (Dallek, 2003: 709).

LBJ and the Gulf of Tonkin Resolution

These moves set the stage for the critical choices to be made by President Lyndon B. Johnson (LBJ) in 1964 and 1965. LBJ was initially very wary of Vietnam, expressing his dissatisfaction with U.S. operations there in a 1963 meeting with high foreign policy officials shortly after President Kennedy's assassination (Woods, 2006: 505). In early 1964 aides to Johnson, most of whom were Kennedy holdovers, ardent anticommunists, Cold Warriors, and supporters of the idea that the United States should expand its use of power in Vietnam, privately drafted a congressional resolution that would give the president a virtual blank check to conduct the Vietnam War as he saw fit (Nelson, 2008: 207). They, like the president, did not want to repeat Truman's failure to ensure formal congressional support for any action they might take. But Johnson, fearing the cost of a controversial war proposal to his Great Society ambitions, and still uncertain of his own convictions in light of the instability of the South Vietnamese government, held back. In early August, however, two incidents involving U.S. surveillance ships off the North Vietnamese coast, one an apparent attack and one later found to have been incorrectly interpreted as such, led the president to ask for and get from Congress the Gulf of Tonkin Resolution. The resolution, essentially a defensive move against Republican criticism of LBJ's inaction in Vietnam rather than a signal of Johnson's intent to take immediate action, enjoyed an 85 percent poll approval rating and wide editorial support (Woods, 2006: 514–16). It empowered him to "take all necessary measures" to repel attacks and prevent aggression against the United States and its regional allies. The resolution passed the House unanimously and passed by a vote of 88–2 in the Senate (Herring, 2001: 806–7).

Despite these domestic political victories, the situation in Vietnam was grim. Outside his advisory circle LBJ was known to be deeply upset about U.S. prospects there (Woods, 2006: 596–97). The South Vietnamese government was in disarray and its counterinsurgency efforts against the Viet Cong were ineffective. By late fall 1964 LBJ was under intense pressure from his closest advisors, the joint chiefs of staff, and much of the American foreign policy establishment, who were worried more about U.S. credibility with its Cold War allies than about the viability of the South Vietnamese government or its military capabilities, to strike the North with a bombing campaign. The "domino theory," first put forward by President Eisenhower, which suggested that to allow one nation to fall to communist insurgents exponentially increased the chances that others would follow, was at this time a driving intellectual force among the foreign policy elite.

Instinctively leery of bombing the North, LBJ asked Under Secretary of State George Ball, who famously embraced the role of "devil's advocate" in the president's inner circle, to summarize the case against increasing U.S. engagement. Ball responded with a persuasive brief against such action which Johnson subsequently pressed against those of his advisors who thought escalation essential to preserve U.S. credibility in the Cold War.

At this moment the president doubted that any escalation of the war to salvage the South Vietnamese government could work (Woods, 2006: 596–99). What is more some who occasionally had his ear strongly discouraged enmeshing the United States in an Asian land war. Ball was one, Vice President Hubert Humphrey another, and Senator Richard Russell, the president's longtime friend and mentor, a third, among others (Greenstein, 2000: 85). But comprehensive telephone records show that LBJ's contacts with such people were far less frequent than they were with National Security Advisor McGeorge Bundy, Defense Secretary Robert McNamara, and Secretary of State Dean Rusk (Burke and Greenstein, 1991: 140).

The domestic political climate at the time was not a source of pressure on President Johnson to increase the use of military force in Vietnam. In January 1965, for example, surveys showed that most members of the U.S. Senate were in favor of a negotiated solution, as were most Americans. LBJ was at the peak of his popularity and had just been elected after a campaign in which he frequently said that Asian boys should fight their own wars. Too, the choices available to Johnson were much broader than just intervention and nonintervention. "In fact there were so many possible strategic options in Southeast Asia in early 1965 that it is unlikely that any two presidents would have proceeded identically" (Greenstein, 2000: 85).

With no time pressure, the political capital of a landslide electoral victory, and abundant congressional and public support for nonmilitary as well as military alternatives, what Johnson could have done but did not do was to commission a rigorous examination of his options in Vietnam. George Ball had persuasively detailed the costs associated with escalation. But he had not been commissioned to lay out the alternatives for debate. It might not have mattered if he had, for Johnson, far less confident of his own foreign policy judgment than he was of his domestic convictions (Kearns, 1976: 256) and determined not to be labeled soft on communism, ultimately felt compelled to heed the advice of JFK holdovers McGeorge Bundy and Robert McNamara that the United States must use its military power to force a change in communist policy (Woods, 2006: 600). Robert Dallek, biographer of both Johnson (Dallek, 1998) and Kennedy (Dallek, 2003) also saw Johnson's lack of self-confidence at this key point as decisive. "With no presidential track record to speak of in foreign affairs during 1964–65, Johnson had a more difficult time limiting U.S. involvement in a tottering Vietnam than Kennedy (who had established himself as a strong foreign policy leader) would have had" (Dallek, 2003: 710).

Johnson certainly did not wish to appear personally weak in the face of communist aggression. But what he admitted to were his fears for the United States and its allies. He believed that a decision against force "would profoundly discourage our closest allies and dangerously encourage our most powerful enemies. Russia and China would try to take immediate advantage of our weakness. The result could be nuclear war. Thus, Johnson could not let Ho unify Vietnam" (Bullion, 2008: 109).

Bombs, Troops, and Retirement

Despite feeling compelled to escalate, LBJ still sought to protect America's Cold War credibility with decidedly limited military action. There would be no full-scale U.S. invasion of the North, no use of nuclear weapons, and (at this point) no mass introduction of American troops. The limits were aimed at protecting Great Society momentum at home, signaling the Soviets and the Chinese that the United States wanted no wider war or nuclear confrontation, while (hopefully) still allowing enough military pressure to motivate North Vietnamese regulars and Viet Cong guerrillas to respect the 1954 Geneva Agreement on a 17th parallel partition. At the same time, the president would have to placate domestic anti-war liberals yet also somehow convince conservative war hawks in Congress of his Cold War bona fides. Obviously, these aims were irreconcilable. Johnson's efforts to integrate them yielded the sometimes deceptive and often garbled public pronouncements on Vietnam that created both his "credibility gap" and his reputation as a poor communicator.

In a January, 1965 meeting with members of Congress and his senior advisors, the president was still uncomfortable with the idea of a larger U.S. role. He "made a strong statement against the outcome that was to emerge only two months later: the introduction of American ground troops" (Burke and Greenstein, 1991: 126). An initially gradual troop build-up would eventually be part of a chain of events set in motion by the North Vietnamese attack on U.S. forces at Pleiku. On February 7, 1965 the president initiated Rolling Thunder, the bombing campaign that he hoped would be enough to achieve his complex set of objectives. Yet as the bombing wore on, the North Vietnamese continued to prevail.

The bombing also sparked the first campus anti-war activities. In the Senate, a small but growing anti-war clique began speaking out. On March 1, a Senate debate on Vietnam that would last for eight years formally began. The president was surprised as well as "hurt and frustrated" by the virulence of this early criticism of his Vietnam policy. He lashed back at his critics in public, but was privately depressed and tormented (Woods, 2006: 606–7). In an April 7 television address to the nation aimed at answering his critics he justified the war in familiar Cold War Munich analogy terms (we will not reward aggression with appeasement) while holding out hope of a negotiated settlement. But he made it clear that the United States would not settle for anything less than an independent South Vietnam: something that later evidence showed Ho Chi Min, who held a stronger hand than Johnson's from the beginning (Perret, 2007), would have to accept only if the United States was willing to use its power to the hilt.

By July of 1965 the bombing campaign had been in effect for five months, and still the North Vietnamese and Viet Cong continued to prevail. It was apparent that bombs would not be enough. There had already been a series of ad hoc troop increases, totaling 60,000 by June. Each was in response to requests by field commander William Westmoreland for troops to protect air bases which since the bombing started had become targets of reprisal. These moves show that the United States had already begun backing incrementally into an ever-larger commitment of U.S. ground troops to Vietnam without ever explicitly intending or formally deciding to do so. The increases were portrayed to the public at the time as moderate and routine.

In March, 1965, the first major news report to use the term "credibility gap" appeared (Woods, 2006: 620). Finally, President Johnson, frustrated yet resolved by now to stand his ground, concluded that a massive increase in troop strength would be essential if the United States was to demonstrate the "will, and force and patience and determination" to prevail. On July 27, 1965, the president announced an open-ended U.S. troop commitment to defend South Vietnam.

In his January, 1966 State of the Union address, the president proclaimed that the United States could afford and should sustain its commitment to both guns (Vietnam) and butter (the Great Society). At this point his public approval in opinion polls still stood at a robust 60 percent. But the bad war news continued. Media coverage of a corrupt and ineffective South Vietnamese government increased. Anti-war sentiment in the Congress and the country intensified. And the president's efforts to explain to the American people how U.S. national interests were served by the war were increasingly ineffective.

Johnson at this point could have had, but did not want, a clarifying debate on the complexities of Vietnam, even though such a debate might have rallied a generally receptive public to his cause. He feared that an open discussion of the true demands and costs of the war would undermine the Great Society. Accordingly, he and those who spoke for him were less than fully candid in their public statements about what would be required to fight the war—announcing troop deployments month by month, for example, rather than announcing the fact that a decision had been made for a doubling of forces by the end of 1966 (Dallek, 1998: 345). The combination of the president's unwillingness to lay out a clear vision of the way forward in Vietnam and the contrast between his public optimism about the war and media reports of domestic dissent and South Vietnamese disarray further eroded his credibility. By August his support score had declined to 47 percent. It remained in the 40s with occasional dips into the 30s for the remainder of his presidency (Greenstein, 2000: 83).

LBJ's open-ended commitment to General Westmoreland would see force levels rise to as many as 535,000 U.S. troops by 1968. But the Tet Offensive that began on January 30 of that year (a military victory for the United States because the Viet Cong lost so many men and captured no significant objectives; but a propaganda victory for the Viet Cong because it brought the bloody war home to many Americans watching television) marked a turning point in U.S. public and ultimately congressional faith in the war effort. Many Americans, confused by the president's explanations, became convinced that LBJ had lied to them, with the result that the president's credibility plummeted. President Johnson himself had also had enough. When General Westmoreland asked for an additional 206,000 troops to "take advantage of the situation" the president balked (Willbanks, March 5, 2008: A23).

Johnson lost faith because he was discouraged by long and bitter experience on so many different fronts. He was discouraged by the lack of military progress before Tet, by the media's misinterpretation of the meaning of Tet, by the testimony of CBS evening news anchor Walter Cronkite, at the time the most trusted man in America, that his post-Tet visit to Vietnam showed insufficient U.S. progress, and by the fact that he and his family had been scarred by anti-war protesters outside the White House, which featured such recurring chants as: "Hey, hey, LBJ, how many kids did you kill today?"

On March 31, President Johnson announced that he would not seek another term as president. On May 10, peace talks on Vietnam opened in Paris. The war would drag on through the Nixon and Ford administrations with a chance for victory still in sight. But to the chagrin of the military, Congress would abandon the effort at what many professional soldiers regarded as the point of success, leading to what some regarded as a self-inflicted defeat in Vietnam in 1975. The evidence in support of this view is in a detailed record of the military effort during the seven years following the Tet Offensive. It consists of declassified transcriptions of the weekly intelligence updates at U.S. military headquarters in Saigon, which were published in book form in 2005 (Sorley, 2005). Entitled *Vietnam Chronicles: The Abrams Tapes*, the work purports to show the "actual progress" of the war during that period. The transcripts record in great detail how the tide of the war steadily turned against North Vietnam as a consequence of strategic and other improvements made by General Creighton Abrams, who replaced General Westmoreland in 1968. In his review of the book, James Schlesinger, defense secretary under Presidents Nixon and Ford, concluded: "That the enemy lost virtually every major military engagement against U.S. forces (after Tet) was 'irrelevant,' as North Vietnamese Gen. Giap later noted, in light of the political attitudes in Washington ... America had abandoned the mission" (Schlesinger, March 18, 2005: W6).

Vietnam Conclusion

Vietnam was a presidential war of choice because it was initiated by a president against a nation that had not attacked the United States. Additionally, the rationale for the congressional resolution of support for the war was not offered from the constitutionally intended position of thoughtful legislative strength because it was not well-grounded. It was based not on a thorough review of the pros and cons of initiating military action but on emotional reactions to alleged North Vietnamese attacks on U.S. destroyers in the Gulf of Tonkin, the second and most important of which (ostensibly occurring on August 4, 1964) never occurred, according to historians (Shane, October 31, 2005: A1). President Johnson cited the supposed second attack to persuade Congress to authorize military action, even though Johnson himself apparently doubted that a second attack had occurred (Bumiller, July 15, 2010b: A6).

As in Korea, emotional reactions to the Cold War atmosphere enhanced by a suspected Soviet-inspired North Vietnamese provocation ensured that congressional skepticism and vigilance would be at a low ebb when the president called for support. Too, by then the Korean precedent had begun to fuel a presumption by many that this was appropriately the president's decision to make whether he asked for support or not, which further discouraged serious congressional oversight. Recently declassified 1968 Senate Foreign Relations Committee transcripts show that Senators became increasingly frustrated at their own ineffectiveness as bad war news accumulated and sharply questioned the veracity of the Tonkin claim. But 1968 was far too late to exercise due diligence (Bumiller, July 15, 2010b: A6).

To most analysts Vietnam continues to look in retrospect like an unnecessary war with painful costs and no rewards; 58,000 American soldiers were killed. According to the Congressional Research Service $686 billion (in 2008 dollars) were expended. The civil rights, education, Medicare, Medicaid, and other legislative achievements of arguably the most effective domestic president of the 20th century were unnecessarily (if not permanently) overshadowed. A significant diminution in public support and trust for the government and the presidency was sparked not only by the lack of success but by the intensity of an anti-war movement that grew more virulent with each passing year.

We must conclude that the president brought this on himself—by backing into an open-ended commitment; by doing so because he had not clarified his war aims and by explaining himself in ways that could not be clearly understood by the mass public, which eventually made it impossible to win domestic credit for the post-Tet military improvements noted above. The U.S. fate in Vietnam would later be sealed by President Richard Nixon, who conceived and almost executed a brilliantly successful U.S. extrication from Vietnam based on "peace with honor," but whose Watergate flaws consumed him and helped ensure the worst possible Vietnam outcome.

Iraq

The decision made by President George W. Bush to invade Iraq in 2003 followed what was perceived as a successful and widely supported incursion into Afghanistan in 2001, undertaken in the wake (also in 2001) of the Islamic Fundamentalist terrorist group Al Qaeda's destruction using hijacked U.S. airliners of the World Trade Center in New York City. The atmosphere in the country as President Bush made ready to invade Iraq still reflected the euphoria of Afghanistan and the seared emotions sparked by the 9/11 attacks.

There was no domestic American public or international clamor for a second war, especially a war on Iraq. "If the United States had never gone to war against Iraq," wrote one expert critic, "most Americans would hardly have cared or even noticed" (Schlesinger, 2004: 37). But the president had bolstered his credibility by his forceful words and deeds in response to 9/11. The American people were for that reason inclined to respond to the persuasion attempts of a man so widely perceived at the time as a strong and trustworthy leader (Broder and Balz, July 16, 2006: A1). They accepted his characterization of the new state of affairs as a "war on terror." They would accept the need to invade Iraq as well.

By all accounts the president, along with many inside his administration and some outside, felt that the post-9/11 climate afforded a rare, not-to-be-missed opportunity to mobilize popular and congressional support for a military effort to topple the Saddam Hussein regime in Iraq. The president's defenders claim that he opted for war as a result of a thorough and careful review of his options in light of U.S. interests (e.g., Feith, July 3, 2008). Others suggest that the president was inclined to war for personal reasons as well: Saddam's attempt on his father's life (Perret, 2007: 353), and because he was eager to display transformative leadership by boldly altering the balance of power in the Middle East (Woodward, 2004; McClellan, 2008). Many agreed with the president that it would be beneficial to rid the world of an unsavory dictator who either previously had, had now, or might soon acquire weapons of mass destruction (Pollack, 2002; Pollack, June 20, 2003: A25). Others saw great potential benefit to establishing a democratic beachhead in the Middle East (Friedman, June 4, 2003). Few analysts, however, saw invading Iraq as a necessary next step in the effort to prevent future attacks by Al Qaeda. To the contrary, many leading Republicans in Congress and foreign policy specialists from previous Republican administrations thought that the benefits of *avoiding* such a war far outweighed the probable costs (Purdum and Tyler, August 16, 2002: A1). These and others saw continued deterrence and containment of Saddam as much safer and potentially more effective than invasion (e.g., Matlock, October 20, 2002: 4, 11). The president was undeterred by these arguments.

Many have asserted that there was little or no formal deliberation inside the Bush White House about the wisdom of initiating a war, or of any systematic effort to anticipate and prepare for worst-case scenarios. The president prided himself on being an "instinct player" who trusted his own judgment, which he famously felt was buttressed by the guidance of a higher power. Many insider accounts portrays an administration that was indifferent or hostile to facts or arguments not supportive of its preferences (e.g., Clarke, 2004; Suskind, 2004; Woodward, 2004; Dilulio, May 23, 2007; McClellan, 2008). In a meticulously documented description of the public relations campaign intended to "sell" the Iraq War to the American people, journalist Frank Rich demonstrates in great detail that from the president's first warning, two months after 9/11, that Iraq would be held responsible for harboring any "weapons of mass destruction" to Secretary of State Colin Powell's dramatic February 5, 2003 televised presentation to the United Nations summarizing the administration case against Iraq to the nation and the world, there was a carefully orchestrated drumbeat of administration commentary, from the president, the vice president, the secretary of state and the secretary of defense, among others, that Iraq had acquired the capability to produce dangerous weapons, had probably already produced some of them, and that it would share such weapons with Al Qaeda and others if it had not already done so, all in a determined effort to harm the United States. Rich concludes his summary with poll evidence showing a dramatic increase—from a low of 6 percent just after 9/11 to highs in the 50s and 60s after Powell's U.N. speech—in the percentage of Americans who were convinced that Iraq had weapons of mass destruction and was allied with Al Qaeda in a determined effort to attack the United States (Rich, 2006a: 57–69).

What, then, was the potential for a full and fair prospective review in the months leading up to the invasion of Iraq? What would have been the prospects for a sustained congressional debate on the merits of the Bush case for war? For a comprehensive airing of the counterargument that Iraq was not linked to Al Qaeda, had no direct role in the attacks on the United States, and was thus no more of a threat to U.S. interests after than it was before 9/11? The prospects were not good.

In support of the debate option was the fact that there was no significant time pressure, no immediate threat to the United States that obviously required either a pre-emptive or a preventive invasion of Iraq (on this distinction, see Schlesinger, 2004: 23–24). What made such a vetting unlikely, however, was not time pressure but the fact that the administration was implacably opposed to an extended debate on the merits. Public shock in response to 9/11 and the natural fear of another terrorist attack were both still palpable, and were assets in what seems to have been a calculated effort to truncate debate. The president, knowing that public fears would recede, apparently sought to extend them by manufacturing a new Iraq-specific sense of urgency (e.g., said President Bush: "Each passing day could be the one on which the Iraqi regime gives anthrax or VX nerve gas or someday a nuclear weapon to a terrorist ally" (The Truth about the War, June 6, 2008: A22)). In his 2002 State of the Union Address the president declared Iraq a part of an "axis of evil" which included nations that armed and sheltered terrorists. In that speech the president also asserted that he would not "wait on events (either fresh provocations or extended debate) while dangers gather."

Congress

The president's approach to Congress combined a wish for its imprimatur with obvious disdain for any expression of its considered opinion. Despite the assertion that he had the constitutional authority to initiate hostilities without congressional approval the administration still thought it prudent to seek a congressional resolution of support, as both Lyndon Johnson and the president's father had done. But President Bush the younger again made clear his aversion to a deliberative process, telling members of Congress: "I want your vote. I'm not going to debate it with you" (Rudalevige, 2006: 220). The Congress obliged, passing the Authorization for the Use of Military Force against Iraq by a margin of 296 to 133 in the House (October 10, 2002) and by a margin of 77 to 23 in the Senate (October 11, 2003).

The Bush strategy for getting the Congress on board was to use the looming mid-term election as leverage. As one senior administration official admitted to a reporter, that timing would make it politically difficult for anyone to vote against it (Bumiller, September 7, 2002: A1).

In his memoir, President Bush identifies several prominent Democrats who voted in support of the resolution, and challenges the claim of some of them that, in Bush's words, "they were not voting to authorize war but only to continue diplomacy." Bush continues:

> They must not have read the resolution. Its language was unmistakable: The President is authorized to use the armed forces of the United States as he determines to be necessary and appropriate in order to defend the national security of the United States against the continuing threat posed by Iraq; and enforce all relevant United Nations Security Council resolutions regarding Iraq.
>
> *(Bush, 2010: 241)*

Bush had a point. Barack Obama's bid for the White House would later be strengthened by the fact that rivals for the 2008 Democratic Party nomination for president, such as Hillary Clinton, had voted for this eventually discredited measure, while Obama had opposed it (albeit before his election to the U.S. Senate, so he did not have as much at stake as those forced to cast a vote in Congress).

But President Bush also allowed that he still has "a sickening feeling every time" he thinks about the failure to find weapons of mass destruction in Iraq, the central rationale for the invasion (Bush, 2010). That cloud still hangs over his presidency. It is clear that there was a rush to judgment. Even if history eventually vindicates this President Bush, the decision-making process that led to the invasion of Iraq was, as in Vietnam, driven more by the manipulation of emotion—fear of another attack on the United States among the public and fear of electoral reprisal among members of Congress—than by sober analysis of evidence and options. There was, in short, a lack of due deliberation at the decision stage. The president did not welcome challenges to his war proposal, and the Congress did not insist on it.

Iraq Conclusion

On a scale ranging from "respectful" (10) to "manipulative" (1) how should we characterize the president's treatment of the Congress and the American people in his effort to persuade them to support the invasion of Iraq? The evidence suggests that the score is not better than 2. In the most comprehensive effort yet undertaken to determine whether high Bush Administration officials portrayed the Iraq threat as graver than it actually was, the Senate Select Committee on Intelligence concluded that Bush and Cheney "repeatedly overstated the Iraqi threat in the emotional aftermath of the Sept. 11 attacks" before the March 2003 invasion (Mazzetti and Shane, June 6, 2008: A1). Supporters and critics of the administration heatedly debated whether or not the president had deliberately lied to the American people (e.g., General McClellan's War, May 30, 2008: A14; The Truth about the War, June 6, 2008: A22). Dismissing that debate as fruitless, another editorial looked forward rather than backward, suggesting what ideal presidential and congressional behavior in future such situations should look like:

> For Congress the lesson is that lawmakers need to double-check intelligence themselves, not simply rely on summaries or administration assurances. Pathetically few members of Congress read the complete 2002 National Intelligence Estimate on Iraq, which detailed misgivings of some intelligence agencies, before they cast fateful votes that authorized the Iraq War … For this and future administrations, the lesson is that White House officials need to weigh and study all available intelligence, not seize only on what supports their preconceived notions. They mustn't present ambiguity as certainty. They mustn't launch preemptive attacks without bulletproof evidence. And never again should they treat war as a marketing campaign, like selling a new brand of toothpaste.
>
> *(Iraq Intelligence Findings Provide Crucial Lessons,*
> *June 6, 2008: 14A)*

Conclusion

The agents of presidential accountability, by unwittingly allowing the precedent of presidential discretion to initiate unprovoked wars to take root, may have put an end to the constitutional experiment in balancing executive encouragement and restraint. As the three cases just reviewed suggest, the costs have been significant. Those who have identified benefits argue that Korea put the Soviets on notice that their efforts to expand would be resisted, and that Vietnam reinforced the same message. For its part, Iraq may someday prove to have been the first step in the eventual democratization of the Middle East. History will decide the ultimate value of these alleged and potential benefits. But the human, monetary, political, and constitutional costs are already clear.

The question of concern next is whether the constitutional imbalance anchored in place by these wars might be partially redressed if not fully repaired. This question has attracted the attention of constitutional scholars (cf., Levinson, 2006; Kleinerman, 2009). But few if any political practitioners (e.g., Baker and Christopher, July 8, 2008) or scholars of American political institutions (e.g., Deering, 2005: 349) believe that anything but modest changes are possible.

In the remainder of this book I seek the kind of closure that can only be achieved by proposing actual solutions to the problems I have identified, despite the impracticalities. That requires that I proceed as if redress is within reach, and ask what it would take to make it happen. In Chapter 5 I propose an institutional mechanism for raising the consciousness of the PAS so that it could pursue novel change experiments when its core membership agreed that it made sense to try. In Chapter 6 I sketch a hypothetical example of how one PAS project related to discretionary war might work in practice.

5

BRINGING THE PAS TO LIFE
The Presidential Accountability Project

Bringing the PAS to life requires institution building: the creation of a private, nonprofit organization, the Presidential Accountability Project (PAP), a think tank designed to work collaboratively with the existing PAS agents and their representatives toward the calibration of presidential power and more coherently managed presidential accountability. Needed is the institutional capacity first to nurture the *idea* of a self-aware presidential accountability system and then to develop the political, conceptual, expert advisory, and case knowledge services needed to develop it. Well conceived, staffed, and implemented, such a project has the potential to help create the strategic vision and the political credibility required to develop and promote a new public policy for balancing presidential power and restraint.

The PAP and its Mission

Such an organization would exist solely to help the members of the PAS devise ways to extract greater public benefit from their actual and potential influence on presidents. We saw in Chapter 3 that each of the agents has an undeniable impact on the incentives of presidents, despite the fact that they do not presently think of themselves as a collective potentially able to deliberately manage such incentives. In its unconscious state the PAS has had both beneficial (e.g., incentivizing great achievements) and unintentionally undesirable impacts (e.g., unchallenged presidential usurpations of power) on the incentives and behavior of presidents. But the consequences of presidential wars of choice, widely perceived as undesirable, suggest that the costs of an unconscious PAS outweigh the benefits. They make clear why there is need for a self-aware version; a group of agents that sees value in the concept of a PAS and is willing to work toward identifying the accountability circumstances in which they see reason to share responsibility and can agree on ways to do so.

Of course, not every agent will be relevant to every accountability question that arises. What is more, their various differences from one another (discussed in greater detail below) ensure that agents will not always be in agreement. But simply working toward increased joint awareness of each others' actual and potential impacts on presidential incentives in various situations is a step capable of reducing unanticipated consequences like those on display in the Truman example in Chapter 2. To develop and promote this self-aware vision for the PAS is the purpose of the institution to be described here.

Toward System Self-Awareness

What if the PAS were "brought to life," in the sense of accepting consciousness of its own existence as an entity that has various impacts on presidential incentives, heretofore rarely orchestrated, that could be better understood and sometimes managed? What if the agents could be persuaded, in particular situations, to be cooperative in the effort to selectively and strategically deploy such influence when it made sense to try?

The PAS as a "System"

My argument is that a voluntarily cooperative and selectively consensual PAS could do a better job of balancing empowerment and restraint, and a better job of anticipating and avoiding unintended/undesired consequences for presidential incentives. The obvious strategy for achieving these things is to seek the enhanced leverage available only through cooperation: the nurturing of a self-aware system. What exactly do I mean by a "system" in this context? David Easton (1965: 21) argues that a "system" can be any set of entities so long as it is "interesting" to explore their relationships. For reasons detailed throughout this book, the seven-agent set that makes up the PAS is at least interesting! Katz and Kahn (1978: 22) shed more light on what I have in mind here by linking the system concept back to *systems theory*, a longstanding interdisciplinary venture (Skyttner, 2005) suggesting that as a body of ideas, *systems theory* "is basically concerned with problems of relationships, of structure, and of interdependencies." If we add a commitment to ongoing communication on shared concerns and selective coordination, we have a checklist that can usefully guide the evolution of a self-aware PAS.

Importantly, any president "integrates" the PAS in her/his own mind (even though it presently does not integrate itself) by trying, for personal reasons, to anticipate what its agents might do in response to various decision options under consideration. Such integration happens when the potential reactions of all accountability agents deemed relevant are jointly assessed by a president faced with a major decision. The decision will be influenced by how s/he expects the particular

PAS subset whose support is needed (but that might seek to thwart action in a given situation) to respond. At such a moment, any president will be acutely attuned to signals regarding how relevant accountability agents view the president's choices. This is one of the precise points at which a conscious PAS can have an impact. As noted in Chapter 2, Truman calculated that he could sidestep a congressional debate about the wisdom of invading Korea with impunity because the emotions of the moment would keep those who could stop him from doing so. It might have been otherwise had a vigilant self-aware PAS been in existence.

Other benefits of systemic self-awareness worth brief note here include greater sensitivity to comparative agent strengths and weaknesses such as those identified in Chapter 3 and openness to the implications for the most apt division of agent labor in particular accountability circumstances. I offer an extended example in Chapter 6, which proposes a method for mitigating congressional weakness with mass public strength by coordinating these two agents in a special procedure aimed at recapturing for Congress a measure of the war-making power when the use of military force is optional.

Potential Objections

There is understandable skepticism among those who doubt that we could realistically ever expect a more robust system of accountability for future presidents because, in the words of one anonymous critic, "it is virtually impossible to coordinate the various elements of the PAS." That is a fair statement of the biggest challenge to this idea. It is why I want to address the most skeptical audience imaginable: current PAS stakeholders. Those who staff the accountability agencies must find the vision of episodic cooperation potentially both worthwhile and feasible before they would even consider taking on the added responsibilities that would sometimes be entailed.

The first task, therefore, is to sell the idea of a PAS to itself; that is, to its members, who, in one way or another, include most of us: the citizens who staff the presidential electorate and who respond to pollsters' presidential support queries, the professional practitioners who operate the Congress in elected and staff roles, the Supreme Court justices and staff, the news media reporters, editors and owners, and the partisan political opposition—elected officials and operatives who must somehow be persuaded to temper their "take no prisoners" instincts with a degree of "loyal opposition" public spiritedness. Last is the "legacy audience": professional historians and political scientists who write presidential biographies, assess the records of presidents and draw conclusions about the significance of each to their times and to American well-being. They too must think about the implications of what they do for the health of the system.

Creating what advertisers call "buy-in" on the part of those so variously and differently motivated will require convincing answers to the following questions.

First, *why should the agents care?* Second, *how would self-awareness and conscious cooperation improve the signals they send to presidents?* Third, *can they commit to caring and still deal with inevitable disruptions to and potential inconsistencies with their established, traditional commitments?*

Why They Should Care

In light of their other, often more pressing, and sometimes contradictory responsibilities, why should they care? They should care because experience has shown that the original constitutional checks and balances incentives must be *supplemented* if precedent created by executive action is not to permanently disrupt the constitutional balance of power envisioned by the framers. It is not that the framers are sacrosanct. The balance that they sought through institutional design was intended to be practical. It let presidents deal with emergencies while restraining them from claiming power beyond necessity by presuming that such action is unconstitutional, and therefore must be compellingly justified to avoid impeachment and conviction (Kleinerman, 2009: 88 and passim). But it has not worked as intended. Neither the formal checks nor the "executive self-restraint" so frequently called for to close the institutional gaps have been enough to sustain that balance (Ceaser, 1979: 62; Matheson, 2009: 149; Pfiffner, 2010: 18).

This means that the supplement must come from creative ways of combining the leverage of both formal and informal agents that can influence presidents. Thus, not only the elections, the Congress, and the Court of the Constitution must be involved, but also public opinion, news media, political opposition, and legacy councils. The failure to stoutly supplement the formal constitutional design with PAS-like support strategies has allowed an unnecessary expansion of the war power.

How Would Self-Awareness Help?

One example of a recurring circumstance in which a self-aware PAS would be useful is during the run-up to a major presidential decision stressed by time pressure and emotion. Self-awareness implies acceptance of certain routines established through PAP services of the sort described later. When time permits (as it did in each of the discretionary wars reviewed in the last chapter) the PAP would seek to promote a routine (borne of sensitivity to the demonstrated costs of failure to have done so in the past) of *prior joint reflection,* to be engaged in by PAS agents that *attempts to control for spontaneous emotional reactions* in deciding what PAS signals of encouragement or restraint should be sent to a president contemplating decision options. Of course, emotion cannot and should not be eliminated. But anticipatory reflection with the examples of previous chapters and the following history in mind can sometimes mitigate the least desirable effects.

There have been many instances in U.S. history when angry and/or fearful national sentiment encouraged what were later considered to be ill-advised presidential decisions: President Adams' decision, in 1798's climate of "tumult and fear," to support passage of the Alien and Sedition Acts (McCullough, 2001: 504);

President Wilson's aggressive support, inspired by war fervor, for "extensive repression" of dissent during and after World War I (Matheson, 2009: 54) and President Roosevelt's 1942 Executive Order 9066, sparked by outrage over Pearl Harbor, incarcerating Japanese aliens and American citizens alike in domestic prison camps (Robinson, 2001) are famous examples. In the Korean case, Cold War emotion led most PAS actors to overlook the implications for the balance of constitutional power of Truman's unsanctioned decision to invade Korea. Thus, nothing emerged to challenge the idea that the president should move without delay to repel the North Korean invasion of the South. In this case (it bears repeating) all that would have been necessary to avoid establishing an unwanted precedent would have been for Congress to insist that it be involved in the decision to send in the troops. In a self-aware environment, news media and opposition politicians in and outside Congress might have pressed Truman to endure the rigors of congressional review, and pressed Congress to insist on it.

National experience with such problems is by now abundant enough that it is not too much to ask that we begin to learn from our mistakes. A disciplined PAS consultation routine might have led to a clarification and coordination of more cautionary accountability signals to the president in this and other past instances, and could do so in the future. Such routines would at a minimum help to reduce the *unwitting* creation of *unintended* incentives.

Added Burdens

Is it unreasonable to ask this very dissimilar set of agents to take on some occasional responsibility for engaging in inter-agent consultation, which amounts to yet another task, and one for which they are unequally and unevenly equipped (how, for example, does the mass public "consult" with the Supreme Court)? No, it is not unreasonable; particularly when it truly matters in the public interest that they do so. A mechanism to address such logistical difficulties with inter-agent consultation, as well as the many other complexities likely to arise, is why there needs to be a PAP. Might occasional consultation be a disruptive experience for agents? Yes. For example, a conscious PAS is likely to increase the frequency with which institutions oriented to "checking and balancing" each other, or at least working in isolation from one another, are pressed to cooperate to send clear signals to presidents at key moments. Yet agents have already cooperated from time to time, albeit spontaneously rather than according to any form of planned coordination. The most famous and extended recent example was Watergate. As noted earlier, Woodward and Bernstein uncovered and published information that partially enabled federal prosecutors, the courts, and the Congress to hold President Nixon to account. More recently, the post-2006 Congress joined an already assertive Supreme Court in pushing back against Bush Administration claims to executive powers independent of Congress (Matheson, 2009: 88–89).

We should not forget the most familiar brand of inter-agent cooperation, which involves not checking but *enabling* presidential plans, as happens (to give an example that would involve many agents) any time Congress and the president cooperate as policy partners to produce and refine major legislation that endures many changes, and enjoys popular support, despite facing decades of political opposition, such as the 1935 Social Security law. The Obama health care law has been challenged and found wanting in lower federal court, has received mixed reviews in the news media and in public opinion polls, and to survive in recognizable form will require the support of the Supreme Court, which has the case before it at this writing.

The differences between these instances of more-or-less self-executing inter-agent exchanges and what is proposed here is the creation of an institution—the PAP—whose mission includes encouraging novel *intentional* coordination (when useful, feasible, and legal) prepared for in advance, and supported by an institutional capacity to (among other things) use historical research to show when such cooperation might and might not have mattered in the past to inform strategies for the future.

In the balance of this chapter I will present what amounts to a "concept paper" spelling out a vision for an operational PAP—the kind of document that would be useful for a group of founders as an orientation to the task of organizational design.

Four Models for the PAP

In preparation for outlining a plan for a PAP organization, it is worth considering what existing organizations have to offer by way of models. This will be revealing of the qualities and characteristics arguably needed to establish a credible institutional facility to support the purposes at hand. No one potential model embodies precisely the features of the ideal PAP. Accordingly, I draw on four organizations, each of which displays one or more of the essential qualities to be embodied in the organizational culture and modus operandi of the PAP: the U.S. Government Accountability Office, the Congressional Budget Office, influential think tanks, and elite management consulting firms.

Government Accountability Office

In 2004 the GAO changed its name from the "General Accounting Office" to the "Government Accountability Office." It did so to reflect the fact that it had long since moved its scope far beyond the private sector accounting firms it had once sought to emulate to a mission of increasing the effectiveness with which the government is meeting its responsibilities, and to help in bringing about improvements (Mosher, 1979: 2). Particularly important guidance for the PAP is GAO's near-autonomous status. Although GAO gets its powers, responsibilities, and resources from Congress, it operates, for the most part, *independently* of Congress: in the exercise of its powers, and in its choice and execution of projects. Though most of its work deals with the executive branch, it is not responsible to that branch. And its potential scope is almost as broad as government itself (Mosher, 1979: 2).

TABLE 5.1 The U.S. Strategy in Afghanistan

GAO-10-655R:

United States Government Accountability Office:
Washington, DC 20548:

June 15, 2010:

Congressional Committees:

Subject: The Strategic Framework for U.S. Efforts in Afghanistan:

The United States and its international partners from over 40 nations have been engaged in efforts to secure, stabilize, and rebuild Afghanistan since 2001. In an effort to establish clear and specific U.S. strategic goals, the President of the United States, in March 2009, outlined the U.S. Strategy for Afghanistan and Pakistan. This strategy emphasizes a strategic goal to disrupt, dismantle, and defeat Al-Qaeda in Afghanistan and Pakistan and prevent their return. The strategy was followed by the completion, in August 2009, of a Civilian-Military Campaign Plan for Afghanistan. In December 2009, the President reaffirmed the U.S. strategic goal and underscored the importance of U.S. efforts to secure and stabilize Afghanistan to help ensure the safety of the United States and the American people.

To assist the Congress in its oversight of U.S. efforts in Afghanistan, this publication and its interactive graphic (1) identify and describe key U.S. and international strategies and plans that collectively guide U.S. efforts in Afghanistan; (2) provide examples and information about key efforts to assist Afghanistan; and (3) identify oversight issues that Congress may wish to consider in its work. During April and May 2010, we presented this strategic framework to Congress as part of our classified briefing on the Afghanistan campaign plans.

The strategic framework includes relevant strategies—the Afghan National Development Strategy, the U.S. Strategy for Afghanistan and Pakistan, and the Afghanistan and Pakistan Regional Stabilization Strategy. It also includes U.S. plans: the Operation Enduring Freedom Campaign plan, the National Security Council Strategic Implementation Plan, and the U.S. Integrated Civilian-Military Campaign Plan (ICMCP). The ICMCP describes three lines of effort—security, governance, and development—to be implemented by U.S. civilian and military personnel. Finally, NATO plans include the NATO Comprehensive Strategic Political Military Plan, and the operational plans for NATO and for NATO's subordinate command—the International Security Assistance Force (ISAF).

By comparison the scope of the PAP is actually *broader* than the government due to its efforts to integrate not only the formal government agents but also the four informal accountability agents that make up the PAS. The GAO has moved to the kind of ambitious assistance to Congress illustrated in Table 5.1's excerpt from a recent report to that body which was intended to help it monitor presidential compliance with the stated aims of U.S. policy toward Afghanistan, which happens to be the subject of the hypothetical scenario set forth in the next chapter.

The PAS includes the Congress. Thus, like GAO, PAP has advisory responsibility to that rule-making body. But unlike GAO its clientele includes six additional agents. That adds layers of complexity, but *only on matters touching shared interest in presidential oversight.* GAO's scope is much broader, ranging from major foreign policy questions like U.S. Afghanistan policy to more mundane financial audits of domestic agencies. GAO is a model for PAP, however, in several other important respects. Like GAO, PAP aspires to be independent of its clients, and also non-partisan, highly professional, and technically knowledgeable and expert in a great variety of specialized areas. GAO also serves as a model for its proven ability to bring analytic competence to bear on unexpected and novel problems.

Finally, GAO has transferrable accountability expertise and an established executive exchange program that offers access to their talents and training that could be useful for PAP staff.

Congressional Budget Office

The Congressional Budget Office (CBO) is also Congress-centered and describes its role as offering objective, nonpartisan, and timely analyses to aid in economic and budgetary decisions on the wide array of programs covered by the federal budget. It also produces the information and estimates required for the congressional budget process. The CBO has built a reputation for solid impartial analysis of economic and policy issues. While the party controlling Congress gets to select the head of the agency, both parties have generally turned to the CBO's respected academics who do not attempt to use the agency to push a political agenda. CBO describes itself as a professional, nonpartisan staff office that does not make recommendations on policy. That nonpartisan stance has been instrumental in preserving the agency's reputation for professionalism and has enhanced the credibility of its products. In addition to its independent analyses and estimates relating to the budget and the economy CBO presents economic budget and policy options and alternatives for the Congress to consider. It routinely discloses the assumptions and methods it uses, which enhances the general perception of its products as objective and impartial.

CBO's substantive overlap with the PAP is minimal. But it offers an important model of how to create and sustain a reputation for analytic integrity in the context of a work environment made contentious and controversial by partisan disagreements. From its inception in 1974, CBO has regularly made both political parties angry, but has managed to sustain its credibility nonetheless, as evidenced by the fact that both sides routinely cite its analytic products (Harwood, March 23, 1993: A2). The PAP will also have to maintain the respect of all sides in the face of predictable unhappiness in some quarters with some of its work, which is what makes CBO a useful model.

But there is an important difference. Unlike CBO (or GAO, for that matter) the PAP must maintain its analytic credibility *despite being partial to one side of an argument.* It must do so because of the role of its Policy Board (discussed below) in advocating standards for presidential accountability rooted not in partisanship but in equally controversial constitutional interpretation.

The mission of the PAP is to work toward the calibration of the balance between the encouragement and restraint of presidents described in Chapter 2. Though far from rigidly "originalist," it tilts more toward the intent of the framers insofar as the theory behind the separation of power is concerned (cf., Kleinerman, 2009: 76–91) than does the status quo. It thus seeks to advance what can fairly be described as a "policy" about presidential power and account-ability, as noted above. This is likely to inspire criticism from those who see things differently: some presidents, particular scholars, journalists, pundits, and others who embrace expansive (e.g., Hamiltonian) theories of presidential power, and who can be expected to offer rival maxims based on different understandings of the Constitution.

These potential differences notwithstanding, if PAP is to achieve respect for the quality of its research and arguments on behalf of its mission that respect must be earned by dint of the same disciplined professionalism in its articulation of principles and in its staff work that characterizes both GAO and CBO. But PAP must also do something that both of those organizations strenuously eschew: maintain analytic credibility despite controversial policy advocacy. Their success at doing precisely that is what makes certain think tanks useful models.

Think Tanks

Unlike GAO or CBO, Washington think tanks are, in large measure, unabashedly politically partisan, or at least philosophically united organizations featuring expert policy analysis and advocacy (Bumiller, January 30, 2008: A12). How do they differ from universities? University scholars are expected to conduct their research first and draw their conclusions second, but this process is sometimes reversed in policy-oriented think tanks. Jonathan Rowe, speaking of one conservative policy advocacy organization in particular, suggested that the term "think" tank was a misnomer. "They don't think; they justify" (Sourcewatch, December 28, 2011).

Not every think tank produces unbiased research and analysis. But what many such organizations have succeeded in doing (that the PAP must also do) is to *show that analysis respected by all sides of any controversy can be nurtured despite an advocacy mission*. Examples of think tanks that often achieve this standard are the models here. They include (but are not limited to) the Brookings Institution, the American Enterprise Institute, and the Center for Budget and Policy Priorities and its founder, Robert Greenstein (Noah and McGinley, July 26, 1993: A12). Like PAP, these are organizations with points of view that they seek to advance through the use of widely respected analytic products.

As he neared retirement after 21 years as president of the American Enterprise Institute (AEI), Christopher DeMuth penned an op-ed piece in which he identified several additional attributes of think tanks worth instilling in the organizational culture of the PAP:

> Think tanks aim to produce good research not only for its own sake but to improve the world ... We are "schools" in the old sense of the term: groups of scholars who share a set of philosophical premises and take them as far as we can in empirical research, persuasive writing, and arguments among ourselves and with those of other schools ... This has proven highly productive. It is a great advantage, when working on practical problems, not to be constantly doubling back to first principles. We know our foundations and concentrate on the specifics of the problem at hand.
>
> *(DeMuth, October 11, 2007: A21)*

DeMuth goes on to note that the spirit of "opposition to the established order of things" is a vital source of the energy and creativity that characterize the best think tanks. "Opposition is the natural proclivity of the intellectual ... and is of course prerequisite to criticism and devotion to reform." It also helps sustain the patience needed to effect real change, which is always uncertain and can take decades to achieve when it does occur. An important source of the credibility and eventual influence of AEI, says DeMuth, was its "fierce" attachment "to the principles of intellectual independence, freedom of inquiry, and open debate." And because they were in "a different line of work from those on the inside" they have "never hesitated to offer blunt criticism when we thought it was justified."

All of the foregoing ideas are relevant, with appropriate tailoring, to what PAP seeks to make of itself. Thus, PAP too will draw energy from the reformist character of its mission; it will also be acutely sensitive to the importance of intellectual independence, critical candor, and patience to its long-term credibility and prospects for influence. And not unlike a philosophically united think tank, PAP will often be in a position to avoid debating first things, focusing directly instead on the application of its clearly advertised principles to specific case problems. This distinguishes PAP from analytic organizations like GAO and CBO, which must often contend with the conflicts embedded in the rival principles behind the options they present to their clients.

Two final points of note emerge from DeMuth's thoughtful essay. The first is relevant to PAP's "deep background" research on past presidential accountability episodes, discussed in more detail below. "Think tanks," he says, "serve as storehouses of ideas, patiently developed and nurtured," waiting for their moments of relevance. Relatedly, PAP will seek out and archive the relevant presidential past in search of lessons to apply to the accountability future as it presents itself.

The second DeMuth point has to do with the importance of clarity: "(We) pay careful attention to the craft of good speaking and writing. Many AEI scholars do technical research for academic journals, but all write for a wider audience as well." It will be essential for all PAP communications (to include speeches, online working papers, a peer-reviewed journal, and a book publication program) to PAS audiences (which range from expert audiences to the mass public) to be able to get arguments and messages that deal with complex questions across to any potential consumer in digestible spoken and written prose. One reason why the impressive corpus of legal and constitutional writings on matters touching presidential accountability is rarely read outside legal and scholarly circles is because of inattention to this maxim.

Elite Management Consulting Firms

In the first part of this chapter I identified PAP as a think tank. I did so because certain think tanks are among the very few organizations that, across dissimilar functional areas, have managed to create extraordinary reputations for themselves as truly exceptional, as the PAP must strive to do. Examples include distinctive colleges and universities (Clark, 2007), some U.S. military groups at certain times in their histories (e.g., the Navy Seals, the Special Forces, the Green Berets, and the Marine Corps), the FBI in its early decades of existence, and the U.S. Forest Service (Kaufman, 2000).

Also part of this elite group is a small number of management consulting firms that have done so as well, and they belong among the models to be studied by PAP founders because they too have learned how to instill cultures of excellence and create impressive reputations for outstanding performance. They are also relevant here because of their *proven expertise in devising methods for changing selected aspects of the performance of client organizations in ways accepted and appreciated by the clients*. This is a useful way of specifying what PAP must be able to do across its highly diverse PAS client base.

Most lists of the best management consulting firms would include such names as McKinsey & Company, The Boston Consulting Group, Inc., Bain & Company, Booz & Company, and Deloitte Consulting LLP. I focus here on McKinsey because it has created a mystique not equaled by other such firms. It is based on achievements worth note and potential emulation by PAP. They include a century of extraordinary client satisfaction, superior self-promotion, excellent recruiting, and unusually comprehensive (and PAP-relevant) IT information systems to support its consultants.

By all accounts McKinsey client satisfaction stems from its rigorous techniques for framing problems and designing analyses, as well as from its methods for working with clients, interpreting results, and presenting highly credible solutions. Its trademark process is said to be sharp, insightful, carefully grounded analyses of its clients' problems followed by persuasive solution proposals. Their consultants use a carefully structured line of attack to frame client problems to make them susceptible to fact-based analysis. Their on-site consulting teams spend extensive amounts of time and energy first connecting with relevant client personnel then identifying and gathering all necessary data (company history, client objectives, in-depth interviews with major actors, document reviews, observation of system functioning, etc.) to enable them to frame problems precisely. McKinsey Partners and research team members engage client leadership and subordinates in the research process as well as the implementation of solutions. Host organizations are invariably impressed by the social facility, articulateness, and the "quick study" intelligence of team members. They also notice their tireless engagement, expertly executed research, the crisp, incisive problem diagnoses, and the cogent presentation of conclusions. The consistently favorable impression created by such disciplined, analytically powerful teams has done much to burnish the McKinsey brand. The success rate of McKinsey's recommended solutions has done nothing to diminish it (Rasiel and Friga, 2001).

As for self-promotion, the firm goes to great lengths to gain the confidence of decision makers not only in its active consulting projects but also in what it believes will be large or strongly growing markets for their services in the future. That is why McKinsey years ago made a strong push in countries such as China and India. Its willingness to invest great amounts of uncompensated time and energy in cultivating new markets in a dignified and measured way is impressive to those national leaders. Its financial stability as well as its self-assurance and professional commitment have all clearly added to its reputation. Interestingly, McKinsey's domestic public image cultivation is tastefully understated, but in a way that is decidedly self-enhancing. The strategy has been described as "a ... (shrewd) search for the spotlight (only) in situations where it really counts; combined with a reclusive attitude" when it does not. "A formal McKinsey interview with the outside world is a rare event" (Rasiel and Friga, 2001).

The pay and prestige of a job with McKinsey explain why the firm continues to be ranked as one of the most desirable employers for graduating MBA students. In many rankings they've actually been first for several consecutive years. Boston Consulting Group and Bain, competitors, also tend to make it into the top rankings—but struggle to challenge McKinsey for the top spot.

Unsurprisingly, McKinsey is extraordinarily careful about hiring, seeking personal impressiveness as well as cognitive talent. The firm is also unusual in that it seeks candidates who might be excluded by other consultancies such as doctors, physicists, and others with PhDs. "The McKinsey mould, it seems, is much broader than at other strategy firms" (Consultant-News.com, October 27, 2003).

The relevance of these attributes to the PAP is clear enough. The professional excellence ideal comes from GAO and CBO, but the McKinsey example usefully suggests that an extra element of dazzle and inspiration is worth striving to create. Though the firm has had 100+ years to develop its reputation, it is important to ask what it takes to achieve extraordinary client esteem from the planning stages through the first day of operations as well as through the decades. The political and constitutional sensitivity of both initial and established relations of PAP officials and analysts to representatives and members of the various agents of accountability organizations makes the McKinsey emphasis on personal impressiveness as well as professional credibility and technical competence worth particular note. If PAP is to inspire enough confidence to lead "client" accountability agents to accept its analysts' advice for adjusting their accountability operations, their ability to establish such bona fides will be paramount. This should influence how PAS positions are described and compensated.

Finally, McKinsey is relevant here because it invests significantly in its knowledge management system to support its field consultants. The PAP will need a system very much like this, but tailored to the specific tasks described in a preliminary way in the next section. The McKinsey system includes generalist researchers, industry- (and function)-specific experts and librarians, and access to journals and databases. McKinsey maintains an organization called the McKinsey Knowledge Centre (McKC) that provides rapid access to specialized expertise and business information. (Wikipedia, February 4, 2012). In addition, consultant-authored internal "practice development" documents capture generalizable insights from client engagements. There are also methods to access individual consultants with expertise from previous client studies or previous employment, for background assistance. The idea is to enable employees to have ready access to relevant facts, information sources, and potentially analogous solutions.

PAP Inception and Organization

Responsibility for the creation of the PAP, which will be a nonprofit 501 (c)(3) private sector corporation, will be vested in a founding Board of Directors. Its first order of business is to take this concept paper and translate it into a grant proposal to fund its second major task: turning the PAP concept into a functioning organization.

Board of Directors

After codifying the PAP mission and purpose through the process of incorporation and after creating the organization and recruiting key managerial and professional people to staff its major functions, the founders will assume traditional Board of Director duties. For example, the Board will retain responsibility for the integrity and implementation of the organizational mission, for ongoing supervision and replacement (when necessary) of the general manager and other officials identified below, for overseeing organizational planning, sustaining the resource base, approving and monitoring all PAP programs and services, and for approving and participating in efforts to establish a suitable PAP public image (Free Management Library, June 4, 2010).

General Manager

The PAP Organization Chart is depicted in Figure 5.1. First on the list below the Board is a general manager, the official charged with what management theorist Chester I. Barnard called "maintaining the organization" (Barnard, 1936). Unlike a traditional CEO, this official (and supporting staff) is charged with administrative,

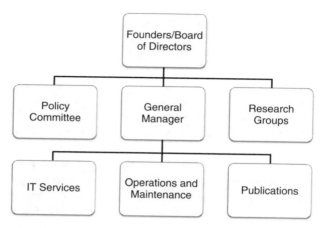

FIGURE 5.1 Organization Chart: The Presidential Accountability Project

not policy-making functions. The latter are reserved for the Board and its expert appointees throughout the organization.

The general manager will perform certain coordinative functions between the Policy Committee and the Research Groups under Board supervision. The office is also responsible for managing recruitment aims and processes established by the Board, for supporting the management and operations of all IT services, personnel operations, and publications groups headed by technical specialists. It takes the lead on organizing conferences and meetings, maintaining buildings and grounds, and has maintenance responsibility for communication and other organizational systems. The details of IT services, Operations, and Publications will not be further elaborated here. In the balance of this chapter we focus instead on the core elements of the PAP concept: the Policy Committee, and the Research Group.

Policy Committee

The lead substantive group is a *Policy Committee*: a permanent working group, whose director is appointed and supervised by the Board. The group is charged with two vital PAP functions: a) ensuring doctrinal "adds and updates" to enhance mission clarity and b) PAS client community building.

Mission Clarification

This work involves integrating (at the discretion of the Board in response to the recommendation of the Policy Committee) compelling new definitional influences into the PAP mission statement. Compelling influences may arise from any of several sources, including PAP research into historical accountability cases, points of view introduced by client accountability agents, the arguments of those who submit articles and books to PAP publication outlets, other relevant scholarly writings, and the lessons taught by ongoing accountability experience. Newly realized implications of the mission statement, as well as new (or newly discovered) sources of ideas not in focus when the original mission statement emerged, will also be subject to scrutiny. Examples would include thoughtful constructs like President Lincoln's "no precedent" doctrine of necessity, Justice Jackson's presidential power formula, and Professor Matheson's "executive constitutionalism" (Matheson, 2009: 155). Too, there will be continuing attention to mechanisms for balancing encouragement and restraint, and to the evolving macro-debate about what constitutes coherent presidential accountability. Any and all proposals for mission refinement will be posted on the PAP web site for comment and discussion, along with invitations to participate in more formal and extensive ways (e.g., periodic update conferences, follow-up submissions to PAP publication outlets, etc.).

It is unlikely that formal changes to the PAP mission statement will be frequent. It is also improbable that changes would force major departures from the search for better constitutional balance. Yet making doctrinal change a real possibility is essential for two reasons. First, it creates a more meaningful incentive to take part in discussion and debate about accountability issues. And because the potential audience (the PAS community) is so broad, the discussion will necessarily extend beyond the community of legal and constitutional scholars without excluding it (indeed, restatement in lay language may make that community's arguments more accessible and influential to this wider audience). Second, a discussion of this kind that is known to "count" for something has a chance to generate publicity for the web-accessible writings relevant to particular debates. This can increase public awareness of the scale and scope of presidential power, to the great benefit of a mass public now underprepared for both of its accountability agent tasks (voting and expressing "public opinion" based on assessments of presidential performance).

PAS Community Building

This is the essential effort first to "sell" the PAS to itself, and then to develop and maintain its sense of community. The PAP Board of Directors, whose membership will include representatives of most accountability agents, will identify colleagues willing to attend an inaugural conference and thereafter to introduce the PAS concept and disseminate information within their respective agent communities. The conference program will include a presentation on the comparative strengths and weaknesses of each of the seven agencies as instruments of accountability (based on the analysis in Chapter 3). Also explained will be the intended role of the PAP as a nonpartisan, research-and-analysis-based service organization dedicated to helping each agency (conceived of as clients) develop strategies for conceptualizing its own accountability mission, address accountability dysfunctions and accomplish "as-needed" voluntary coordination with other agents. Pursuant to the latter, an inter-agent steering committee will be proposed, as will annual PAS (all-agent) conferences.

Also to be broached is the idea of establishing on-site agent–liaison offices and mechanisms to facilitate developing relationships with the PAP and each other. Liaison arrangements will vary by agent characteristics. For example, formal and informal accountability agents such as Congress, the Supreme Court, and the political parties have fixed central locations able to house liaison activities. News reporters and historians, on the other hand, both widely dispersed across many organizations, would house liaison activities at national association sites.

The American people currently have no organization properly constituted and equipped to serve as their "central headquarters." That is why I reiterate in passing here a proposal initially made elsewhere for different but compatible reasons (Buchanan, 1991: 157; Buchanan, 2004b: 82–95). It is that a foundation be created to serve as a national center for promotion of the political interests and needs of the American people as a democratic citizenry. As noted earlier, the people are the source of sovereign power and the linchpin of the PAS. The president is the electorate's most important representative and its most widely shared political focus. That is why the people's role in the PAS must be among the concerns of such an organization. The Congress and the parties cannot serve the people in this particular capacity because they are electorally self-interested. Needed is a disinterested professional organization centered exclusively on those for whom representative democracy was created (Dahl, 1998: 46, 52). Called the *American Citizens' Foundation* (ACF), it will, like other accountability agent headquarters, situate its liaison and other PAP activities amidst its other priorities and organizational units (described in the cited references).

Agent Development Sessions

Some agent representatives will be lukewarm to the PAS idea. Others will be opposed. Both groups will be asked to join with less skeptical peers in attending a second series of briefing–and–discussion sessions aimed at illustrating the potential value of participation to representatives of each accountability agent in separate, agent-specific sessions. Here are brief descriptions of session topics for each of the accountability agents. The intent is to engage the agents in reflection on their own accountability problems, and to suggest how the PAP might be able to help.

Congress: Accountability and the Re-election Incentive

We have seen that Congress often avoids challenging presidents, especially in foreign policy, due to the anticipated electoral costs to members of doing so. This is problematic because it can take the best-equipped accountability agent in the PAS out of the equation. Congress has more formal authority and a larger collection of tools for influencing presidents than any other accountability agent. Many have concluded that there is no easy fix for this problem (e.g., Mann and Ornstein, 2006; Rudalevige, 2006). That suggests the proposition that is to be at the center of this session's discussion and debate: *The political cover of public opinion has been and will again be necessary to embolden Congress to use its plenary powers to ensure the respect of presidents.* The Research Group will introduce wars of choice as examples of congressional reluctance to deal forcefully with presidents. And it will offer examples (e.g., the Army McCarthy hearings, the McCarthy censure, the Irvin Committee hearings on Watergate, and the Clinton impeachment and Senate trial) where public opinion has been brought to bear on specific questions, crystallizing the congressional will to act in ways less likely without it. The policy trial proposal (Chapter 6) applies this principle to wars of choice.

Supreme Court: Power Balance, Pedagogy, and Partisanship

Of all the agents of accountability the Supreme Court has done the most to articulate written standards for holding presidents accountable in specific cases with decisions that, taken as a body of work, shows movement toward striking balances between the encouragement (e.g., the "sole organ" theory) and the restraint (e.g., the Bush era detainee cases) of presidential power. Justice Jackson's Youngstown opinion also set a precedent for what might become an ongoing pedagogical role for the Court by articulating a graduated presidential power standard linked to the consistency of presidential assertions with the will of Congress. A potential complication arises from charges of partisanship cited in Chapter 3 and raised again in a recent book by Justice Stephen Breyer (2010) who, with the increasingly activist Roberts Court in mind, stresses the importance to the Court's legitimacy of judicial restraint. Three questions for Supreme Court representatives arise from the corpus of presidential power cases and the legitimacy issue. First, given the president's role in the rise of the national security state and the history of Court support of presidential power: is there too much encouragement and not enough restraint? Relatedly, what is the proper balance, and what can be the Court's role in striking it? These questions will be discussed in light of a brief Research Group staff presentation summarizing Court cases touching presidential power. Second, is it reasonable or possible to encourage the Court to undertake additional pedagogy in the Jackson mold? Any Justice is free to do so in any presidential power opinion she or he writes. But few have. Why? Finally, is the appearance of judicial partisanship a threat to the legitimacy of presidential power rulings?

How Can Constructive Opposition Be Fostered?

As noted in Chapter 3 opposition to the executive by the rival political party is essential to democracy, but it serves the PAS only when its criticism is credible enough to be taken seriously by both president and citizens. Credible criticism can create useful incentives for presidents and can lead to compromise: a value espoused by recent "loyal opposition" concepts (Stolberg, February 21, 2009). The accountability value of opposition declines precipitously, however, when defeating the president becomes more important to it than forging compromise on policy. Then opposition does little more than seek to advance one side in a power struggle. That spirit was on display when Senate Minority Leader Mitch McConnell (R, KY) told the *National Journal* in October, 2010 that "The single most important thing we want to achieve is for President Obama to be a one-term president" (Tucker, October 26, 2010). The Research Group will present historical evidence mapping the ebbs and flows of constructive versus destructive political opposition. The question for this session is: what if anything can give opposition politicians the incentive to be constructively critical on a more consistent basis?

Reviving Accountability Journalism

There would be insufficient presidential performance information to serve as grist for the PAS mill without vigorous investigative journalism. But from the point of view of most presidents after Nixon, the scrutiny encouraged by Watergate was overwrought and had to be stopped, and they began restricting access (Woodward, 1999). Thereafter, presidential pushback went much further. Summarizing his book-length analysis of how the press was "poisoned" by presidential media strategies begun under Nixon and advanced by his advisors who served in the Reagan, Clinton, and Bush administrations, Mark Feldstein concluded:

> In all, the post-Watergate turnaround was breathtaking. Three decades after Nixon's resignation, his acolytes had completed a stunning reversal, expanding executive power while taming the news media. After the "erosion" that followed Watergate, Vice President Cheney said proudly, "we've been able to restore the legitimate authority of the presidency." Thanks to sophisticated propaganda, hardball intimidation, sensationalist distractions, and deregulatory bribery, Nixon's men had poisoned the press in a way their mentor never dreamed possible. Richard Nixon would have been proud.
>
> *(Feldstein, 2010: 365)*

Leading print news outlets would eventually apologize to their readers for what they came to see as insufficiently critical coverage of Bush Administration rationales for the invasion of Iraq. But in a media era dominated by declining print newspaper circulation, profit-driven TV news conglomerates, and TV and web-based partisan (Fox and MSNBC) "criticism" of presidents, what are the prospects for consistently high-quality accountability reporting by professional journalists? How can they be strengthened?

The Biographers' Tale: Unintended Consequences

The celebration of great presidents has incentivized extraordinary presidential efforts to achieve great things against long odds. This has yielded positive results, but it has also led some presidents to ignore contemporary criticism in the expectation of historical vindication. As the Research Group briefings on past presidents will show, the record is mixed. But the implications for presidential incentives have gotten little attention. This session considers those implications. The question: can presidential historians and biographers practice their craft with greater sensitivity to the incentives they help to nurture?

Citizen Preparedness and Impact

Citizens "staff" both the formal "presidential election" agency and the informal "public opinion" agency within the PAS. In the absence of an American Citizens' Foundation, who can represent the people in this agent development session that deals with both their roles in the PAS? Two groups would fill this bill. One is a collection of academics and foundation officers with established interest and expertise in citizen development. The other is a group of randomly selected "ordinary citizens," recruited to apply the necessary "reality test" to the notions of those who want to increase the quality of their functioning within the PAS. Quality is of the utmost concern here because, again, the president–public relationship is the most important in American representative democracy. Only citizens have the moral authority to legitimize and either directly or indirectly (through their influence on other accountability agents) both empower and restrain the president.

The strategic problem is that majorities are under-prepared for these tasks. This is widely understood, but occasions little remedial effort. Elected officials have little or no incentive to "improve" voters and many political scientists consider it either "rational" for citizens to be politically ignorant and indifferent (Riker and Ordeshook, 1968) or argue that "information shortcuts" enable voters to perform their civic duties adequately without significant investments of time and energy (see Kuklinski and Quirk, 2000 for a critique of this practice). Yet citizens are too important to the PAS to be left in a virtual "state of nature" when all who seek to influence them, including presidents and those within all the other agencies of the PAS, develop and apply professional skills to the task. Many political actors benefit from citizen political ignorance and indifference. But neither the people nor a political system ostensibly designed to protect their interests are beneficiaries. The system can only help citizens willing to help themselves by increasing their investments in presidential citizenship.

The Research Group presentation will place two items on the discussion agenda for this session. One is the inadequacy of political socialization in America for any level of citizen functioning, including presidential citizenship. The other is a general proposal to increase the use of coordination mechanisms (such as noncommercial forms of public interest polling and the policy trial device discussed in Chapter 6) intended to focus, inform, and deploy authoritative citizen input to affect national political decisions.

Research Group

Some Research Group activities have been mentioned, but it remains to describe its overall mission more fully. First, the group will be organized into six teams, corresponding to the various accountability agents. Thus, there will be teams for Congress, Court, citizens, media, history, and opposition, made up of relevant subject matter experts. Second, the work of the Group and of each team is broken into two overlapping parts: basic and applied research and client applications.

Research

The research mission is to create and maintain a knowledge management system akin to that developed by McKinsey but organized by accountability agent and targeted to accountability issues. This will initially involve synthesizing relevant secondary research literature into agent categories and making its relevance to the PAP mission explicit. As one example, a detailed review of Supreme Court opinions touching on the presidency (along with published secondary works covering similar ground) will be done, then interpreted to conclude what the Court has contributed to (or subtracted from) the "empower–restrain" balance doctrine to date. As another example, the history of citizen development efforts in the United States from the founding to the present will be compiled and a set of propositions extracted concerning what is and is not possible by way of enhancing civic competence, in search of lessons concerning how to achieve what is possible. Working histories of the accountability performance of each agent will shed valuable light on current practices and the potentials for improvement.

Once the "state of the art" has been identified for each agent, more specialized original research can be conducted. Some of this research may involve responses to agent requests, illustrating the potential overlap between research and client applications. For example, news reporters frequently ask whether contemporary partisan oppositional intensity and style are similar to other historical eras, and with what impact on the value of opposition to accountability. Such an inquiry could prompt a Media Team study that increased understanding of how and why the utility of opposition has varied.

Other research questions are most likely to arise from within. An obvious question of concern to those familiar with the comparative strengths and weaknesses of accountability agents detailed in Chapter 3 is the extent to which various agents have engaged in cooperative accountability strategies that allowed the strength of one agent to compensate for the weakness of another. Some familiar examples involve spontaneous rather than orchestrated cooperation. One case in point is the interactions of news reporters, courts, and Congress during the Watergate affair. Another is explained by Matheson (2009: 88): "for much of the Bush presidency Congress was substantially passive in the face of the administration's claims to executive power, but the Supreme Court set limits to such claims, in turn prompting Congress to take action."

Another Research Group function is to track the accountability performances of agents in the "here and now" in search of problems that invite reflection and discussion of possible solutions. One such problem is the politicization of congressional oversight, illustrated in Chapter 3 by the 109th and 110th Congresses. In these congresses, partisan majorities were easy on co-partisans and hard on opposition presidents. This adulterates the application of accountability into a double standard. It seems ill-advised to allow partisanship to distort the workings of accountability to this extent.

Another interesting problem is the "accountability gap" disclosed by the post-2006 Bush Administration, during which the lack of a re-election incentive (22nd Amendment) and the lack of supermajority votes needed to override vetoes and impose cloture trumped and disabled both majority public opinion and majority congressional opinion, leaving the president unchecked, accountable only to history. Is this a gap that somehow should be closed? It seems a question worthy of debate, followed by an advisory opinion issued by the Congress team.

Conclusion

Finally, the "war power" problem introduced in the early pages of this book remains unresolved. After Korea, it expanded to include Vietnam and Iraq, neither of which featured serious congressional involvement in the choice of war. There has been no adjustment to the congressional abdication of the war power. As shown again in the Libya incursion the War Powers Resolution of 1973 is ineffective and like it the proposed War Powers Consultation Act of 2009 leaves the Truman precedent in place.

It would take strong, nonpartisan medicine to get this issue back on the national agenda, but an act of creativity by a PAP Research Group with credibility similar to the GAO or CBO might be able to start a discussion. Suppose, for example, that the Research Group were asked to improve upon politically feasible but ineffective remedies like the War Powers Act, by addressing this intellectual exercise: "What would it actually take to re-engage the Congress in decisions about discretionary wars?" It might answer: "Use an established constitutional procedure—impeachment—to put a proposed policy of initiation or escalation of a war, rather than the president, on trial." The sixth and final chapter, which follows, combines political fact and fiction to develop this idea as an example of how the Research Group, in response to this most intractable of accountability problems, might attempt to "think outside the box."

6

PROSPECTIVE ACCOUNTABILITY FOR WARS OF CHOICE

Policy Trials

Nonessential wars like Vietnam and Iraq proposed for questionable reasons and legitimized by congressional resolutions based on unverifiable claims and misleading public appeals have imposed significant costs on the polity. How might such costs be avoided or reduced in the future? There is an established constitutional procedure—impeachment—that can be adapted to the task of putting a prospective military action (not the president) on trial before such action is taken. A policy trial would be a deliberative proceeding, a reasoned debate on the merits, invoked and controlled by Congress, if a president either requested congressional authorization or signaled the intent to use the military *for reasons legislators deemed debatable*. Policy trials would be triggered only by a president's proposal or apparent intent to order *optional* military deployments, not by time-sensitive emergencies created by attacks on the United States. For that reason such trials involve no challenge to the presidential discretion that makes truly necessary emergency action possible. This can be an effective way to authoritatively re-engage Congress in prospective decisions concerning whether or not to deploy the military, as the case study presented below will show.

Afghanistan: An Escalation of Choice

In the fall of 2009, while President Barack Obama was considering whether or not to send another large contingent of U.S. troops to Afghanistan, a substantial body of elite and mass opinion concluded that another presidential troop deployment was not essential and potentially contrary to the national interest. Unpersuaded, the president decided to increase an already sizable U.S. troop presence; in effect "upping the ante" in a war that had been initiated on October 7, 2001 by the Bush Administration in response to the 9/11 terrorist attacks on New York City.

He was moved to do so because the U.S. position had deteriorated. Beginning in 2002, the Bush administration diverted U.S. military, intelligence, economic, and diplomatic power from Afghanistan to Iraq. As a result the Taliban was able to regroup and again seriously threaten the Afghan government. As the situation worsened all agreed that it posed an increasing threat to U.S. interests. But there was substantial disagreement concerning how the United States should respond. The decision would be made by President Obama (Rubin, February 1, 2010).

Vice President Joseph Biden was only the highest profile figure to argue that a sizeable troop increase was neither essential nor the best approach to the problems posed by the resurgence of the Taliban and, to a lesser extent, Al Qaeda in Afghanistan. Insider accounts make it seem likely that if Biden had been president that step would not have been taken (Baker, December 6, 2009b: A1; Alter, 2010: 383). It seemed to Biden and others, such as the U.S. ambassador in Kabul, Karl W. Eikenberry, that there were significant questions about the adequacy of President Hamid Karzai of Afghanistan as a strategic partner, and that there were alternatives to sending in additional troops; alternatives that might yield better results at a lower cost (Schmitt, January 26, 2010a: A1). Karzai was already widely perceived as a major problem when in the fall of 2009 Eikenberry dispatched his top-secret cable strongly advising against reliance on a partnership with Karzai, who "shuns responsibility" for defense, governance, and development and has a "record of inaction" on corruption (Alter, 2010: 385). By April, 2010, after deciding to partner with him, President Obama had come to appreciate how serious a problem Karzai was. The president made a special trip to Kabul to chastise him for his failure to rein in corruption. Press accounts of administration unhappiness with the Afghan leader increased. Soon, Karzai struck back, going so far as to threaten to join the Taliban if his Western allies did not let up on their public criticism and pressure. He then ostentatiously met with President Mahmoud Ahmadinejad of neighboring Iran, who used his visit to Kabul as an opportunity to deliver a blistering diatribe against the United States.

Karzai would remain a major worry to the Obama Administration. But by then it was already too late to withdraw the extensive new investments of troops and resources it had made in its effort to defeat the Taliban and create a viable Afghan state. So the administration suspended its public criticism and resigned itself to working with him (Cooper and Landler, April 10, 2010: A1). As Fareed Zakaria put it, the United States could not replace him and could not succeed without him (Zakaria, April 12, 2010a: A17). As former Secretary of State James Baker put it, Karzai remained "the only game in town" (Baker, March 24, 2010 presentation, LBJ School and Library). That was still true when, in August of 2010, Karzai and the United States clashed over corruption again (Trofimov, August 4, 2010: A8).

Daunting questions remained. Could the expected U.S. military success possibly be followed by the establishment of a viable, centralized Afghan state required to allow the United States to withdraw? Would the American people, who had long been "growing tired of the war and might not accept many more years of extensive

American commitment" (Baker, October 14, 2009a: A1) keep faith with their president, given the widespread belief that stabilizing the situation in Afghanistan would require U.S. support of all kinds well beyond Mr. Obama's promised start date of July, 2011 for beginning to bring home the troops?

All Optional Deployments are Equal

The president's decision to up the ante in Afghanistan was optional, not essential. It was an expression of presidential preference rather than an unavoidable response to unarguable necessity. That is why the elective escalations of existing wars like Afghanistan (in which the original 2001 justification was no longer compelling, or escalation the only option for dealing with the new realities) should be treated like any other preference for optional military deployment: a proposal requiring the prior approval of Congress.

Why Prior Approval?

There are three reasons why prior approval should be sought in these circumstances: first, because exclusive presidential control is *not* truly necessary; second, because so many past presidents in similar circumstances who did not subject their preferences to rigorous challenge decreased their chances for success; and, third, because *not* seeking the considered prior approval of Congress and the people risks more rapid loss of support if things go wrong.

Presidential Control Unnecessary

Prior congressional approval is advisable first because in such circumstances exclusion of the Congress is not justifiable. There is no need for exclusive presidential control of the decision. Presidential control is essential only when there is urgent need for timely action. Optional deployments rarely involve significant time pressure. Emergencies that justify peremptory presidential action are typically responses to direct military aggression against the United States. There is usually insufficient time and few calls for prior congressional approval. Examples include the Civil War after Fort Sumter, World War I after German U-boat attacks on American shipping, and World War II after the Japanese attack on Pearl Harbor. There was similar aggression in the 9/11 airline hijackings by terrorists controlled by Osama Bin Laden from a base in Afghanistan that demolished the twin towers in New York, killing 3,000 Americans.

But if direct and immediate aggression against the United States is absent, and particularly if there is significant public and congressional opposition outside the president's immediate circle to initiating or increasing U.S. military action (decidedly true for Iraq in 2002 and Afghanistan in 2009, present but not intense for Vietnam in 1965, not present for Korea before the 1950 U.S. invasion), then there is both time for debate before decisions are made, and reason to broaden the range of authoritative input.

Inadequate Policy Analysis

The four presidential war initiatives addressed in this book (Korea, Vietnam, Iraq, and Afghanistan in 2010), all of which featured optional major, unprovoked (or not recently provoked) U.S. military action, did not provide for or allow full review of all the relevant considerations and/or options in the internal deliberations that preceded presidential action. As shown in Chapter 4, for example, there was no documented attention to non-Cold War North Korean motives in Truman's deliberations that might have affected how the war council interpreted the challenge. For his part, President Johnson escalated the war in Vietnam despite what he knew to be marginal prospects for success in part to avoid the disapproval of anti-communist war hawks in and outside his administration. George W. Bush made clear his primary reliance on his own "gut" instincts and his disregard for congressional opinion and the views of external national security experts before invading Iraq.

Barack Obama's decision-making process about Afghanistan was in most respects very different. A rich, detailed yet selective, and useful portrayal of Obama's mindset and his conflicts with the military, which also makes clear that much of what happened remains classified, is Alter's (2010: 363–94). The most orderly and authoritative chronological account of his pre-decision advisors' meetings available at this writing is offered by Baker (December 6, 2009b: A1). He and Alter both reported that the meetings involved graduate-seminar-level depth on the circumstances in both Afghanistan and Pakistan, and the most exhaustive such deliberations since the Cuban Missile Crisis. Baker reported that Obama was open to conflicting opinions, and that as new information unfolded and the debate wore on, everyone, including the president, changed their beliefs about the mission and the strategy due to the persuasiveness of the discussions. Alter added that "there was always a gravitas inside the Sit Room [described below] befitting the seriousness and complexity of the decisions" (Alter, 2010: 381).

Still, both Baker and Alter point out that one highly important question was *not* addressed: whether or not to withdraw from Afghanistan. In light of the reported thoroughness of the discussions of all the other options across no fewer than ten meetings it is surprising that in the second meeting with his war council on September 30, 2009, *the president closed the door on any discussion of pulling out of Afghanistan*: "I just want to say right now, I want to take off the table that we're leaving Afghanistan" (Baker, December 6, 2009b: A1). The president was undoubtedly motivated by his own repeated promises on the campaign trail to upgrade the U.S. effort in Afghanistan (which he had done on a smaller scale in the early months of his administration) and also by his conviction that Al Qaeda and other terrorist groups had potential access to Pakistani nuclear weapons, and thus posed an existential threat to the United States. He was said to have been motivated in part by a "new classified study of what would happen to Pakistan's nuclear arsenal if the Islamabad government fell to the Taliban" (Alter, 2010: 370–74). Nevertheless, a thorough review of U.S. options would require a consideration of the "no change" possibility. It would also require a careful airing and refutation of the arguments for troop withdrawal before ruling it out. Process experts would surely expect that such options (along with alternatives to troop increases for protecting U.S. interests) be fully vetted before any decision to approve a major military escalation was made. But the commander-in-chief chose not to permit that debate.

Another critical consideration, in some ways just as important, was also ruled off-limits by the president: the level of American public support required to sustain a major new military venture (Alter, 2010: 376). President Obama, like many of his predecessors, felt it was wrong to bring up political considerations in the Situation Room, the presidential decision center beneath the West Wing of the White House, where foreign policy decisions from Kennedy's in the Cuban Missile Crisis to Obama's in the Afghan troop surge have been made. This does not mean that the president and his political team did not consider this issue: they surely did. It does mean, however, that the *potential public role* in the success of the venture was not part of the discussion. Thus it had an unknown impact on the advice given to the president by his counselors.

These presidential decisions to rule important topics "out of bounds" are the principal reason why the decision-making process should expand beyond the president and his chosen advisors in non-crisis situations. First, the possibility of "group think" is always present in an advisory body whose discussions are led by a senior authority figure like the president (Janis, 1972). Even when participants are encouraged to speak their minds they are often reluctant to do so. This is also why the terms and ground rules governing the debate, including the subjects that may or may not be discussed, should not be dictated by the president. These are core arguments in support of the policy trial concept.

Of course presidential decision making can be flawed during the handling of unavoidable crises as well elective conflicts. But there is little to be done about that in such circumstances. Indeed, the greater the threat to a nation's survival the more likely are war leaders and citizens to feel bound together by the common effort to prevail. Even egregious battlefield mistakes, like those sometimes made by Prime Minister Winston Churchill in his desperate effort to fend off the Nazi onslaught, must be tolerated. Churchill's strategic choices, described by a recent chronicler of his war leadership as very mixed indeed (Hastings, 2010), were overlooked out of necessity. Recrimination becomes secondary to survival in such circumstances; leader support a matter of do-or-die patriotism.

But when a conflict is optional, not time-sensitive, and does not threaten national survival, public response to the president who "owns" it is likely to be far more critical, and public support for the war directly contingent on the publicly perceived level of timely battlefield success in relation to costs. In such circumstances, there can be hell to pay for a president who comes to be seen as having failed to get the decision right in the first place, and who then compounds that by failing to win decisively at an early date.

This dynamic is set in motion by the fact that congressional and public "buy-in" is so thinly and tenuously grounded at the start. Despite the emotionally charged congressional resolutions and supportive opinion polls that have sometimes followed the initial call for war, the people and their representatives feel no enduring sense of either shared purpose or responsibility for what happens after that. That is the president's problem.

Fragile Political Support

This is the basis for the third argument for treating optional deployments as special cases. Unless Congress and the people have a stake in the decision, such that responsibility for it is understood by all to be shared with the president, Congress, and the people, all but the president will have little incentive to endure unsatisfying war news resolutely. In fact, public and congressional support for the wars of choice discussed in Chapter 4 was eroded by bad war news. Once the Chinese entered the Korean War, American support plummeted. In Vietnam, massive troop deployments were yielding little progress and were tolerated only until the (mis)perceived victory of the enemy in the Tet Offensive abruptly exhausted public patience. There were significant pockets of doubt from the beginning about the wisdom of invading Iraq, and support for the war had declined to barely half those polled by the time President Bush was narrowly re-elected. The U.S. troop "surge" that improved the chances for a successful outcome did not substantially improve the president's standing before he left office. Even if a stable and democratic Iraq eventually emerges, the question of whether happy endings should excuse unprovoked attacks will still divide American public opinion to some extent.

Unsurprisingly, presidents have often sought to avoid such debates, and any need for public support, by recourse to secret uses of force, at least when a problem of small-enough scale made that option seem feasible. Stephen Kinzer (2006) documents many instances in which potential condemnation of U.S. "regime change" operations in places like Nicaragua (Taft, 1909) and Iran (Eisenhower, 1953) was sidestepped by using covert operations.

The widely perceived failure of the three highly public conflicts discussed in Chapter 4 and the discomfort prompted by the Obama Afghan initiative collectively invite consideration of a novel approach to reaching decisions about optional initiation or escalation of large-scale military ventures: a turn toward power sharing. The argument is that discretionary war should require the prior approval of the two most important agents within the PAS: the Congress and the American people, convened in a unique way (the policy trial method to be described later) in response to any presidential proposal to take unprovoked military action on a large scale.

Why Congress Needs the People

The involvement of Congress in such ventures is obligatory, since Congress alone has the constitutional power to declare war. Why, then, must the American people be involved? Why should they not simply leave it to their elected representatives to make such decisions in consultation and/or debate with the proposing president? The answer is clear: the record shows that the modern Congress will not challenge a president bent on war without political cover provided by their voting constituents. Congress, in fact, rarely moves on any big controversial question unless pressed by clear, stable and electorally consequential public opinion (Buchanan, 2004a: 96–107). A Congress that won't stop a controversial presidential war without the kind of constituency pressure that ended its support for Vietnam will certainly not be willing to put a president's call for war on trial in its absence.

Why is this case? Consider first Congress's modern record in dealing with foreign and national security policy. Historians and constitutional scholars have been unhappy with the failure of Congress to aggressively protect its constitutional war powers against presidential encroachment (e.g., Schlesinger, 1973, 2004; Fisher, 2004a; Wills, 2010). In fairness, however, Congress has not been entirely deferential to presidents in this area. For example, it has from time to time under certain well-specified conditions—opposition party control, the size of a proposed deployment, and the state of international obligations—imposed significant checks on presidential war power. Howell and Pevehouse (2007: 223) and other authors also show that the Congress has aggressively challenged presidential war policy. For example, it badgered Truman, Johnson, and Bush, more or less continuously, affecting war policy to greater or lesser degrees in all three cases. But Congress has not seriously challenged a major presidential military initiative since before the U.S. entry into World War II. Thus, the question: under what conditions would Congress be willing to insert itself into the decision-making process concerning elective military action *before* troops are dispatched?

This question arises because most recent congressional assertions of its constitutional authority over the president in the area of war power involve *retrospective* accountability (i.e., the application of restraints or punishments *after* presidents have acted). And although such "after the fact" accountability is essential to representative democracy, not least to inform the judgment of history and to prepare voters for the next election (Buchanan, 2004b: 51–52), it lacks what is proposed here: action by the Congress to vet a proposal *before* a president may start a nonmandatory war. As noted in Chapter 3, Congress is the only accountability agent with the constitutional power to impose prior restraint on presidential action. To paraphrase Senator Arthur Vandenberg's famous assertion: [Congress should be in on] "the policy takeoffs instead of merely ... the crash landings" (Rudalevige, 2006: 276). But as Howell and Pevehouse note, it is rare for Congress to use its powers to restrain a president *before* a conflict actually begins (Howell and Pevehouse, 2007: 21).

Political Will

A serious pre-invasion congressional vetting of any prospective decision for war would certainly be constitutional. It might increase the likelihood of durable public support for the war, and it could be designed to increase the quality of the decision-making process. But the Congress has shown no recent inclination to initiate a review of its own. It is only when outsiders forced the issue—either presidents demanding resolutions of congressional support or public opinion signaling implacable opposition to the Vietnam War—that Congress was moved to act at all.

Conventional wisdom concerning the fecklessness of Congress in such cases is succinctly captured by former JFK speechwriter Ted Sorensen, who observed: "Congress already has enormous power, if it only had the guts to use it" (quoted in Roberts, 1974: 27). More recently, reflecting on the modern legacy of presidential wars of choice pundit George Will made the same point: "Congress' constitutional powers relevant to war-making have atrophied from disuse" (Will, May 5, 2008: A9). And in an interview shortly before his death, former JFK and LBJ defense secretary Robert McNamara lamented the absence of congressional oversight of ultimately unsuccessful Vietnam War policy during the Johnson Administration. "I think the Congress, particularly with respect to war, should play a greater role than it does ... In some way, the Congress should retain a lasting and a continuing interest in war" (Woodward and Goldstein, October 25, 2009: F1).

Perhaps it should, but scholars of Congress are not optimistic that it will happen anytime soon. For example, after reviewing the history of the matter, Christopher Deering concluded that "despite the intentions of the founders, the politics of war and foreign affairs are very much transformed relative to the century following the adoption of the Constitution ... a dramatic resurgence of congressional influence in war and foreign affairs is highly unlikely" (Deering, 2005: 372, 373). Similarly, after their book-length assessment of the current state of the institution, Thomas Mann and Norman Ornstein wrote that "We wish we could ... restore Congress to what it should be and at times has been. Unfortunately, there is no quick fix ... the lesson for our purposes is that major change within Congress is most likely to originate outside" (Mann and Ornstein, 2006: 226; 227).

Incentives

What is it that so consistently prevents Congress from asserting its power on matters of peace and war? The answer is collective action and self-interest problems that leave individual members of both houses with no incentive to join together to vigorously challenge the president on such politically fraught decisions. The reason is that such decisions threaten their hold on elective office. When confronted with these choices they tend to function defensively. Said Texas Rep. Ron Paul, "Congress would rather give up its most important authorized power to the president and the U.N. than risk losing an election if the war goes badly" (quoted in Rudalevige, 2006: 276). Related to re-election are the kind of partisan incentives described in Chapter 3, illustrated by the tendency of Republicans to uncritically support President Bush's Iraq policy. Why, then, did many congressional Republicans not oppose President Obama's decision to order troop increases in Afghanistan and drone attack increases in Pakistan? Both parties supported the president's expansion of the drone attacks as "a potent weapon against terrorism that put no American lives at risk" (Shane and Schmitt, January 23, 2010: A1). But it was Republicans in greater numbers than Democrats who supported the decision to increase troop deployments to Afghanistan by 30,000.

Republican support for the president's troop increase decision did not reflect a sudden emergence of bipartisanship. The president, after all, had been unable to attract a single Republican vote on his health care initiative, a longstanding Democratic Party priority, largely for strategic partisan reasons. The Republicans sided with the president's troop initiative, however, because it was consistent with what had been Bush Administration policy, and because they knew that most Democrats in Congress were opposed. There was therefore no challenge to the Republican Party's recent "ownership" of national security issues. On this issue, Republican policy and partisan interests were both served by supporting a president who was defying his own party (Henninger, January 14, 2010: A14).

Most noteworthy for present purposes, however, is the absence in these Bush and Obama examples of support for the hypothesis ventured by James Madison in Federalist 51, that "the great security against a gradual concentration of the several powers in the same department, consists in giving to those who administer each department the necessary constitutional means, *and the personal motives*, to resist encroachment of the others" (Wills, 1982: 262, emphasis added). As the Bush–Obama examples show, this particular personal motive is most decidedly missing. Nowhere inside Congress was there apparent concern for the incentive that the founders hoped their "separation of powers" design would at least encourage if not guarantee: institutional loyalty strong enough to impel members of Congress to set lesser personal motives aside to defend against executive encroachment on their constitutional prerogatives.

Prospective Accountability

Since World War II, constitutionally mandated "ambition against ambition" has not been enough to get the Congress to seize the initiative when the issue involved the war power. Again, a Congress that will not stop a war without sustained popular pressure (e.g., Vietnam) surely will not move to prevent or limit the start or escalation of a war without overwhelming public encouragement. The only law to date intended to impose a measure of prospective accountability aimed at checking discretionary presidential war making was the War Powers Resolution of 1973. Passed due to unhappiness with Vietnam, the Act requires (among other things) the president to consult with Congress "in every possible instance" *before* putting American troops in harm's way: an explicit reach for prospective influence. Not unexpectedly, every president since Nixon has regarded the resolution as unconstitutional. Further, each of these presidents conducted one or more military operations with either perfunctory or no consultation with Congress. As Michael Nelson observes, "(t)he main lesson of more than three decades of experience under the resolution is that law cannot substitute for political will if Congress intends to curb the president's role in war making" (Nelson, 2008: 221).

A bipartisan proposal, advanced in 2008 by two former secretaries of state, has sparked little controversy and so far has been ignored. It too reaches for prospective influence. But it would be just as unlikely to work as the War Powers Act if adopted. It sought to replace that measure with something called the War Powers Consultation Act. The proposed legislation (except in emergencies) "require(s) the president and congressional leaders to discuss the matter before going to war" (Baker and Christopher, July 8, 2008: A23). Like the 1973 law this proposal is prospective in intent, and it would go beyond the War Powers Act by creating a special congressional committee and staff to implement the consultations. The Congress would be required to vote on a resolution of approval within 30 days of a president's deployment of force, failing which any member of Congress could propose a resolution of disapproval. But that resolution would have the force of law only if passed by both houses of Congress and then only if a near-certain presidential veto could be overridden.

The problem with this initiative was identified by the proposing Commission's vice-chair, Rep. Lee Hamilton (R–IN): "Presidents will do what they want to do, and they have the constitutional power to do it. What we hoped to ensure is that they hear other points of view before they do" (Broder, July 9, 2008, online). In one way or another, Presidents Truman, Johnson, Bush, and Obama each did hear "other points of view." But although these presidents informally "consulted" with a few members of Congress before acting, none was moved to invite any member or members of Congress to participate in their internal war deliberations. These examples show that without an uncharacteristically vigorous assertion of existing congressional war and budgetary powers to *require* that prospective military action be put on trial *before the president is authorized* to dispatch troops, presidential consultation with Congress will be meaningful only if the president wants it to be.

Prerequisites to Change

The prospects for changing this reality cannot be described as promising. But that need not deter attempts like this to identify what it would actually take to bring it about. Most if not all major reforms begin as improbable "what ifs." As acknowledged in Chapter 1 significant change is always politically difficult. But it is not impossible to make it happen. What would it take here?

In the first place, change would require an adjustment to what has since 1950 been complete presidential dominance of the "national security state" which was spawned by the Cold War and extended by the Terror War. As has been noted, executive dominance arose due to the perceived need for timely and forceful action in response to crises (Deering, 2005; Wills, 2010). But because they allow time for reflection before acting *wars of choice can be viewed as falling outside the crisis imperative that led Congress and the American people to accept total presidential control of the war power.* I argue that *voluntary* military action is a unique kind of choice that is the logical place to experiment with an *equally unique form of power sharing* that can benefit the national interest without weakening the presidency. The obvious first question is: what now keeps presidents from ceding even this limited ground?

The answer is a series of disincentives put in place by the circumstances surrounding Truman's initiation of the Korean War. First, since Truman's peremptory action presidents have no incentive to share the war power with Congress unless it uses its plenary power to force it. Second, Congress will *not* force it without reliable, re-election-protecting political cover from the people. And, third, the people cannot be expected to supply political cover without the signal of a formal public debate on the question of whether or not to start or increase U.S. involvement in a war, a debate in which they are cued by media and political elites that they have a decisive role to play.

These are the missing incentives that leave the president unchallenged. The key point to notice, however, is that only the people can create them. That is because *only they have the leverage to get the Congress to put pressure on the president.* That is why (to answer the question posed at the beginning of this chapter section) the people must be involved. But to create popular leverage there must be a method for deploying the people, a "coordination mechanism" capable of bringing their moral and political leverage to bear in a way authoritative enough that both the Congress and the president have the incentive to come into compliance with their clearly expressed will. Presidential and congressional elections are examples of such coordination mechanisms. The policy trial is intended to serve as another.

Policy Trials

Unlike the War Powers Act and the War Powers Consultation proposal discussed above, what follows was not crafted with political feasibility in mind. The failure of the War Powers Act and the timidity of the proposed War Powers Consultation Act suggest that anything noncontroversial enough to be politically feasible will not be strong enough to work. So before worrying about feasibility, we must first ask what can actually be strong enough to work without altering the Constitution. The policy trial proposal is designed to address the "missing incentives" problem.

One step in that direction is to establish a formal procedure that features a real debate on the merits and not merely rally events designed to build what Chapter 4's cases suggest will be little more than temporary emotional support for a president's war policy. Ultimately, policy trials can be among the "correction factors" promoting the calibration of presidential power away from unnecessary expansion, as discussed in Chapter 1.

Mechanics

The model for a policy trial is the impeachment process, as described in Article 1 sections 2 and 3 of the Constitution, except that what is on trial is a prospective war policy, not the president. The power to establish a policy trial process is in Article 1 Section 4, which grants each House the right to determine the rules of its own proceedings.

The process, set in motion by a majority vote of the House, would impose special rules of order designed to create a formal public debate on the pros and cons before any congressional resolution or declaration of war is possible, and before the president is authorized to deploy military force. Invoking the procedure signals the president that he and his representatives must formally defend the proposal against well-prepared opponents with the Chief Justice presiding and, in a departure from the impeachment process, both the House and the Senate empaneled as the jury.

The gravity of the choice (in the fictional case below, the options are to escalate or pull out of Afghanistan) and the luxury of time to fully consider the pros and cons using the best available information (actually present in the cases of Afghanistan, Vietnam, and Iraq, partially accessible in the case of Korea) justify a temporary, decision-specific suspension of traditional deference to the president. Deference now leaves presidents free to pre-empt (Obama), evade (Truman), obstruct (Bush), or manipulate (Johnson) congressional debate as they see fit. It is clearly understood that invocation of a policy trial does not alter the traditional presidential power to act unilaterally in time-sensitive emergencies and crises.

The Role of the Public

Finally and most importantly, invoking the procedure signals the American people that something rare and serious is afoot. They will pay closer attention than usual to the (inevitably televised) proceedings because the news media and political elites will tell them that if history is any guide, their reaction will play a vital role in determining the outcome.

In fact, on this count, there is nothing new here. Public opinion has often been highly influential, indeed decisive, in the resolutions of a wide variety of high-profile formal congressional proceedings. Examples include the Army McCarthy hearings, the McCarthy censure, the Irvin Committee hearings on Watergate, and the Clinton impeachment and Senate trial. Public opposition to U.S. engagement in World War II led Congress to pass two Neutrality Acts (in 1935 and 1937) that prevented a frustrated President Roosevelt from helping the allies before the U.S. entry into the war.

These examples suggest that policy trials would be decisive. They would be decisive because, as in the examples, they would be preceded by highly explicit "role-sending" publicity which would put the people on notice that their collective judgment about a major decision facing Congress is likely to carry great weight.

If history is any guide, such role sending, particularly when followed by deliberative policy trial proceedings, would almost certainly crystallize a public consensus that is informed, coherent, and sturdy enough both to influence and politically protect members of Congress, most of whom will follow the public's lead.

Who Benefits, and How?

Finally, is this is an attack on the presidency? No, and here is why: first, policy trials are a way to ensure a more rigorous mode of policy analysis than presidents have undertaken in these circumstances by themselves. There are no guarantees, but there is also no denying that a policy that is carefully vetted before adoption has a better chance to work than a military venture that is rushed through under emotionally evocative circumstances. That is why a more cautious procedure helps all concerned: including the president, the Congress, and the people. Just as important, policy trials can be a way to head off untenable military initiatives. An agreement to stand down and think carefully before embracing a war option can make it easier to expose questionable proposals before they are launched. That too would clearly serve the interests of all.

Especially helpful to the president is a way to create shared responsibility and durable support: things that presidents acting alone to initiate wars have been unable to achieve. This can happen when all three principals—President, Congress, and the people—after careful review agree that a particular elective war is in the national interest. A president who persuades the people and the Congress through a disciplined policy review rather than through an informal rally campaign is much more likely to implicate them psychologically; that is, to create "buy-in" for a policy, if it must have their approval to be enacted. This also implies something else that helps all three principals: credit sharing when things go right and blame sharing if things go wrong—as can happen even to carefully vetted policies. Importantly, blame sharing can reduce political system-draining recriminations of the kind that followed Korea, Vietnam, and Iraq. In sum, blame or credit sharing for optional acts mutually agreed upon after careful review is the scenario best able to approach rational policy democratically arrived at.

Finally, there is in this proposal an opportunity to re-engage the Congress—in a limited but significant way—in national security decision making. This should be of interest to those who have expressed dissatisfaction with the rise of the national security state and what they regard as its elevation of an unnecessarily dominant president (e.g., Fisher, 2004a, Fisher, 2004b; Deering, 2005; Bacevich, 2010b; Wills, 2010) and other supporters of the original constitutional design who especially dislike the war powers marginalization of the Congress (Rudalevige, 2006: 261–85). And the carefully circumscribed situations in which the president would be required to share power under my proposal should be reassuring to those who fear and reject anything that would compromise complete presidential control in authentic emergencies.

I will offer an illustration of how the first policy trial can be made to work in practice in the fictionalized recasting of the 2009 Afghanistan troop increase decision presented as the last and longest section of this chapter. First, however, let me explain the policy trial triggers, which show why Afghanistan is a fitting case upon which to base my illustration of the policy trial process. Then, as the last step before presenting the policy trial debate, we look at the state of play at the time the president made his decision to up the ante in Afghanistan. That is the base upon which the fiction will rest.

Policy Trial Triggers

Afghanistan is a fitting case because it features the six characteristics, listed in Table 6.1, that make a military proposal from the president a candidate for a policy trial. *First*, the initiation/escalation of what are substantial troop deployments must truly be *optional* rather than essential (with "essential" meaning that there is an immediate and undeniable threat to national security requiring an immediate military response that leaves no time for such a procedure). Although President Obama called Afghanistan a "war of necessity" due to the need to prevent the Taliban from recreating for Al Qaeda the sanctuary that it had in the 1990s (see below for more detail), informed critics on the right and left saw many plausible alternatives to a large troop deployment to address that problem, making the troop increase option a clear matter of choice rather than necessity to a significant body of opinion (Schmitt and Shane, September 8, 2009: A1). *Second*, the prospects for military success will be uncertain; such that there are no guarantees of victory to offset what will inevitably be significant costs. This was decidedly true at this writing in Afghanistan because, as one high-profile editorial put it, "there will never be enough American troops on the ground to defeat the Taliban or provide security for Afghans" (Mr. Obama's Task, November 19, 2009: A26) and also because the capacity of the Afghans to defend themselves against the Taliban without U.S. help was still the subject of concern after the president's decision. In short, success simply could not be reliably forecast at the moment the president decided to escalate U.S. troop involvement. Moreover, the link between securing Afghanistan and guaranteeing the prevention of additional major terrorist attacks within the United States was never a certainty,

TABLE 6.1 Policy Trial Triggers

- Troop deployment is optional, not essential
- Military success is uncertain
- There is public, elite ambivalence/reluctance
- There is potential for unintended expansion
- Congress is otherwise excluded from decision
- There is ample time for policy trial procedures

not least because the terrorist threat had metastasized well beyond the borders of Afghanistan. *Third,* there was limited-to-nonexistent enthusiasm for an expanded troop deployment on the part of nonexpert political elites and citizens. To be sure, the proposal at the moment of choice was not hotly controversial. It was at the time a second-or-third-tier issue. But it had generated disagreement and significant opposition, as measured by media reports of elite pushback and public opinion polls (Baker, October 14, 2009a: A1; Schmitt and Shane, September 8, 2009: A1; On Afghanistan: A Negative Shift, May 25, 2010).

Fourth is some potential for later, unintended expansion of U.S. involvement. President Obama added 30,000 U.S. troops to the 68,000 already in place by the end of 2009. The United States was partnered with a corrupt government and an inept army facing an Afghan insurgency that, in the words of Maj. Gen. Michael Flynn, the head of military intelligence, "can sustain itself indefinitely" (Filkins, February 21, 2010: wk 1). It seemed highly unlikely that the United States would be able to hand over complete control to the Afghan government or military within many years after the July, 2011 drawdown start date. And it could not be ruled out that pressure to up the military ante would be felt in order to avoid an embarrassing collapse of the effort. For example, the May, 2010 Times Square bomber episode made it apparent that Pakistan-based terrorist groups could still reach and threaten the United States. That led the Obama war council to begin seriously contemplating a "boots on the ground" expansion to Pakistan, which to that point had been off-limits (Perlez, May 9, 2010b: A6).

Fifth is the likelihood, borne out in this case as in those discussed before, that *Congress would be excluded* from administration deliberations and decisions unless it insisted on being involved. President Barack Obama's actual consultations with Congress seem from the outside to have been as perfunctory as those of his "wars of choice" predecessors while confronting a similarly portentous moment of choice. Obama's choice did not involve the *initiation* of a war. But it did involve choosing among the options of abandoning, downsizing, or escalating an existing military conflict that had lost public support and that to escalate would, given the unsettled circumstances in Afghanistan, represent a "high stakes gamble" for the president and the nation (Baker, December 6, 2009b: A1). The *sixth* and final important similarity between his circumstances and those faced by his WOC (War of Choice) predecessors was that President Obama had ample time to consider his options. Indeed he would be criticized by those (mostly Republicans) who were eager for a speedier decision to escalate, some of whom accused him of "dithering."

Scheduling a Policy Trial

How is such an event to be placed on the national agenda? Since Congress rarely moves on big controversial questions without public support, the public may first have to decide if a policy trial is necessary before Congress can be expected to initiate it.

The Campaign for a Policy Trial

If called upon to do so, the American people are best able to make such a poll-tested decision in response to the equivalent of a national political campaign that had debated whether or not to put a president's prospective war policy on trial. Such an approach would resemble the kind of nonelectoral political campaigns that preceded the 2010 success of the Obama health care initiative and the failure of the Clinton health care initiative in 1993. Given sufficient controversy there will be members of Congress with the skill, the motivation, and the access to resources needed to finance, organize, and deploy a campaign able to compete with the president's.

Antagonists vs. Protagonists

The president and his allies can of course be counted on to campaign aggressively both on the merits of their proposal as well as against any departure from established deference to presidential control of the war power. They will argue that such a trial would only weaken the presidency and ultimately make the nation more vulnerable to its enemies. For their part, trial proponents too will be forced to confront the president's prestige and available expertise, which will make it hard to make the case against military action on the merits. But they will also be able to argue that the costs of previous elective wars (Korea) or elective war escalations (Vietnam) have consistently outweighed most if not all benefits to the national interest. In cases like Afghanistan, Iraq, or Vietnam, with no particular time urgency, the debate can be lengthy. If the president enjoys majority support early and holds it there will be no trial. If the issue is controversial enough, a split public decision might be sufficient to motivate Congress to act.

Unlike formal trials (whether legal trials, impeachment trials, or the proposed policy trials) where rules of order and procedure specify what is in and out of bounds, a campaign of any sort is as noisy and as emotionally manipulative as participants feel the need to be, constrained only by the risk of alienating the public, in what is likely to be an intense effort to prevail. The serious prospect of such an unfettered campaign might itself discourage presidents without real conviction that a prospective war both serves the national interest and can be won (President Lyndon Johnson, for example, felt sure of the former but not of the latter).

Reality: Presidential Escalation in Afghanistan

President Obama's attitudes toward the wars in Iraq and Afghanistan were made clear while he was an Illinois state senator. That was when he first expressed opposition to the invasion of Iraq, while leaving the door open to other military ventures. He made that willingness clear in the fall of 2002, as the Bush Administration rallied the country for an invasion of Iraq. He appeared at an anti-war demonstration in Chicago and said "I'm not opposed to all wars. I'm opposed to dumb wars" (Wilson, January 19, 2010: A1). Later, during his 2008 campaign for the nomination of his party and for election to the presidency, he vowed, if elected president, to send more troops to Afghanistan. He promised repeatedly to pursue Al Qaeda along the border with Pakistan. "By the time he reached the point of decision, his lack of room to maneuver was mostly of his own making" (Alter, 2010: 363). In the spring of 2009 then President Obama called the 2001 American invasion of Afghanistan, which was a response to the 9/11/2001 attack on the New York City Trade Center by Al Qaeda that killed thousands of Americans on their own soil, a "war of necessity." In March he ordered 21,000 additional troops to Afghanistan (Alter, 2010: 365). Later, in the fall of 2009, due to setbacks in U.S. fortunes despite the initial troop increase, plus questions of whether a corrupt Afghan regime could be a reliable war partner against the Taliban or Al Qaeda, Mr. Obama was pressured by military leaders to again substantially increase U.S. troop deployments to Afghanistan. After an elaborate three-month, ten-meeting decision-making procedure he concluded that he should send in 30,000 additional troops, while seeking 10,000 additional NATO troops. That is what he did.

Obama's Arguments for Escalation

Faced with what amounted to a choice for or against a major escalation of (and, at least in theory, the possibility of choosing to withdraw from) the Afghan War, President Obama initiated a far more searching internal deliberative process than anything Truman, Johnson, or Bush had undertaken before ordering optional large-scale troop deployments. In the fall of 2009, he began (as noted) a procedure that would extend across three months to ten meetings with various groups of foreign policy and military advisors to consider his decision. The process was prompted by the August 20, 2009 Afghan election, which because of ballot stuffing raised questions about the president's initial game plan and the viability of the U.S. relationship with such a government "partner" as Hamid Karzai, the winner of a disputed election, branded at home and abroad as corrupt, that gave him another term as president of Afghanistan.

The lessons President Obama drew from his lengthy study of the Afghan problem, culminating in his explanation of the reasons for his troop increase decisions, were initially stated in two key speeches, beginning with his December 1, 2009 West Point address, which I quote here and below at length:

> When I took office, we had just over 32,000 Americans serving in Afghanistan compared to 160,000 in Iraq at the peak of the war. Commanders in Afghanistan repeatedly asked for support to deal with the reemergence of the Taliban, but these reinforcements did not arrive. And that's why, shortly after taking office, I approved a long-standing request for more troops. After consultations with our allies, I then announced a strategy recognizing the

fundamental connection between our war effort in Afghanistan and the extremist safe havens in Pakistan. I set a goal that was narrowly defined as *disrupting, dismantling, and defeating* al-Qaeda and its extremist allies, and pledged to better coordinate our military and civilian efforts. Since then, we've made progress on some important objectives. High-ranking al-Qaeda and Taliban leaders have been killed, and we've stepped up the pressure on al-Qaeda worldwide. In Pakistan, that nation's army has gone on its largest offensive in years. In Afghanistan, we and our allies prevented the Taliban from stopping a presidential election, and although it was marred by fraud, that election produced a government that is consistent with Afghanistan's laws and constitution. Yet huge challenges remain: Afghanistan is not lost, but for several years, it has moved backwards. There's no imminent threat of the government being overthrown, but the Taliban has gained momentum. Al-Qaeda has not reemerged in Afghanistan in the same numbers as before 9/11, but they retain their safe havens along the border. And our forces lack the full support they need to effectively train and partner with Afghan security forces and better secure the population. Our new commander in Afghanistan, General McChrystal, has reported that the security situation is more serious than he anticipated. In short, the status quo is not sustainable.

The president went on to extol his policy review:

The review has allowed me to ask the hard questions and to explore all the different options, along with my national security team, our military, and civilian leadership in Afghanistan, and our key partners. And given the stakes involved, I owed the American people and our troops no less. This review is now complete. And as commander-in-chief, I have determined that it is in our vital national interest to send an additional 30,000 U.S. troops to Afghanistan.

(Obama West Point Speech, December 1, 2009)

Obama's Cost–Benefit Analysis

The most thorough available account of Mr. Obama's decision-making process made it clear that the president's decision involved his own cost–benefit analysis (Baker, December 6, 2009b: 1). He had been supplied with estimates showing a $1 trillion price tag if the Afghan war lasted ten more years. And he had walked among the graves at Arlington National Cemetery and visited severely wounded soldiers at Walter Reed Hospital, in a self-forced confrontation with the human cost of war.

Just two weeks before hearing then-Afghan commanding General Stanley A. McChrystal's August, 2009 warning that the war effort would fail without a substantial increase in troops the president had referred to Afghanistan as a "war of necessity." When he announced his strategy at West Point he avoided that phrase. His policy review had convinced him that a troop increase was an essential recommitment to the war on Al Qaeda. But it would be temporary, with the troop drawdown to begin in July, 2011, because the larger struggle for Afghanistan "had to be balanced against the cost in blood and treasure and brought to an end." The president's "high stakes gamble" was that a "quick jolt of extra forces could knock the enemy back on its heels enough for the Afghans to take over the fight" (Baker, December 6, 2009b: A1).

As for what the indicators of success and failure would be, General McChrystal's troop increase proposal, leaked to Bob Woodward just a week after the initial September 13, 2009 Obama war council meeting (in an apparent attempt by the Pentagon to force the president's hand; see Alter, 2010), explained why succeeding in Afghanistan required more troops: to permit a strategy shift from a focus on disabling the Taliban—considered impossible by the group despite Obama's repeated public claims to the contrary—to capturing and stabilizing population centers so as to protect resident civilians while preparing Afghan military and police to protect those gains when U.S. forces withdrew.

Obama's specification of July, 2011 as the month in which withdrawal would begin was a message to the military. Jonathan Alter (2010) reports that the internal pressure brought to bear by the president to bind the military to that time frame was extraordinary, and that the defense secretary and the generals signed on unequivocally. Nevertheless, many people, both in and outside the administration, at the time and subsequently, have publicly either qualified or doubted the validity of that pledge. The president himself was less than fully clear about what the pledge meant. At his joint press conference with President Karzai in Washington on May, 12, 2010, for example, in response to a reporter's question that framed his initial pledge as having been to "remove most troops" by that date, he was equivocal. He made it clear that troop drawdowns would *begin* then, but did not address how rapid the withdrawal would be. By November 2010, in an effort to convince both Afghans and the Taliban that the United States would not leave en masse, the president had "tweaked" his departure message to suggest that while U.S. troop departures would still begin in 2011 it would be 2014 before the United States would hand over the defense of Afghanistan to the Afghans themselves (Bumiller, November 10, 2010c).

Nevertheless, the president's objectives, as articulated in the following selection from his December 2009 speech to West Point cadets, apparently still reflected his thinking:

> As cadets, you volunteered for service during this time of danger. Some of you have fought in Afghanistan. Some of you will deploy there. As your commander-in-chief, I owe you a mission that is clearly defined and worthy of your service. And that's why, after the Afghan voting was completed, I insisted on a thorough review of our strategy. *If I did not think that the security*

of the United States and the safety of the American people were at stake in Afghanistan, I would gladly order every single one of our troops home tomorrow ... I make this decision because I am convinced that our security is at stake in Afghanistan and Pakistan. This is the epicenter of violent extremism practiced by al-Qaeda. It is from here that we were attacked on 9/11, and it is from here that new attacks are being plotted as I speak. This is no idle danger, no hypothetical threat. In the last few months alone, we have apprehended extremists within our borders who were sent here from the border region of Afghanistan and Pakistan to commit new acts of terror. And this danger will only grow if the region slides backwards and al-Qaeda can operate with impunity. We must keep the pressure on al-Qaeda. And to do that, we must increase the stability and capacity of our partners in the region. Of course, this burden is not ours alone to bear. This is not just America's war. Since 9/11, al-Qaeda's safe havens have been the source of attacks against London and Amman and Bali. The people and governments of both Afghanistan and Pakistan are endangered. *And the stakes are even higher within a nuclear-armed Pakistan, because we know that al Qaeda and other extremists seek nuclear weapons, and we have every reason to believe that they would use them. These facts compel us to act along with our friends and allies. Our overarching goal remains the same: to disrupt, dismantle, and defeat al-Qaeda in Afghanistan and Pakistan and to prevent its capacity to threaten America and our allies in the future. To meet that goal, we will pursue the following objectives within Afghanistan. We must deny al-Qaeda a safe haven. We must reverse the Taliban's momentum and deny it the ability to overthrow the government. And we must strengthen the capacity of Afghanistan's security forces and government, so that they can take lead responsibility for Afghanistan's future.*

(*Obama West Point Speech, December 1, 2009, emphasis added*)

The president shed some additional light on his concept of the goal in Afghanistan in his December 10, 2009 Nobel Prize acceptance speech, but this time he did so with the human costs of the venture in focus. As if to justify such costs, he also evoked the nobility of the contributions made by the U.S. military to global security since World War II. And he acknowledged both the opposition and the pain that accompanies any war. I quote below from that speech:

(Afghanistan is) a conflict that America did not seek; one in which we are joined by 42 other countries—including Norway—in an effort to defend ourselves and all nations from further attacks. Still, we are at war, and I'm responsible for the deployment of thousands of young Americans to battle in a distant land. Some will kill, and some will be killed. And so I come here with an acute sense of the costs of armed conflict. We must begin by acknowledging the hard truth: We will not eradicate violent conflict in our lifetimes. There will be times when nations—acting individually or in concert—will find the use of force not only necessary but morally justified.

... as a head of state sworn to protect and defend my nation, I cannot be guided by (the examples of King and Gandhi) alone. I face the world as it is, and cannot stand idle in the face of threats to the American people. For make no mistake: Evil does exist in the world. A non-violent movement could not have halted Hitler's armies. Negotiations cannot convince al Qaeda's leaders to lay down their arms. To say that force may sometimes be necessary is not a call to cynicism—it is a recognition of history; the imperfections of man and the limits of reason.

... I begin with this point because in many countries there is a deep ambivalence about military action today, no matter what the cause. And at times, this is joined by a reflexive suspicion of America, the world's sole military superpower. But the world must remember that it was not simply international institutions—not just treaties and declarations—that brought stability to a post-World War II world. Whatever mistakes we have made, the plain fact is this: The United States of America has helped underwrite global security for more than six decades with the blood of our citizens and the strength of our arms. The service and sacrifice of our men and women in uniform has promoted peace and prosperity from Germany to Korea, and enabled democracy to take hold in places like the Balkans. We have borne this burden not because we seek to impose our will. We have done so out of enlightened self-interest—because we seek a better future for our children and grandchildren, and we believe that their lives will be better if others' children and grandchildren can live in freedom and prosperity.

So yes, the instruments of war do have a role to play in preserving the peace. And yet this truth must coexist with another—that no matter how justified, war promises human tragedy. The soldier's courage and sacrifice is full of glory, expressing devotion to country, to cause, to comrades in arms. But war itself is never glorious, and we must never trumpet it as such.

So part of our challenge is reconciling these two seemingly irreconcilable truths—that war is sometimes necessary, and war at some level is an expression of human folly. Concretely, we must direct our effort to the task that President Kennedy called for long ago. "Let us focus," he said, "on a more practical, more attainable peace, based not on a sudden revolution in human nature but on a gradual evolution in human institutions."

(Obama Nobel Prize Acceptance Speech, December 10, 2009)

Finally, the president continued to press his case and avow his commitment to victory in the following excerpt from his May 22, 2010 West Point commencement speech.

We face a tough fight in Afghanistan. Any insurgency that is confronted with a direct challenge will turn to new tactics. And from Marja to Kandahar, that is what the Taliban has done through assassination and indiscriminate killing and intimidation. Moreover, any country that has known decades of war will be tested in finding political solutions to its problems, and providing governance that can sustain progress and serve the needs of its people.

So this war has changed over the last nine years, but it's no less important than it was in those days after 9/11. We toppled the Taliban regime—now we must break the momentum of a Taliban insurgency and train Afghan security forces. We have supported the election of a sovereign government— now we must strengthen its capacities. We've brought hope to the Afghan people—now we must see that their country does not fall prey to our common enemies. Cadets, there will be difficult days ahead. We will adapt, we will persist, and I have no doubt that together with our Afghan and international partners, we will succeed in Afghanistan.

(Obama Commencement Speech, May 22, 2010)

Prelude to Fiction

With President Obama's actual decision and selections from his most prominent public explanations of it before us (as background for what follows) the fictional policy trial can proceed. The trial blends the reality of what was happening when the president made his decision with the reality of events that have transpired since then (up to the time of publication). I use real facts and real arguments on both sides (usually indicated by citations to sources) where possible to ensure realistic complexity. Fictionalized are the events, procedures, and human interactions needed to create and deploy the policy trial narrative efficiently. The factual back-drop will surely be superseded by new developments by the time this book appears. That need not detract from the point of the exercise, which is to show how the process could be made to work to the benefit of the constitutional balance.

Fiction: The First Policy Trial

The story begins *after* the ten fall 2009 in-house Obama Af–Pak meetings. But it starts *before* the president's December 1, 2009 West Point speech excerpted above. The president had recently initiated a meeting with House Speaker Nancy Pelosi to give her advance notice of his decision to increase the number of U.S. troops in Afghanistan (fact). Just two days after his meeting with Pelosi he was surprised to receive a phone call from her requesting yet another meeting that she insisted be held before the president publicly announced his decision (the blending of fiction with fact now proceeds, with the latter identified by citations).

Obama, who had studied the issue for months and had already written his West Point speech, was frustrated at the timing and the nature of Pelosi's request. She had made her own lack of enthusiasm for a troop increase abundantly clear at their initial meeting and had informed him then that he could not count on the votes of Democrats to finance the troop increase (Baker, December 12, 2009b: A1). Now she wanted him to endure another meeting, this time with her and other leading Capitol Hill Democrats, to consider an idea that she said might allow him to avoid a break with his own party over war policy. The president was skeptical: "I'll listen, but don't expect me to change my mind," he said.

That afternoon, three senior congressional Democrats met with President Obama in the Cabinet Room at the White House. Senate Majority Leader Harry Reid began the discussion. "As you know, Mr. President, a majority of Democrats in both the House and the Senate is opposed to the idea of sending more troops to Afghanistan. We do not believe such a policy can succeed in a place made famous as 'the graveyard of empires' (Jones, 2009; Kakutani, July 14, 2009: C1). We fear that the escalation of a war that half the American people are already describing as 'not worth the cost' would undermine the historic opportunity we now have to build a new domestic policy legacy worthy of great Democratic presidents and Congresses of the past."

House Majority Leader Steny Hoyer broke in: "May I read you something, Mr. President?" Obama nodded and Hoyer read the words of President Lyndon B. Johnson, spoken to a young Harvard professor who had accompanied him to Texas in 1969 to help him write his memoirs:

> Oh I could see it coming all right. History provided too many cases where the sound of the bugle put an immediate end to the hopes and dreams of the best reformers: The Spanish-American War drowned the populist spirit; World War I ended Woodrow Wilson's New Freedom. World War II brought the New Deal to a close. Once the war began, then all those conservatives in Congress would use it as a weapon against the Great Society.
>
> *(quoted in Kearns, 1976: 252)*

"Mr. President, we sure don't want anything like that to happen to you or to us," concluded Hoyer. "We know that you believe your policy to be right for America," he added. "But we fear that without adequate public support from the beginning and most important, support that is strong enough to last as long as the war takes to win, we could be setting ourselves up for failure.

"Like Truman, Johnson and Bush, you have a choice. They made choices for wars that destroyed their presidencies. We are here to suggest that you don't have to do that. There are ways to protect America from terrorist attacks without escalating the war in a sink-hole like Afghanistan."

At this point, Nancy Pelosi, the second most powerful person in the room, interrupted. "There may also be a way to create more enduring support for your plan than presidential speeches alone have been able to do in the past. We are here to ask that you consider an idea that would either strengthen the commitment of the American people and the Congress to your policy or, to be blunt, get you to modify or abandon it. The idea is called a policy trial, and we think it can help resolve the fix we are in, with a president hell-bent on a plan that already divides the country right down the middle." Pelosi took a folder from her briefcase and handed it to the president. "Here is a brief document that explains how a policy trial would work. As you'll see, it is modeled procedurally on the impeachment process described in the Constitution because that affords a convenient, pre-existing and legitimized mechanism. But make no mistake: only the proposed escalation policy is on trial, not you as president."

The president had heard enough. Dropping the folder on the table, he said testily, "As for public support, my information is that some people may be reluctant about Afghanistan but they are far from taking to the streets with pitchforks (Hiatt, May 24, 2010: A19). Besides, I know that I can convince them that this is the right thing for us to do because I just spent three months with the best experts available making sure that it *is* the right thing to do! You'll see the proof that the American people understand this after I've had a chance to explain the policy up at West Point … Now, god damn it, what's this about putting my policy on trial? I'm president of the United States and commander in chief of the armed forces! I know that I have to keep the support of the people, but that's my problem and my responsibility, not yours! Would you seriously want to provoke a constitutional crisis by trying to force me to do something like this? I don't think so. For that matter would you risk a confrontation that could tear the Democratic Party apart right in the middle of our best opportunity in years to press our agenda at home? I can't believe that either."

Pelosi turned to look at Reid, who, as if on cue, began speaking with restrained urgency: "Of course not, Mr. President! Believe me; we don't want either of those things! The truth is that we think this idea is actually the best way to keep our nation together, protect your presidency, and protect our shared agenda. Keep in mind, sir, that you could win such a trial; in fact you probably will. And the fact that you were willing to undergo it could put you in a much stronger position to endure bad war news if it comes than your predecessors were! And let's face it, sir; this war has the potential to serve up a lot of bad news!"

The pensive but still-irritated president began tapping his finger against his front teeth as Reid continued: "The scenario we have in mind is this. First, you as president would do what you're about to do anyway: give your speech explaining why you want the country to support an escalation of the war in Afghanistan. But instead of that being the end of it, we—that is, the 'principals' in the American system—the president, the Congress, and the people—would agree to use the special circumstances of the current situation to *try an experiment* that could help us to avoid the bitter and costly consequences that followed previous discretionary presidential wars in Korea, Vietnam and Iraq.

"What makes our current situation such a good fit for this experiment? The main thing is that the escalation you propose is, to put it bluntly, *not obviously essential to our survival or well-being*. Forgive me, sir, but those are the facts. There is no overwhelming majority agreement in Congress or the country, such as existed after the Japanese attack on Pearl Harbor on December 7, 1941. At this point, with 9/11 so far in the rear-view mirror, what you propose to do is better described 'optional' or even 'not required.' This is the considered opinion of many of your fellow country men and women. It is the judgment of at least half the Congress, half the American people, a majority of your own political party and even of some who are on your own national security team! They feel this way partly because what you propose to do is not a response to a new invasion or any other potentially overwhelming threat. Yes, there is the continued Al Qaeda threat, and there is also the chance that Pakistani nuclear weapons can fall into the wrong hands. These things must of course be dealt with. *But they do not necessarily require a massive new troop deployment to deal with effectively*. There may be other as or even *more* effective ways of managing these problems. That, at least, is the way many of us see it.

"What is more, there is no particular time urgency for sending in more troops. As you said yourself when Cheney accused you of 'dithering' over a decision, General McChrystal told you he needed no additional troops until January, 2010. That's why you felt free to take three months to study the matter! And the fact that we can easily capture some more time is also what makes it possible for us now to call for a formal and much more public debate than you just orchestrated inside your administration, with significant portions of your discussion classified (Alter, 2010: 375). A public hearing can be portrayed as a logical next step beyond your extensive internal deliberations, because going public in this way will give you the chance to ask for explicit, well-briefed and carefully considered national support for your decision—the very thing that LBJ and George W. Bush needed but didn't have when the going got tough in Vietnam and Iraq. We're talking about 'buy-in and blame sharing' here; shared responsibility for decisions to initiate optional military action. We're also talking about *binding all three constitutional 'principals'—again, the president, the Congress, and the American people—to the struggle*, with the understanding that not just the president but *all of the principals should share responsibility* for seeing their initial agreed-upon commitments all the way through to the result, whether that result is pleasant or painful. That is the way grown-ups do things in the real world and that mind-set is the most important thing that the policy trial experiment is designed to foster.

"Speaker Pelosi noted the possibility that a debate between you and your representatives and respectful and well-prepared opponents of your proposal in Congress might conceivably persuade a public audience to strongly oppose an escalation of the troop level. If that happened, the result might be to motivate Congress to use its plenary power to prevent enactment of the policy. To be sure, that possibility exists; for that matter, it exists right now whether there are policy trials or not. But as I told you, I believe you would win this debate, and I imagine that you think so yourself. If you do, we expect that you will have won a sturdier brand of public support than you could hope to achieve without having braved a disciplined public face-to-face argument with real critics of your proposal. That would be something worth having and worth watching! Maybe your predecessors would have been skittish about such a confrontation; but they would love to have had the kind of support that could come from winning a public debate like that.

"Finally, Mr. President, I hope it is clear that we want very much to form a partnership with you on this project. We don't want to defy you. But we are convinced that the interests of the president, the Congress, and the American people are all better served by a bold experiment like this than by a repetition of failed past procedures that might fail again, and we hope very much that you can be persuaded to agree. We believe our chances for a durable consensus that might increase the chances for success or, failing that, do a better job of weathering a setback will be greater if we're all on the same page from the start. For reasons spelled out in the policy trial document that Speaker Pelosi gave you, we and our constitutional advisors believe that your emergency war powers are undisturbed by this plan. But I would be remiss if I didn't make it clear that if you refuse to cooperate and claim a constitutional right to press forward without our cooperation we would plan to take our case to the people. You can read about that option in the speaker's document too under the heading, 'Scheduling a Policy Trial.' We're well aware that even if we went to the people you might still convince them that we are wrong to challenge the president and in that way you might avoid a policy trial. But if you refuse, we intend to go public; and a public fight would obviously not enhance our ability to work together after that.

"I'm sure all this sounds radical, confrontational, and even unthinkable to you right now. But you must try to understand how we see this situation we are in, how intensely we fear the consequences for our country and our party if you press ahead in Afghanistan without the superior cover and grounding a *truly public* process can offer. We fear the potential adverse consequences so intensely that we are willing to risk coming over here and speaking to you like this. Our courage was strengthened by the fact that you are an unusual person and president, someone with the self-confidence to debate political and policy opponents publicly and privately, as you have done with partisan and policy opponents on health care and other issues in ways no other president has tried before (Stolberg and Pear, February 26, 2010: A1). You're also someone who is capable of thinking outside the box; or at least a person who is able to consider this proposal on the merits without moving immediately and reflexively to assert your authority, like so many who have been in your position would probably do. I'm repeating myself, but to us the odds of success seem better this way than by taking another trip down the same slippery slope."

By the time the Majority Leader had finished speaking his lengthy piece President Obama was externally more subdued, but internally still incredulous and angry at what he had heard. He was also beginning to feel weary. "Thank you Nancy, Harry, and Steny for your candor about these strong feelings you share. This is indeed a lot for me or any other president to swallow. I'm not sure you fully appreciate the magnitude of what you're asking of me. But as you acknowledged, I now must give my speech. Let me say that I hope you will listen very carefully to what I have to say at West Point. And before you take any public action of the sort you have described, not to say threatened, I hope you will give me a chance to study your document and think about it and also about what you have said here today." With that, the president rose from his chair and the meeting was adjourned.

The next morning the president went early to the Oval Office to think quietly and privately about the meeting of the day before, and his options for dealing with it. He wanted to sort them out before consulting Rahm, David, Joe, or anyone else about the best course of action. His first instinct was a visceral unwillingness even to consider surrendering what was clearly his constitutional authority. That, he knew, is exactly what Bush, Cheney, Nixon, maybe even JFK and FDR would have done. But he also had known all along that Afghanistan could end up being a pivotal definer of his presidency. In the face of such potentially defining moments, he was proud of his willingness to gamble, because he believed it to be the only way to give his best judgments a chance to prevail, to solve an intractable problem, to get something important accomplished. His careful in-house study of his Afghan options was a novelty in its own right. And as he thought about what the congressional trio had said to him, he also felt confident that he would prevail in either a public confrontation or a formal trial, just as he had prevailed in his highly improbable quest for the presidency. If he did not prevail in a campaign-style debate about whether to have a policy trial, he reasoned, he could always do what his predecessors had done: simply assert the war power and count on conservative support in Congress (most Republicans and some Democrats would be solidly behind him) and, in the end, still carry the day. Many believed, along with the *Wall Street Journal* editorial board, that "(a) commitment to a hard, at times unpopular, fight is the mark of Presidential leadership" (Afghan Staying Power, June 15, 2010: A16).

On the other hand, was that the smartest thing to do? If he won in a formal policy trial, Pelosi's analysis might actually be right—it would not only take his bipartisan image and reputation for self-confidence to the next level; it could strengthen his hand in the long run by creating some acceptance for the idea of blame sharing as a hedge against the unpredictability of war. After all, wars like Afghanistan do have a history of producing difficult long runs.

After reading the Pelosi policy trial document, Obama concluded that a campaign to beat down the congressional opposition was a sure loser. Reid had it right: it would destroy the Democratic Party brand for the rest of his presidency, and it could have more devastating effects than anything the Tea Partiers or even Barry Goldwater had done to the Republicans.

So President Barack Obama decided to take part in a policy trial without first fighting to avoid it in a campaign against Congress. The former constitutional law professor was secure in his belief that participating voluntarily would still leave him in a position to assert his authority if necessary, whatever the trial might produce. But it wouldn't come to that because he knew he could win.

The Special Proceeding

The Chief Justice of the United States gaveled the special meeting of a joint session of the United States Congress to order. "This is an unprecedented event, organized by authority of the United States House of Representatives, in agreement with the

United States Senate, under Article I Section 5 of the Constitution of the United States, which grants each House of Congress the right to determine the rules of its own proceedings. This particular proceeding is hereby designated as a *policy trial* by the authority vested in me for this purpose by the Special Joint Congressional Committee charged with organizing this event. It is the wish of a majority of the members of the House of Representatives, in agreement with a majority of the Senate, that we use this proceeding to invoke and conduct a debate on the merits of the Afghan troop escalation policy proposal of President Barack Obama, as set forth in a speech to United States Military Academy Cadets on December 1, 2009.

"It is the further wish of the members of both Houses that we employ some but not all of the procedures described in the Constitution for the management of impeachment trials. For example, that explains my presence in the chair as arbiter of the proceeding. But there are certain highly important distinctions between what we do here today and the actual impeachment process that must be absolutely clear before we proceed. The most important difference is that the President of the United States is not on trial during this proceeding. What is on trial is his intent to increase troop deployments to Afghanistan by some 30,000 troops. But this proposal is only on trial in the sense that we will hear a carefully organized debate on the merits of what the president wants to do. And after the television audience of American citizens has weighed in by means of a special polling procedure with its reaction to the debate, the Congress, in its collective wisdom, will decide what, if anything, it wants to do at the conclusion of the trial.

"Another important difference between this proceeding and an impeachment trial is that the ending here may be inconclusive. Congress may decide to formally endorse the president's policy. It may assert its constitutional plenary power to prevent the president from implementing the policy. Or it may make no formal resolution of any kind. What happens at the conclusion of this proceeding is entirely at the discretion of the United States Congress, presumably in consultation with the president and in light of the wishes of the American people.

"A third important distinction between the impeachment process as described in the Constitution and this procedure is that instead of a two-step process initiated in the House and resolved in the Senate, this will be a joint session from beginning to end, with both Houses empanelled as the jury, the American people as their advisors, and with me as procedural overseer.

"By prior agreement of the president and the Joint Committee, proceedings are divided into three categories: proposal, rebuttal, and closing statements. Each side in this debate will be represented by a principal and three advisors. The president has chosen to represent himself as principal and to be advised by Defense Secretary Robert Gates and Representative Ike Skelton, Democrat of Missouri and chairman of the House Armed Services Committee. The principal of the opposition side will be Representative Nancy Pelosi, Democrat of California and speaker of the House of Representatives. She will be assisted by Senator Russell Feingold, Democrat of Wisconsin, and Professor Andrew Bacevich of Boston University (2010b).

The President's Proposal

"Mr. Chief Justice, ladies and gentlemen of the Congress, my fellow Americans. I am here voluntarily, because I welcome the chance to make the case for my Afghan troop increase policy in detail. I especially welcome this unprecedented opportunity to defend the plan in response to well-prepared and principled critics, and to do so in the presence of the two most important audiences in this nation: the American people and their representatives in the United States Congress. To my mind, the value of an event like this is that it can solidify a shared understanding of the problem we face, and do so in a way that strengthens our national commitment to measures that are absolutely essential to successful management of the most dangerous threat to our national security that we currently face (Shanker and Bumiller, June 17, 2010: A10).

"As you know, that threat stems from the many fanatical nonstate terrorist groups, spearheaded by Al Qaeda, which enjoy safe haven along Pakistan's border with Afghanistan. Al Qaeda is still bent on the destruction of our way of life. Its ability to linger in this area lets its strategists support the efforts of other extremist groups who attack and kill American troops in Afghanistan, while seeking to recapture Afghanistan as a launching pad for more 9/11 type attacks on the United States.

"The safe haven in Pakistan also positions Al Qaeda and other terrorist leaders to search out and potentially to exploit opportunities to gain access to that nation's nuclear weapons. Bear in mind that Pakistan will soon be the world's fifth largest nuclear power (Sanger and Schmitt, February 1, 2011: A1). Pakistanis are stockpiling these weapons mainly to deter what they see as their biggest threat: India. India has superior conventional forces which Pakistanis see as the principal threat to their security. The problem from our perspective is that the terrorists in Pakistan are not fully under the Pakistani government's or the military's control. Terrorist strength and autonomy in the northwest tribal region inside Pakistan increase the vulnerability of its nuclear arsenal. This is the most significant threat to the United States and our allies and it therefore must be our greatest concern.

"I did not reach the decision to deploy more troops lightly. After the most careful deliberative process undertaken by any president since the Cuban Missile Crisis (Alter, 2010) I concluded that the single most effective method available for addressing the threat of terrorists with nuclear weapons in control of Afghanistan is to assist and help protect the governments of both Afghanistan and Pakistan. The only reliable way to do that, I believe, is to substantially increase the U.S. military presence in the region. This is something I promised to do in my campaign for this office; and this will be the second and larger of my deployments. I intend to keep our forces there just long enough to allow the governments of Afghanistan and Pakistan to secure their ability to control such threats with only civilian economic and technical assistance from international sources as back-up.

"A larger troop deployment is essential because it will be both a stabilizing presence and a facilitator of all our other efforts to help strengthen Afghanistan and undermine Al Qaeda and other terrorist groups in Pakistan. It stabilizes by increasing the security of Afghan citizens and their government. And greater security makes all our other efforts in the region—military training, technical and financial aid, intelligence, the effort to negotiate a settlement with the Taliban and other insurgents, citizen outreach, and other community development projects—that much more effective at serving our interests as well as the interests of our allies. This in a nutshell is why we need more troops in the region.

"Our strategy is to use the military to clear and hold key Afghan cities like Marja and Kandahar of hostile forces, then to deploy Afghan police and civil servants to provide services and build the legitimacy of the central government. We are also engaged in developing the Afghan military and national police capabilities (Fick and Nagl, February 21, 2011: A17). When these activities have succeeded, the Afghan government will be secure, and the U.S. may withdraw troops without compromising its security. This will encourage the Afghan people to increase their resistance to the Taliban, both forcibly (Chandrasekaran, June 21, 2010a: A1) and through informal political action such as decision-making councils, which have been described as 'nation-building from the ground up' (Gall, June 20, 2010b: 5; Gall, February 5, 2011: A4). And there are efforts to co-opt mid and low-level insurrectionists while also angling for higher-level agreements through military pressure and the independent efforts of President Karzai.

"Let it be clear that my plan is to *gradually* transfer control and defense functions to the Afghans *as they are able to assume the responsibility. The withdrawal start date of July 2011 does not mean a massive U.S. pullout starts then and ends soon thereafter.* It means that the withdrawal that *begins* then will proceed at a rate determined by conditions in the field. There will be no wholesale withdrawal of U.S. troops from the main fight against the Taliban in 2011. There will be a gradual transition, beginning in the more stable northern and western areas of the country. And the drawdown will include NATO troops as well as U.S. troops (Klein, June 28, 2010: 20). But the bottom line is this: *We must not and will not leave a regional situation in which Afghanistan and Pakistan are unstable and vulnerable* (Wood, August 25, 2010b). Again only a large U.S. force will be able, with the help of allies, to impose stability long enough for local authorities to *lock down* the ability to sustain it on their own. Again, *that is why we need to increase our troop strength.* We simply cannot stop the threats posed to our national security without doing so. Given the dangers we seek to avoid nothing could be more squarely in the national interest of the United States.

"The hostile forces in that dangerous part of the world cannot be disabled from offshore, long-distance platforms alone. We need boots on the ground.

"I see my time is up, so this concludes my opening statement."

"Thank you, Mr. President," replied the Chief Justice. "Speaker Pelosi, the floor is yours."

"Thank you, Mr. Chief Justice. The first speaker for the opposition brief will be Senator Russ Feingold of Wisconsin, who will offer our opening statement." The senator rose and strode to the podium in the well of the House chamber, placed a manila folder on it and adjusted the microphone. He took several sheets of paper out of the folder, and glanced through them. Then, setting his notes aside and grabbing the sides of the podium, he raised his head and gazed at the large audience of Congress men and women, news reporters, and television cameras. After a long pause, he began to speak in slow, measured tones.

Opposition Rebuttal

"Mr. President, Mr. Chief Justice, Madam Speaker, fellow legislators, ladies and gentlemen. As all of you know, we of the opposition share the president's objective of ending or at least more effectively managing the threat to our national security posed by the growing network of terrorists who respond to the direct leadership or are inspired by the example of Al Qaeda. That is the problem we all want to solve. Our disagreement with him is over means, not ends. Our analysis, which like his is based on extensive consultations with many respected, experienced experts, leads us to conclude that a large new deployment of troops to Afghanistan is not the best way; indeed is not likely to be an effective way, to address the threat posed by terrorists to our national security. This afternoon I will present four reasons why the president's policy is unlikely to work. Then I will suggest an alternative approach to dealing with our problem.

"The first reason why a large troop deployment will not work is because you, the American people, are not united behind the idea. Polls show clearly that you are now and long have been closely divided between support and opposition to the war itself as well as to an expanded U.S. military presence in Afghanistan (pollingreport. com/afghan.htm). Wars cannot be based on narrow, uncertain majorities. As former Secretary of State Henry Kissinger wrote recently, 'it is essential to avoid the debilitating cycle that blighted especially the Vietnam and Iraq wars, in which the public mood shifted abruptly … from widespread support to … calls for an exit strategy with the emphasis on exit, not strategy' (Kissinger, June 24, 2010: A21). Our national experience shows that wars cannot be successfully waged without the kind of deep and long lasting commitment displayed by the American people during World War II. Wars are unpredictable. They involve painful costs in lives and dollars. And they can last for years. The military already refers to Afghanistan as 'the long war' (Bacevich, June 27, 2010a: B1). As the president just said, and as Generals McChrystal and Petraus have also said, the July 2011 withdrawal initiation rate will be dependent on conditions on the ground. What that really means is that to see this war through to a successful conclusion could take far longer. Before you endorse the president's policy you should ask yourselves if you are ready to sustain your support and commitment indefinitely, for five, ten, fifteen, or more years despite high costs, setbacks, and sacrifices, through thick and thin. If you, the people will not resolve to offer that kind of support, Congress cannot be expected to do so and the president's policy will be on thin ice.

"Second, successful counterinsurgency in an unstable, corrupt, and poor country like Afghanistan requires nation building. In Afghanistan, corruption is so pervasive as to require a complete change in the culture of government. As one recent news report put it: 'Afghan government is awash in corruption, with virtually every public transaction here carrying a price. Corruption is so rife, and the Afghan government so predatory, that American officials believe that it is one of the primary factors driving Afghans into the arms of the Taliban insurgency' (Rubin and Filkins, July 1, 2010: A12). Recently uncovered evidence proved what we already knew: that the problem extends to the very top of the Afghan government (Rosenberg, August 12, 2010: A1). That means the U.S. must hold insurgents at bay with little help from a skeptical population that wants its political leaders held accountable while a thoroughly corrupt elite political culture refuses to reform itself despite U.S. prodding to do so. Afghanistan's leaders are enriching themselves while Afghan citizens, who trust neither their leaders nor the Americans, leave our soldiers to fight and die without their help. Ordinary Afghans will not risk their lives for either the Americans or their own government until it is clear who will prevail. But the Americans cannot prevail without their help (Filkins, February 27, 2011: br1). It has not been possible to make corruption a top public priority while the help of key officials in the Afghan government, known to be corrupt, is still needed to defeat the insurrection (Chandrasekaran, September 13, 2010b: A1; Filkins and Mazzetti, August 26, 2010: A1). This can only delay the speed with which Afghan military and civic institutions and governance capabilities are strengthened to the point of nationwide credibility, and job-creating economic development is established. The problem is that it is only after evidence of these changes has become convincing that popular trust and support for the government can be expected to emerge. Only then will Afghanistan be strong enough to sustain itself against insurgents without outside help. This would take many years; possibly a decade or more.

"Here is an example of the challenge on the economic side. Afghanistan's recently discovered mineral wealth, though enticing to the world's mining companies, would take many years to develop due to lack of necessary infrastructure, political stability, and project and worker safety from insurgent attacks (Risen, June 18, 2010: A4). The experts say that to create the stability needed to achieve these things in a country like Afghanistan would require full reintegration of insurgent forces into civil society, changes in the elected national leadership, elimination of all political corruption and possibly even substantial alteration of deeply entrenched and decentralized tribal cultures and traditions.

"These are things that the Obama Administration hopes to show measurable progress toward in a mere 18 months, as is implied by the president's stipulation of a July, 2011 beginning of a transition to Afghan takeover and redeployment of U.S. troops out of Afghanistan. In fact, such a nation-building venture would require not the one hundred thousand troops which the president's proposed 30,000 troop surge would achieve, but *several hundred* thousand troops. And it would take a decade or more rather than one or two or even five to seven more years (Jones,

2008: 10; Biddle, July/August, 2009: 4; West, 2011). In the face of these realities, some of the president's critics say: Mr. President, *either convince the people and Congress to get all the way in with their eyes wide open, or get all the way out.* You can't have it both ways. Ambivalence just emboldens our opponents to outwait us (Ajami, June 28, 2010: A21).

"Third, even if we got all the way in and accepted the huge costs necessary to convert Afghanistan into a functional modern state, it still would not solve our terrorist problem. Al Qaeda's leadership is based in the remote tribal areas of Pakistan today. But the Al Qaeda movement is based 'in the soul of thousands of Muslim youth from Bridgeport, Conn. to London,' connected by the 'virtual Al Qaeda—the Internet' (Friedman, June 23, 2010: A23). Look at the rise of Al Qaeda-like cells around the world, in places like Algeria, the Sahel, Somalia, and Yemen that are successfully recruiting such youths. Consider the Al Qaeda strategy of recruiting of non-Muslin youths—especially converts to Islam whose appearances and names would not arouse the same suspicions as those from Islamic countries might (Hoffman, January 16, 2010: A17). And think of the rise of 'home grown' terrorists in the U.S inspired by the same Al Qaeda ideals, such as the 'Times Square bomber' Faisal Shahzad, or the U.S. Army major, the psychiatrist Nidal Malik, who is accused of killing 13 fellow soldiers at Fort Hood, Tex. Both are said to have been influenced by the charismatic cleric Anwar al-Awlaki, once based in Maryland, but now in Yemen, whose mixture of 'scripture and vitriol' is said to have enticed young Muslims into a dozen plots against U.S. targets to date (Shane and Mekhennet, May 9, 2010: 1). Our terrorist enemies now recruit people who can easily and legally enter and travel in the U.S. to plot and mount attacks (Gorman, September 10, 2010: A3).

"This means that we cannot stop Al Qaeda's efforts to destroy American domestic or international targets with our army massed in a single country. Put another way, we should not allow the recently estimated 100 to 500 Al Qaeda members in Pakistan and Afghanistan (Barnes et al., August 13, 2010: A1; Sanger and Mazzetti, July 1, 2010: A12) to tie up 100,000 American troops. We should make more efficient use of our military resources than this. We might, as President Obama contends, send a discouraging signal to all those who identify with their mission by converting Afghanistan from a failed to a successful state. But again, we lack the popular support and political will to make the huge commitment of blood and treasure needed to do it. Even if we had those things and were able to succeed in Afghanistan, there are no guarantees that this would prevent some small terrorist cell from reigniting worldwide terrorist zeal and momentum with a single act, like smuggling a suitcase-sized nuclear bomb into New York City and detonating it, a potential said to be the greatest fear of many national security analysts (Etzioni, 2007; Stewart, February 10, 2010, online).

"My last point in response to the president's proposal concerns the threat posed by the vulnerability of Pakistan's nuclear weapons to capture by terrorists. The president's concern is understandable, because the threat is real. But he believes that a large U.S. military presence gives us our best chance to keep the nukes from falling into the wrong hands (Alter, 2010: 374–75). In this, he is wrong. The fact is that our military presence in Afghanistan over a period of almost a decade has done nothing to change what are essentially internal conditions that place Pakistan's control of its own nuclear force in jeopardy. More U.S. troops next door can't change those conditions because they are of Pakistan's own making. And Pakistan won't allow a sizeable U.S. military presence inside its borders to help fix the problem.

"Pakistan has the most serious terrorism problem of any country in the world today (Zakaria, September 13, 2010b: A15). It got into this fix because of a decades-long cultivation of terrorist groups for use as proxies in its struggle against India in places like Kashmir and Afghanistan. The Pakistani military and its intelligence organization, the ISI, have spawned a deeply rooted terrorist culture in and outside their national borders that now bids to metastasize out of the government's control. Many different groups of terrorists are allowed to thrive in Pakistan's tribal North Waziristan province in Northwestern Pakistan. Some, like the Haqqani Network, have long been allied with the Pakistani military and intelligence agency even as they attack NATO forces including Pakistan's ally, the United States, in Afghanistan. This is why many Afghan officials and elites regard Pakistan, not Al Qaeda or Haqqani, as the 'real aggressor' (Spanta, August 23, 2010: A13). But others, such as the Pakistani Taliban, an offshoot of the Afghan Taliban that Pakistan itself created to take over Afghanistan after the Soviet withdrawal from that country in 1989, have turned hostile to the government in Islamabad (Landler and Bumiller, May 1, 2009: A4; Perlez, June 3, 2010c: A6). A spring, 2009 Taliban offensive in the Swat Valley in Western Pakistan showed these Islamic militants able to claim territory just 60 miles from the seat of Pakistani nuclear power: Islamabad (Lander and Bumiller, May 1, 2009: A4). That sparked grave fears in the U.S. that the nuclear arsenal was at risk (Sanger, May 4, 2009: A1). The Pakistanis were far less worried. 'This is not South Vietnam,' said Husain Haqqani, the Pakistani ambassador to the United States. 'The Taliban need to be fought, but they're not about to take over Pakistan and overcome a one-million-strong military' (Landler and Bumiller, May 1, 2009: A4). A Pakistani counteroffensive in the Swat valley did wrest the valley from Taliban control soon thereafter (Nordland and Perez, May 28, 2010: A8). But to date, such skirmishes have not dissuaded Pakistani military and intelligence leaders from sustaining their decades-long ties with terrorist groups that attack U.S. troops in Afghanistan, even though the U.S. considers such militant instability the most significant threat to Pakistani nukes.

"Now let me come back to the point I made earlier: that the Pakistani estab-lishment, including the military, the ISI, and the democratically elected president, *puts limits on the extent to which the U.S. is allowed to help with this problem*. We have been trying for years but without much success (Sanger and Broad, November 18, 2007: 1). There are strict limits on what Pakistan will allow the U.S. to do to protect the Pakistani government or to ensure the safety of its nuclear arsenal, about which they are very protective and secretive (Sanger, May 4, 2009: A1). The painful fact is that the Pakistani people intensely dislike the U.S. because the drone attacks in their border regions kill civilians as well as terrorists. Pakistanis were appreciative of U.S. help during their recent terrible flooding, but their basic dislike of U.S. military policy endures (Schmitt, August 15, 2010b: 5). That creates political pressure on Pakistani leaders to pretend they are not complicit in the drone attacks. It also means they might not survive the populist backlash if they allowed the United States to deploy its troops on Pakistani soil to root out Al Qaeda and company from the remote tribal areas. But they would not want U.S. forces in Pakistan even if the public were sympathetic because the Pakistani military and ISI intelligence elite as well as President Zardari (Zardari, December 10, 2009: A35) *all want to sustain their own control of Pakistan's nuclear arsenal as well as its political destiny*. They do not want to become a protectorate of the United States. Instead they want help from those they can control. They get such help from the terrorist groups with which they are allied, and over which they are still said to exert great sway (Gall, June 14, 2010a: A8). These groups serve as their proxies in various important ways. Terrorist groups that they support in Afghanistan, such as the large fighting force controlled by Sirajuddin Haqqani, for example, have been unleashed against India's assets and personnel in that country. India worries Pakistani leaders far more than the chance that their nukes might fall into Al Qaeda's hands, which they see as remote. Pakistan wants U.S. help, *but they also want the freedom to make the contradictory deals with both the Americans and the terrorists they perceive as essential*. It is in this sense that they continue to work both sides of the terrorist street, and play a double game. On the one hand, it wants the U.S. as its ally in Pakistan's own internal war with Islamist insurgents potentially capable of toppling the current civilian government, which would indeed put its nukes at some risk of terrorist takeover (Biddle, July/August, 2009: 8). But on the other hand, Pakistani officials also see their powerful terrorist allies (especially the Haqqani network) as essential in light of the widely expected early U.S. exit from the region. That is why they feel *justified* in playing a double game. Pakistan covets a leading role for itself in the stabilization of Afghanistan once the Americans are gone, something that armed allies like the Haqqani Network, which runs a large part of the anti-Karzai, anti-U.S. insurgency in Afghanistan, and which itself might become part of Afghanistan's ruling coalition in a deal with Hamid Karzai, could help to ensure (Perlez et al., June 25, 2010: A1). Something like this might even happen before America leaves, in which case we could find ourselves with 100,000 troops on the ground and no one to fight (Shane, June 27, 2010b: wk 1). In light of such byzantine complexities U.S. officials have apparently concluded that pressuring Pakistan to attack the Haqqani network because the latter attack U.S. forces is counterproductive: it only strains a relationship the U.S. must sustain in its own interests despite all the complexities and contradictions (Barnes et al., August 13, 2010: A1).

"Whether the war continues or not, however, this stubborn fact remains: There is little the U.S. can do in any direct way to prevent Pakistan's nuclear weapons from falling into the wrong hands. Given Al Qaeda's relative weakness compared to Pakistan ally Haqqani, the latter's susceptibility to Pakistani influence if not control, and that nation's fear of India, it is possible that even though the two have worked together closely Haqqani would respond to a Pakistani demand that it repel any Al Qaeda move to seize its nuclear weaponry. That may be why the Pakistani military establishment remains so convinced that it can control its own nuclear destiny without U.S. help. The U.S. has been able to buy some influence on Pakistan with economic aid and external military assistance from our drones. But a settlement could make both seem unnecessary, greatly reducing U.S. leverage. Even if the war in Afghanistan continues, pushing Pakistan too hard could lead it to sever its ties with the U.S., leaving America without influence.

"In the end, the Pakistani national security elite remain dominant over the elected civilian government headed by President Asif Ali Zardari. The national security elite are well-positioned to resist U.S. political pressure. It is possible that weakness brought on by massive flooding or a sharp increase in the internal threat posed by homegrown Islamist militants could change their thinking (Wright and Gorman, August 17, 2010: A9). But unless that actually happens, they will do whatever it takes, up to and including cutting ties to the United States, to maintain control of their nuclear arsenal in order to deter the threat from their major strategic obsession: India.

"*I come finally to our own recommendation.* If a large troop deployment to Afghanistan is not the answer to our national security problem, and it is not, then what is? We believe that it is to shift away from the expensive and largely ineffective counter-insurgency strategy embraced by the administration, to an off-shore anti-terrorist policy that emphasizes the strengthening of our worldwide intelligence capacity in consultation with allies. Our alternative strategy also would emphasize increases in the size and sophistication of our rapid deployment strike capabilities. We would use our intelligence, special operations military strike forces, and covert operations skills and resources to anticipate, meet and disrupt terrorist challenges threatening to the United States whenever and wherever they arise around the world (Shane et al., August 15, 2010: 1). To do this effectively, the U.S. could keep a small, specialized force of military and intelligence personnel in Afghanistan and elsewhere. It is interesting to remember that this very option was considered and rejected by the president's national security team during his three month Af–Pak policy review; and according to media reports, the president's people are still divided on this question (Spiegel, June 23, 2010: A12). Perhaps we can be persuasive enough in this forum to encourage the president to seriously reconsider this option!

"The drones we use in Pakistan are an example of the anti-terrorist approach that we recommend. The drones have been the most effective tool that we have deployed to date against terrorists. We should focus our efforts entirely on Pakistan and on other terrorist host states with the ability and the will to threaten U.S. security. After our troops come out, we should use force in Afghanistan again if and only if Al Qaeda is again able to pose threats to the U.S. from its soil, and then we should employ only counterterrorist techniques. If the attempts by Afghanistan and Pakistan to forge a coalition peace government bear fruit, the odds of this being necessary could drop substantially (Perlez et al., June 25, 2010: A1).

"For all these actual and potential reasons, it makes no sense to send another large contingent of U.S. ground forces to Afghanistan. In fact, the president should throw his support behind the idea of a negotiated settlement in Afghanistan in hopes of being able to pull out our forces already there. What would be our desired end-state upon leaving Afghanistan? With or without an agreement with the Taliban, it might go something like this: 'An Afghanistan that provides no safe haven to terrorists bent on attacking the U.S., ensures equal rights to all its citizens and maintains its sovereignty with international help but without foreign troops on its territory' (Serwer, June 25, 2010). This is the position we will defend in our concluding statement. Thank you, Mr. Chief Justice."

With that, the senator gathered his papers, stepped away from the lectern, and walked briskly to the opposition table where Speaker Pelosi and Professor Bacevich, both smiling broadly, were seated.

"Are you ready to close, Mr. President?" inquired the Chief Justice. Barack Obama, already approaching the lectern from his table on the other side of the chamber, nodded impassively and, with a single sheet of paper in his left hand, stepped up to the microphones and began to speak.

President's Closing Statement

"Thank you, Mr. Chief Justice, and thank you, ladies and gentlemen, for your patient attention to both of our opening statements. I congratulate Senator Feingold for his careful preparation and his heartfelt presentation. As I will make clear in my closing statement, we agree on more than he or members of the audience may think.

"I will address each of the four points the senator made, as well as his proposed alternative to my plan. Let me begin with his point that 'even if we got all the way in and accepted the huge costs necessary to convert Afghanistan into a functional modern state, it still would not solve our terrorist problem. Attacks against the U.S. could and would continue.' This point is actually closely related to his proposed solution, which, as he says, 'would emphasize increases in the size and sophistication of our rapid deployment strike capabilities. We would use our intelligence, special operations military strike forces, and covert operations skills and resources to anticipate, meet and disrupt terrorist challenges threatening to the United States whenever and wherever they arise around the world' (Shane et al., August 15, 2010: 1). The interesting fact here is that we agree! What the senator proposes is, in fact, already being done. We are doing just what he recommends wherever threats are known to us right now. I won't get into details, but in partnership with allies and host countries we are forcefully addressing threats around the globe (DeYoung and Jaffe, June 4, 2010: A1; Miller, August 25, 2010: A1).

"But I must disagree with his assumption that what he proposes is an *alternative* to stabilizing Afghanistan with a troop increase. In fact, because of the situation in Pakistan, we must do both! Given that nation's nuclear capabilities, its rivalry with India for influence in Afghanistan, its heated internal dissident, terrorist threats, bitter disagreements among the Pakistani elite, the ambitions of regional neighbors Iran and China, Pakistan's own history of self-protective alliances with terrorist organizations such as the Haqqanis and Al Qaeda in havens it provides in its own province of North Waziristan, and especially given Pakistan's unshakeable belief that the U.S. will eventually abandon the 'graveyard of empires' as all other occupying forces have done (Perlez, February 10, 2010a: A1), several things are clear.

"*First*, this is the most dangerous and unsettled region in the world today, and therefore one we cannot ignore, or deal with exclusively from afar. *Second*, there is no way the U.S. can tip the balance in favor of Afghan self-determination and ultimately Pakistani self-protection without a *sizeable* short-term increase in our military presence. Al Qaeda has not re-emerged in Afghanistan in the same numbers as before 9/11, but it retains its safe havens along the border. *And our forces in place presently lack the full support they need to effectively train and partner with Afghan security forces while securing the population.* Both Generals McChrystal and Petraeus have asserted that the surest way to reverse jihadist momentum in Afghanistan in preparation for the eventual U.S. drawdown is the temporary infusion of 30,000 troops.

"Keep in mind too that stability in the region is threatened not only by jihadists in Afghanistan and Pakistan, but also by the possibility of nuclear war between Pakistan and India, both of whom are now busily increasing their nuclear arsenals (Sanger and Broad, April 12, 2010: A1). Neither U.S. nor international forces are now permitted to have "boots on the ground" within either of those states; but the odds of nuclear attacks are greatly reduced if an international contingent *friendly to both sides* is in place in the region. A civil war within Pakistan, which is not beyond the realm of possibility, could leave its nuclear weapons in the wrong hands. And the potential for a new, more radical yet still nuclear Pakistan supported by stronger nearby nations with certain antipathies to the U.S. and its allies is at least conceivable. China, for example, already has a rapidly developing 'civilian' nuclear power relationship with Pakistan (Page, September 21, 2010: A15). Such prospects are increased by chaos like that created by the monsoon floods in Pakistan, which have forced it to divert troops to disaster relief, thus downsizing plans to combat Taliban and Al Qaeda militants (Gall, September 14, 2010c: A4). Those floods were recently described by United Nations Secretary General Ban Ki-moon as the most formidable national disaster he has ever seen (Khurrum, August 16, 2010, online).

"In making these points about possible futures I do not seek to 'borrow trouble' where none presently exists. No, I mention these things here for a different reason: to show how the options proposed by my critics *overlook the broader long-term interests of the U.S. and its allies* in the security and stability of Central Asia as a whole which is seriously threatened by the political fragility of its two most vulnerable states. That *forces* those of us responsible for U.S. national security to ponder such unpleasant possibilities, and to think about what should be done to reduce their likelihood.

"I know that there is in many quarters a reflexive suspicion of America, the world's sole military superpower, and a conviction among some well-intentioned analysts here at home that 'parochial self-interest laced with inertia' drives America to find reasons to maintain a global military presence (Bacevich, 2010b: 225). But let me remind you that it was an attack on the U.S. that brought our forces to Afghanistan. And it is threats to regional stability and a peaceful world order that can be controlled but not eliminated that lead me to believe that the international community may need to be involved in the effort to protect the gains achieved for Afghanistan, Pakistan, and other regional actors when most of our troops have returned home. If it occurred such an arrangement would be in the tradition of the post-World War II model that left allied military installations in various parts of the world at the invitation of host nations.

"In the near term, however, the biggest contribution the U.S. can make to regional security and stability in Central Asia is to convince all concerned that it will not withdraw all its troops while Afghanistan and Pakistan are under duress. Consider, for example, the situation that existed in Iraq at the time the U.S. ceded primary responsibility to the Iraqis for their own security. At that time the Iraqis had not resolved the stalemate produced by their recent national elections. They feared that if an already months-old stalemate were not resolved, civil war might again break out and once again there would be no protection from harm for ordinary citizens. In that environment, Iraqis knew that only the U.S., which had left a substantial troop presence in place for a year after the scheduled withdrawal of the majority of its forces, was in a position to offer a credible guarantee that they would not again be subject to the pain and terror of anarchy (Feldman, August 28–29, 2010: W1).

"History shows that things do calm down if it is clear that hostile forces will be thwarted by outside help until local authorities can ensure safety on their own. The U.S. has no wish to prolong its stay in Central Asia. But the Afghan–Pakistan nexus remains a dangerous place and the American people must understand that we cannot simply pull back behind our borders while that remains the case. Professor Bacevich of the opposition team has not spoken at this forum but he has written a book in which he makes numerous valuable points about waste and overkill and selfish interests driving the U.S. defense establishment in undesirable fiscal and policy directions. In response I say that where he is right, let us fix it! We probably do not need as many U.S. troops stationed in Europe as we currently have (Bacevich, 2010b: 227). We don't need a nuclear stockpile as large as we have, and we have already negotiated nuclear stockpile reductions with the Russians (Perry and Shultz, April 11, 2010: wk 11). We cannot afford to finance weapon systems we no longer need, and Secretary Gates is orchestrating record defense budget cuts in response to that fact (Dreazen, May 10, 2010a: A8). And as I said before I became a candidate for this office, we did not need to invade Iraq!

"On the other hand, we did need to help stabilize the post-World War II world. And you, the American people, must understand that, in our own interest and the world's we do need to help stabilize today's troubled Central Asian region. So we should make adjustments in our national security arrangements where it makes sense. But we must guard against "throwing the baby out with the bath water," which is what cutting things we need to keep would be like.

"Of course, this burden cannot be ours alone to bear. The threat is shared and therefore the economic and human costs of maintaining international peace must also be shared. As I said at West Point the other day, since 9/11, Al Qaeda's safe havens have been the source of attacks against London and Amman and Bali. The Russians see a possible return to Islamic fundamentalism in Afghanistan as a threat to their security and are offering help to Afghanistan (Boudreaux, August 19, 2010: A10). Islamist attacks on NATO coalition supply routes passing through Tajikistan, a former Soviet Republic, further alarm the Russians, and show how easily insurgents can metastasize throughout Central Asia (Trofimov and Cullison, September 21, 2010: A10). So it is not only the people and governments of Afghanistan and Pakistan that are endangered. And again, the stakes are higher for all within a nuclear-armed Pakistan, because all know that Al Qaeda and other extremists seek nuclear weapons, and there is every reason to believe that they would use them. These facts compel us and our allies to muster the resources needed to create and sustain political order.

"Senator Feingold has warned that we are in no position to finance a program of 'nation building' in Afghanistan. I agree. Fortunately, nothing on that scale will be required of us in Afghanistan, because, as the senator also pointed out, that nation has the mineral riches to finance its own nation building once the Taliban and Al Qaeda have been sufficiently subdued. As I have said, I am convinced that the troop increase makes our military contribution to the Afghan mission achievable in less than two years. We won't have to get 'all the way in,' as Senator Feingold put it. After that we will settle into a smaller role involving technological support, diplomacy, and only a residual military presence (along with allies) intended to help the Afghan authorities discourage militant internal or external agents unwilling to press their claims through the electoral process or diplomatic channels. This has been our pattern in Europe, Japan, Korea, Iraq, and elsewhere. It will be the same in Afghanistan. We must face the fact that our interests as well as a lawful international order require it.

"And so I appeal to those of you in this chamber and to the people of America who hear or read these words to *support me* in this effort to do what is right in the service of world peace and our highest national interests. I have candidly disclosed what is likely to follow the troop increase policy that sparked this proceeding. I have stated plainly that we have no choice but to continue to do *what it takes* to help sustain a *still tenuous* world order based on security, responsibility, justice, and peace. I acknowledge the point of Speaker Pelosi and others that these ventures cannot succeed without the enduring support of the American people.

"Finally, please remember what I said at West Point: That the United States of America has helped underwrite global security for more than six decades with the blood of our citizens and the strength of our arms. That is what we seek to do today in Central Asia. Our service and sacrifice have promoted peace and prosperity from Germany to Korea, and enabled democracy to take hold in places like the Balkans. We have done this not because we seek to impose our will. We have done it out of enlightened self-interest—because we seek a better future for our children and grandchildren, and we believe that their lives will be better if others' children and grandchildren can also live in freedom and prosperity. Thank you and may God bless the United States of America."

"And thank you, Mr. President," said Chief Justice Roberts. "I have been informed that the speaker of the House of Representatives, Ms. Nancy Pelosi, will offer the closing statement for the opposition. Madam Speaker."

Opposition's Closing Statement

"Thank you, Mr. Chief Justice. I will be brief. The president has spoken forcefully, but he has sought to broaden the argument beyond the issue in dispute in this policy trial. Let me remind him and the audience that the issue before us today is not our future interests in Central Asia but whether to endorse or disapprove of his plan to send 30,000 additional troops to Afghanistan. Senator Feingold has set out compelling reasons why such an increase cannot be expected either to diminish the terrorist threat to our homeland or to reduce the vulnerability of Pakistan's nuclear arsenal to hostile takeover. Professor Bacevich of our 'challenge' team (Bacevich, 2010a) and others (Zakaria, September 13, 2010b: 15) have made the point in their writings that the actual threat posed by Al Qaeda is substantially diminished (Shane, February 28, 2011: A1). The probability that an attack within the U.S. on a scale comparable to 9/11 could happen again has been authoritatively and dispassionately described as "unlikely." That was among the conclusions of a report issued by the National Security Study Group of the Bipartisan Policy Center in Washington, DC. The report was written by terrorism analysts Peter Bergen and Bruce Hoffman, and the group was chaired by two former leaders of the 9/11 Commission, Congressman Lee Hamilton of Indiana and Governor Tom Kean of New Jersey. Terrorist threats remain, the report concludes, but they are far more likely to be of the homegrown variety (Gorman, September 10, 2010: A3). The relevant point for this policy trial is that the likeliest terrorist threats today *cannot be addressed by increasing our troop presence in Afghanistan!* At a time of vast budget deficits, when Defense Secretary Gates is moving to cut billions from the defense budget, the untold additional costs in blood and treasure certain to follow a large troop increase are *not necessary* and therefore simply *not justified.* A large troop increase at this point solves nothing.

"Let me also remind the president that we already have 70,000 troops in Afghanistan. If troops alone could prevent nuclear war between India and Pakistan, that number should be sufficient to do it. More likely, what prevents nuclear war there is what prevented it between the U.S. and the Soviet Union during the Cold War: 'mutually assured destruction'—the certainty that a devastating nuclear attack will provoke a devastating nuclear response. Such a deterrent requires no outside help.

"If our focus in this proceeding wasn't limited to President Obama's proposal to add 30,000 more troops to our deployment in Afghanistan, I would be advocating a substantial reduction in our current Afghan force size. In fact others are doing just that. Another study group, this one sponsored by the New America Foundation, has issued a report written by an ad hoc group of former government officials, leading academics, and policy experts. The report advocates a substantial reduction of our Afghan troop presence (vanden Heuvel, September 7, 2010: online). Its major thrust is to present an alternative to the White House/Petraeus strategy on the grounds that it misinterprets the essential nature of the conflict. Instead of being a struggle between the central government and the Taliban, it is in fact a civil war, being fought over the question of how political power should be allocated across ethnic, geographic, and regional lines. This bipartisan group of experts advocates a plan that guards against the resurgence of Al Qaeda (one of what it calls the two top U.S. priorities) by selective use of the methods discussed earlier by Senator Feingold, and which the president says we are already using.

"The second vital U.S. interest, according to this group, is to protect Pakistani nuclear weapons. But these analysts are far more sanguine than the president is about that problem. Let me quote, in conclusion, from their report: 'Fortunately, the danger of a radical takeover of the Pakistani government is small. Islamist extremism in Pakistan is concentrated within the tribal areas in its northwest frontier, and largely confined to its Pashtun minority (which represents about 15 percent of the population). The Pakistani army is primarily Punjabi (roughly 44 percent of the population) and remains loyal. At present, therefore, this second strategic interest is not seriously threatened' (*A New Way Forward*, Afghanistan Study Group, 2010, online).

"In closing, we suggest that the certain costs of the president's proposal are not justified by the potential gains. There are more promising and far less costly avenues to meeting our key objectives than a large troop increase. Therefore we recommend to you, the American people, that you *oppose* the president's suggested troop increase, and that you make your opposition to it emphatically clear, in writing, to your Senators and Representatives in the Congress, and to the polling organizations that will be contacting many of you over the next two weeks. If, as we expect, your opposition to this plan takes the form of a strong majority, I as speaker of the House, and Senator Feingold as a member of the Senate Foreign Relations Committee will each introduce into our respective chambers a resolution of disapproval of the president's troop increase plan. Thank you all very much for your participation in this historic event."

Conclusion

Here is where this fictional account of the first policy trial and the final chapter of this book both end. I deliberately bring the proceeding to a close *before* the outcome is known so that it does not deflect attention from the central point: that concentrating national attention on a disciplined debate on the merits will position the American people and the Congress to make well-grounded decisions that a president may agree with, but in any case cannot ignore. As a result the people and their leaders will be better equipped to accept informed and shared responsibility for the consequences of the policy decision, whether those consequences prove to be popular or not.

NOTES

Chapter 1

1 Some early reviewers of the reform ideas presented in this book asked for detailed implementation strategies, and they were right to do so. Such strategies must indeed be developed to guide the effort to put the ideas into practice. But detailed strategic blueprints would be premature here. The first order of business is to show the *plausibility* and the *promise* of the Presidential Accountability Project and the policy trial proposals described in Chapters 5 and 6. Spelling out the strategies for winning a chance for these ideas to prove themselves will be the next step, to be taken under separate cover.

Chapter 2

1 Other informal agents may also influence presidents in important ways that amount to holding them to account. But they have done so less consistently. Examples include governmental commissions like the Baker Hamilton Iraq Study Group. Such commissions are often ignored, as the Baker group was (see Shane, December 28, 2006: A24). Others have sought to be influential in ways thought by some to be outside the bounds of propriety (e.g., major parts of the president's political base, such as the Christian Right for President Bush, or big labor for President Obama). Sometimes even foreign governments, such as those allies that declined to participate in the invasion or occupation of Iraq, may influence presidential decisions. For example, the Bush Administration moved away from unilateralism toward a multilateral approach to dealing with the nuclear threats posed by North Korea and Iran in the second term, arguably in part due to feedback from allies. In these cases, the president has no presumptive obligation to respond, but may perceive it as in his or the country's interest to do so.
2 The leaders of the early republic—including John Adams, Thomas Jefferson, James Madison, Benjamin Rush, Benjamin Franklin, and George Washington—were convinced of the need for centralized citizen development because many of them were acutely sensitive to the historic fragility of republican regimes. Accordingly, they believed that tax-supported, state-sponsored schools and universities were vital necessities if the United States was to avoid a similar fate. Their motives were defensive: to

equip citizens to help to safeguard liberty from tyrants and demagogues (Brown, 1996: 85, 105, 111). In a bill providing for a public education system, submitted to the Virginia legislature in 1779, Thomas Jefferson offers a classic statement of the citizen capabilities needed to effectively oversee elected officials (reproduced in Cremin, 1970: 440). Preeminent is the prevention of tyranny, which, despite well-conceived governmental forms, experience shows to be probable unless "the minds of the people at large" are "illuminated" with enough of historical experience to "know ambition under all its shapes." They are also encouraged to "use their natural powers to defeat [ambition's] purposes." Thus, "illumination" (knowledge of the history of political tyranny and of the forms of government best able to restrain it, plus knowledge of the sources of their own political tradition and of the rights and liberties secured by the revolution) and "encouragement" (the cultivation of a socialized attitude: *vigilance against tyranny*, which to fulfill required "full information of [the performance of currently elected leaders] through the channel of the public [news]papers [which should] penetrate the whole mass of the people") are the two most important educational means to this great end. Given the limited safety of even the best governmental forms, the *spirit of watchfulness* in the population at large is of decisive importance. "In Jefferson's view, that spirit cannot be presumed—as the *Federalist Papers* seem to imply—but must be cultivated and its grounds carefully articulated" (Pangle and Pangle, 1993: 108, 111, 114). Jefferson's effort to pass his bill in Virginia failed, as did his effort to market it as a national model.

3   There is a small but growing scholarly literature on the concept of accountability— mostly dealing with the accountability of elected officials in representative democracies—that is useful to an effort to sort out the presidential case. But because it emphasizes a strict holding to account, with certain punishment for failure to meet expectations (Pitkin, 1967; Schedler, 1999; Grant and Keohane, 2005; Borowiak, 2007, 2011; Lewin, 2007), it is of limited use to our grasp of how the accountability system for presidents currently works. Nevertheless, it has relevance to how it can be improved. Much is made in the theoretical literature on accountability of what amounts to holding the feet of elected officials to the fire. For example: "In a democracy, the politicians should be accountable to the citizens. Our understanding of democracy is that it is a system where the citizens have the power to dismiss the government; democracy includes the right of the people to 'kick the rascals out'" (Lewin, 2007: 4). And consider: "Accountability, as we use the term, implies that some actors have the right to hold other actors to a set of standards, to judge whether they have fulfilled their responsibilities in light of these standards, and to impose sanctions if they determine that these standards have not been met. Accountability presupposes a relationship between power-wielders and those holding them accountable where there is a general recognition of the legitimacy of 1) the operative standards for accountability and 2) the authority of the parties to the relationship (one to exercise particular powers and the other to hold them to account). The concept of accountability implies that the actors being held accountable have obligations to act in ways that are consistent with accepted standards of behavior and that they will be sanctioned for failures to do so" (Grant and Keohane, 2005: 29–30). Borowiak (2007) offers one of the relatively few conceptualizations of accountability that can be construed as leaving room to reward good performance when he says, "Central to this understanding is the idea that to be accountable is to have to answer for one's actions and to face sanctions depending upon that answer *and one's performance*" (Borowiak, 2007: 999, emphasis added). In other words, sanctions can be positive or negative *depending* on how well or poorly an incumbent performs. The way *sanctions* and *performance* are used in this definition of accountability implies a concern not just with discouraging undesirable actions—the usual emphasis in this literature—but also with *encouraging desirable* performance. Similar is Pitkin, who notes that the purpose of holding any representative to account is to

give the office holder the *incentive* to *act in certain ways expected or demanded by those represented* (Pitkin, 1967: 55–57, emphasis added). By this doctrine, acting in the prescribed ways implicitly yields rewards; unacceptable actions invariably invite punishment.

Chapter 3

1 Exceptions to proximity bias would include attribution of responsibility to presidents for an event that dominated a presidency, such as Herbert Hoover's failure to win re-election in 1932 due to the Great Depression, or for an early action that sparks the undying enmity of an intense minority large enough to spell re-election defeat, as happened to George H. W. Bush in the 1992 election due to his failure to keep his pledge never to raise taxes.

2 For example, the Bush Administration successfully resisted efforts to force it to disclose the records of Vice President Cheney's 2001 energy policy task force meetings with energy executives, a move ratified by the U.S. Supreme Court in 2004. They used an Executive Order (number 13233, issued in November, 2001) to keep White House records of former presidents from scholars and journalists, effectively overturning the Presidential Records Act of 1978, which transferred ownership of presidential documents to the federal government (Davis, December 15, 2007: A17). And they "quietly" signed an agreement in the spring of 2006 with the Secret Service (in the midst of the Jack Abramoff lobbying scandal) declaring that "records identifying visitors to the White House are not open to the public" (Yost, January 6, 2007: A15). Previously the Secret Service had often released such logs in response to requests from outside groups and news organizations. Since that agreement, a federal judge has ruled that White House visitor logs were public records and had to be released. But appeals have so far mooted that judgment (Shenon, December 18, 2007: A27).

Chapter 4

1 Chapter 4, an expanded version of an article entitled "Presidential Accountability for Wars of Choice" (*Issues in Governance Studies*, 22, December, 2008) (Buchanan, 2008b) is reprinted by permission of the Brookings Institution, Washington, DC.

REFERENCES

ABC News. March 19, 2008. Interview with Vice President Richard Cheney.

Abramowitz, Michael. December 15, 2006. Truman's Trials Resonate for Bush. *Washington Post*, p. A3.

———. May 13, 2007. Bush's Relations with Capitol Hill Chilly. *Washington Post*, p. A5.

Accountability Act. March 30, 2007. *Wall Street Journal*, p. A14.

Achen, Christopher H. and Larry M. Bartels. 2004. *Pocketbook Voting and the Limits of Democratic Accountability*. Paper presented at the annual meeting of the American Political Science Association, Chicago, IL.

Ackerman, Bruce. 1991. *We the People*. Cambridge, MA: Harvard University Press.

———. 2005. *The Failure of the Founding Fathers*. Cambridge: Harvard University Press.

———. 2010. *The Decline and Fall of the American Republic*. Cambridge, MA: Harvard University Press.

Afghan Staying Power. June 15, 2010. *Wall Street Journal*, p. A16.

Afghanistan Study Group. August 16, 2010. *A New Way Forward: Rethinking U.S. Strategy in Afghanistan*. http://www.afghanistanstudygroup.org/

Ajami, Fouad. June 28, 2010. Petraeus and Obama's Uncertain Trumpet. *Wall Street Journal*, p. A21.

Aldrich, John H. 1995. *Why Parties?* Chicago, IL: University of Chicago Press.

Alter, Jonathan. 2010. *The Promise: President Obama Year One*. New York: Simon & Schuster.

———. May 24 and 31, 2010. Secrets From Inside the Obama War Room. *Newsweek*, pp. 29–33.

Amar, Akhil Reed. 2005. *America's Constitution: A Biography*. New York: Random House.

Ambrose, Steven. 1990. *Eisenhower: Soldier and President*. New York: Simon & Schuster.

American Political Science Association. 1950. *Toward a More Responsible Two-Party System*. New York: Rinehart.

Arnold, Douglas H. 2004. *Congress, the Press, and Political Accountability*. Princeton, NJ: Princeton University Press.

Associated Press. February 8, 1997. Democrat Advised Burning Watergate Tapes. *Dallas Morning News*, p. 4A.

———. December 16, 2006. Democrats Push for Iraq Study Group Recommendations. USA Today.com.

Bacevich, Andrew J. June 27, 2010a. Endless War, a Recipe for Four-Star Arrogance. *Washington Post*, p. B1.

Bacevich, Andrew J. 2010b. *Washington Rules: America's Path to Permanent War.* New York: Henry Holt.

Baker III, James A. March 24, 2010. *An Evening with James Baker.* Lyndon B. Johnson Presidential Library. Austin, Texas. http://www.lbjlibrary.org/join-us/pastevents/2010/evening-baker.html

Baker III, James A. and Warren Christopher. July 8, 2008. Put War Powers Back Where They Belong. *New York Times,* p. A23.

Baker, Peter. October 14, 2009a. Biden No Longer a Lone Voice on Afghanistan. *New York Times,* p. A1.

———. December 6, 2009b. Inside the Situation Room: How a War Plan Evolved. *New York Times,* p. A1.

Baker, Peter and Helen Dewar. February 13, 1999. The Senate Acquits President Clinton. *Washington Post,* p. A1.

Barnard, Chester I. 1936. *The Functions of the Executive.* Cambridge, MA: Harvard University Press.

Barnes, Julian E., Stobhan Gorman, and Tom Wright. August 13, 2010. Pakistan Fight Stalls for U.S. *Wall Street Journal,* p. A1.

Barron, David J. and Martin S. Lederman. 2008a. The Commander-in-Chief at the Lowest Ebb: Framing the Problem, Doctrine, and Original Understanding. *Harvard Law Review* 121: 693, 704.

———. 2008b. The Commander-in-Chief at the Lowest Ebb: A Constitutional History. *Harvard Law Review* 121: 949.

Basler, Roy P., ed. 1990. *Abraham Lincoln: His Speeches and Writings.* New York: Da Capo Press.

Beinhart, Peter. January 10, 2010. Amid the Hysteria—A Look at What Al Qaeda Can't Do. *Time Magazine.* http://www.time.com/time/magazine/article/0,9191,1952315,00.html

Berke, Richard L. December 14, 1998. Many in G.O.P. See No Fallout For 2000 Vote. *New York Times,* p. A1.

Bernstein, Barton J. 1989. The Truman Administration and the Korean War. In Michael J. Lacey, ed. *The Truman Presidency.* New York: Cambridge University Press, pp. 410–44.

Biddle, Stephen. July/August, 2009. Is It Worth It? The Difficult Case for War in Afghanistan. *American Interest,* p. 617. http://www.the-american-interest.com/article.cfm?piece=617

Binkley, W. E. 1937. *President and Congress.* New York: Random House.

Black, Conrad. 2007. *Richard M. Nixon: A Life in Full.* New York: Public Affairs Press.

Black, J. Stewart and Hal B. Gregersen. 1997. Participative Decision-Making: An Integration of Multiple Dimensions. *Human Relations,* 50: 859–78.

Blumenfeld, Laura. July 2, 2010. Obama's National Security Officials, on the Night Watch. *Washington Post.* www.washingtonpost.com/wp-dyn/content/article/2010/07/02/AR2010070202983_pf.html

Borgida, Eugene, Christopher M. Federico, and John L. Sullivan, eds. 2009. *The Social Psychology of Citizenship.* New York: Oxford University Press.

Borowiak, Craig T. 2007. Accountability Debates: The Federalists, The Anti-Federalists, and Democratic Deficits. *Journal of Politics* 69: 998–1014.

———. 2011. *Accountability and Democracy: The Pitfalls and Promis of Popular Control.* New York: Oxford UP.

Boudreaux, Richard. August 19, 2010. Russia Pitches in to Battle Taliban. *Wall Street Journal,* p. A10.

Bradlee, Benjamin C. June 17, 1992. Watergate Leaves No Answers, Only Memories. *Austin American-Statesman,* p. A21.

Bravin, Jess. June 26, 2008. How Bush Misread War-Powers. *Wall Street Journal,* p. A10.

Breyer, Stephen. 2010. *Making Democracy Work: A Judge's View.* New York: Knopf.

Broder, David. March 11, 2006. An Ugly Nativism Poisoned the Ports Debate. *Austin American Statesman,* p. 11.

——. January 4, 2007. Suggester in Chief. *Washington Post*, p. A17.

Broder, David S. and Dan Balz. July 16, 2006. How Common Ground of 9/11 Gave Way to Partisan Split. *Washington Post,* p. A1.

Broder, John M. July 9, 2008. Report Urges Overhaul of the War Powers Law. *New York Times*. http://www.nytimes.com/2008/07/09/washington/09powers.html

Broder, John M. and Robin Toner. December 10, 2006. Report on Iraq Exposes a Divide Within the GOP. *New York Times*, p. 1.

Brody, Richard A. 1991. *Assessing the President.* Stanford, CA: Stanford University Press.

Brooks, David. May 7, 2006. Marshmallows and Public Policy. *New York Times*, Section 4, p. 13.

Brown, Richard D. 1996. *The Strength of a People: The Idea of an Informed Citizenry in America 1650–1870.* Chapel Hill, NC: University of North Carolina Press.

Brownstein, Ronald. 2007. *The Second Civil War: How Extreme Partisanship Has Paralyzed Washington and Polarized America.* New York: Penguin Press.

Bryce, James. 1891. *The American Commonwealth*, Vol. 1. New York: Macmillan and Co., pp. 73–80.

Brzezinski, Zbigniew. 2007. *Second Chance: Three Presidents and the Crisis of American Superpower.* New York: Basic Books.

Buchanan, Bruce. 1978. *The Presidential Experience: What the Office Does to the Man.* Englewood Cliffs, NJ: Prentice-Hall.

——. 1987. *The Citizen's Presidency.* Washington, DC: CQ Press.

——. 1991. *Electing a President: The Markle Commission Research on Campaign '88.* Austin, TX: University of Texas Press.

——. 1996. *Renewing Presidential Politics: Campaigns, Media and the Public Interest.* Lanham, MD: Rowman & Littlefield.

——. 2000. Regime Support and Campaign Reform. In Larry M. Bartels and Lynn Vavreck, eds. *Campaign Reform: Insights and Evidence.* Ann Arbor, MI: University of Michigan Press, pp. 173–200.

——. 2004a. *Presidential Campaign Quality.* Saddle River, NJ: Pearson-Prentice Hall.

——. 2004b. *The Policy Partnership: Presidential Elections and American Democracy.* New York: Routledge.

——. 2008a. *Presidential Accountability for Wars of Choice.* Paper presented at the 2008 annual meeting of the American Political Science Association.

——. December, 2008b. Presidential Accountability for Wars of Choice. *Issues in Governance Studies*, 22: 1–15. http://www.brookings.edu/papers/2008/1230_war_buchanan.aspx

——. 2008c. *The Founders' Plight: Presidential Accountability Without Citizens.* Working Paper, Department of Government, University of Texas at Austin.

——. 2010. *Appraising Presidential Performance: A Test of the "Values and Targets" Hypothesis.* Paper presented at the annual meeting of the American Political Science Association, Washington, DC.

Bullion, John L. 2008. *Lyndon B. Johnson and the Transformation of American Politics.* New York: Pearson Longman.

Bumiller, Elisabeth. September 7, 2002. Bush Aides Set Strategy to Sell Policy on Iraq. *New York Times*, p. A1.

——. January 30, 2008. Research Groups Boom in Washington. *New York Times*, p. A12.

——. January 22, 2010a. U.S. to Provide Spy Drones to Pakistan. *New York Times*, p. A8.

——. July 15, 2010b. Senate Records Show Doubts on '64 Vietnam War Crisis. *New York Times*, p. A6.

——. November 10, 2010c. U.S. Tweaks Message on Troops in Afghanistan. *New York Times*. http://www.nytimes.com/2010/11/11/world/asia/11military.html

Burke, John P. and Fred I. Greenstein. 1991. *How Presidents Test Reality.* New York: Russell Sage Foundation.

Burnham, Walter D. 1994. Pattern Recognition and "Doing" Political History: Art, Science, or Bootless Enterprise? In Lawrence C. Dodd and Calvin Jilson, eds. *The Dynamics of American Politics: Approaches and Interpretations*. Boulder, CO: Westview Press.

Burns, James MacGregor. 1973. *Presidential Government*. Boston, MA: Houghton Mifflin.

———. 2009. *Packing the Court: The Rise of Judicial Power and the Coming Crisis of the Supreme Court*. New York: Penguin Press.

Burstein, Paul and William Freedenburg. 1978. Changing Public Policy: The Impact of Public Opinion, Antiwar Demonstrations and War Costs on Senate Voting in Vietnam War Motions. *American Journal of Sociology*, 84: 99–122.

Bush Gave a Bit. May 11, 2007. *Wall Street Journal*, p. A1.

Bush, George W. January 3, 2007. What the Congress Can Do for America. *Wall Street Journal*, p. A13.

———. 2010. *Decision Points*. New York: Crown.

Calmes, Jackie. December 16, 1998. House Divided: Why Congress Hews To the Party Lines on Impeachment. *Wall Street Journal*, p. A1.

Canes-Wrone, Brandice. 2006. *Who Leads Whom? Presidents, Policy, and the Public*. Chicago, IL: University of Chicago Press.

Carnerale, Mary Lu. October 12, 2007. Democratic Leaders in Congress Seek to Pass Energy Bill without Formal Conference Committee. *Wall Street Journal*, p. A8.

Carroll, James. 2006. *House of War: The Pentagon and the Disastrous Rise of American Power*. New York: Houghton Mifflin.

Casey, Steven. 2008. *Selling the Korean War: Propaganda, Politics, and Public Opinion in the United States 1950–1953*. New York: Oxford.

CBS News.com. 2010. Exit Poll for House Race. http://www.cbsnews.com/election2010/exit.shtml?state=US&jurisdiction=0&race=H&tag=content

Ceaser, James W. 1979. *Presidential Selection: Theory and Development*. Princeton, NJ: Princeton University Press.

Chandrasekaran, Rajiv. June 21, 2010a. U.S. Eager to Replicate Afghan Villagers' Successful Revolt Against Taliban. *Washington Post*, p. A1.

———. September 13, 2010b. Karzai Rift Prompts U.S. to Reevaluate Anti-Corruption Strategy in Afghanistan. *Washington Post*, p. A1.

Clark, Burton R. 2007 (1992). *The Distinctive College*. New York: Transaction Publishers Reprint.

Clarke, Richard A. 2004. *Against All Enemies: Inside America's War on Terror*. New York: Free Press.

CNN. 2004. CNN.com Election 2004. http://www.cnn.com/ELECTION/2004/ October 28, 2006. Interview with Stephen Breyer. http://www.cnn.com/2006/POLITICS/10/27/activist.judges/index.html

Cohen, Adam. August 15, 2006. Has *Bush v. Gore* Become the Case That Must Not Be Named? *New York Times*, p. A22.

Consultant-News.com. October 27, 2003. You Have to Hand It to McKinsey. http://www.consultant-news.com/article_display.aspx?p=adp&id=1017 (accessed February 4 2012).

Cooper, Michael and Mark Landler. April 10, 2010. U.S. Now Trying Softer Approach Toward Karzai. *New York Times*, p. A1.

Corwin, Edward S. 1957. *The President: Office and Powers 1787–1957*. New York: New York University Press.

Cremin, Lawrence A. 1970. *Education: The Colonial Experience 1607–1783*. New York: Harper & Row.

Cullison, Alan and Maria Abi-Habib. May 24, 2010. Afghan Raids Show Taliban Will Persist Amid Losses. *Wall Street Journal*, p. A9.

Cumings, Bruce. 2010. *The Korean War: A History*. New York: Modern Library.

Curry, Tom. December 5, 2006. Pelosi: "We Won't Cut Off Funding" for Iraq. MSNBC.com/id/16057734.

Dahl, Robert A. 1990. Myth of the Presidential Mandate. *Political Science Quarterly* 105: 355–72.

———. 1998. *On Democracy*. New Haven, CT: Yale University Press.

Dallek, Robert. 1998. *Flawed Giant: Lyndon Johnson and his Times 1961–1973*. New York: Oxford University Press.

———. 2003. *An Unfinished Life: John F. Kennedy 1917–1963*. Boston: Little, Brown.

Davis, Charles N. December 15, 2007. Protect the Nation's History. *Austin American-Statesman*, p. A17.

Deans, Bob. November 11, 2007. Democrats Outflanked. *Austin American-Statesman*, p. G3.

Deep Throat's Legacy: Watergate, the Press and the Presidency. June 2, 2005. *Wall Street Journal*, p. A12.

Deering, C. J. 2005. Foreign Affairs and War. In P. Quirk and S. Binder, *The Legislative Branch*, New York: Oxford, pp. 349–81.

Delli Carpini, Michael X., and Scott Keeter. 1996. *What Americans Know About Politics and Why It Matters*. New Haven, CT: Yale University Press.

Dellinger, Walter and Christopher Schroeder. March 14, 2007. The Purse isn't Congress's Only Weapon. *New York Times*, p. A23.

DeMuth, Christopher. October 11, 2007. Think-Tank Confidential. *Wall Street Journal*, p. A21.

Dewey, John. 1927. *The Public and its Problems*. New York: Henry Holt.

DeYoung, Karen and Greg Jaffe. June 4, 2010. U.S. "Secret War" Expands Globally as Special Operations Forces Take Large Role. *Washington Post*, p. A1.

Dhume, Sadanand. May 3, 2010. Why Pakistan Produces Jihadists. *Wall Street Journal*. http://online.wsj.com/article/SB10001424052748703866704575223832888768098.html

Dilulio, John. May 23, 2007. John Dilulio's Letter. *Esquire*. http://www.esquire.com/features/dilulio

Dionne, Jr., E. J. December 19, 2006. "The Real America" Redefined. *Washington Post*, p. A29.

Donald, David Herbert. 1995. *Lincoln*. New York: Simon & Schuster.

Dowd, Maureen. January 6, 2007. Monkey on a Tiger. *New York Times*, p. A31.

———. May 12, 2010. The Evil of Lesser Evilism. *New York Times*, p. A23.

Dreazen, Yochi J. May 10, 2010a. Gates Talks of Tough Choices Ahead. *Wall Street Journal*, p. A8.

———. May 17, 2010b. Afghan Violence Blocks Reconstruction Plan. *Wall Street Journal*, p. A15.

Dreazen, Yochi J. and Greg Jaffee. December 15, 2006. Call to Add U.S. Forces is Resisted at Home, in Iraq. *Wall Street Journal*. http://www.freerepublic.com/focus/f-news/1753885/posts

Easton, David. 1965. *A Systems Analysis of Political Life*. New York: Wiley.

Edwards, George C. III. 2003. *On Deaf Ears: The Limits of the Bully Pulpit*. New Haven, CT: Yale University Press.

Elkins, Stanley and Eric McKitrick. 1993. *The Age of Federalism: The Early American Republic, 1788–1800*. New York: Oxford University Press.

Etzioni, Amatai. 2007. *Security First: For a Muscular, Moral Foreign Policy*. New Haven, CT: Yale University Press.

Feith, Douglas J. July 3, 2008. Why We Went to War in Iraq. *Wall Street Journal*, p. A11.

Feldman, Noah. August 28–29, 2010. A Very Long Engagement. *Wall Street Journal*, p. W1.

Feldstein, Mark. 2010. *Poisoning the Press: Richard Nixon, Jack Anderson, and the Rise of Washington's Scandal Culture*. New York: Farrar, Straus and Giroux.

Fenno, Richard E. Jr. 1978. *Home Style: House Members in their Districts*. New York: Scott-Foresman.

Ferling, John. 2004. *Adams vs. Jefferson: The Tumultuous Election of 1800*. New York: Oxford.

Ferris, Timothy. 2010. *The Science of Liberty*. New York: Harper.

Fick, Nathaniel and John Nagl. February 21, 2011. The "Long War" May Be Getting Shorter. *New York Times*, p. A17.

Filkins, Dexter. February 21, 2010. The Prize in Marja: Momentum. *New York Times*, wk 1.

———. February 27, 2011. The Next Impasse: Review of "The Wrong War," by Bing West. *New York Times* Book Review, p. 1.

Filkins, Dexter and Mark Mazzetti. August 26, 2010. Key Karzai Aide in Graft Inquiry is Linked To C.I.A. *New York Times*, p. A1.

Fiorina, Morris P. 1996. *Divided Government*, 2nd ed. Boston, MA: Allyn and Bacon.

———. 2006. *Culture War? The Myth of a Polarized America*, 2nd ed. New York: Pearson Longman.

Fisher, Louis. 2004a. *Presidential War Power*, 2nd. ed. rev. Lawrence, KS: University Press of Kansas.

———. 2004b. *War and Responsibility*. Lawrence, KS: University Press of Kansas.

Free Management Library. June 4, 2010. Overview of Roles and Responsibilities of Corporate Board of Directors. http://managementhelp.org/boards/brdrspon.htm#anchor185116 (accessed February 4 2012).

Freidel, Frank. 1990. *Roosevelt: A Rendezvous With Destiny*. Boston: Little, Brown.

Friedman, Barry. 2009. *The Will of the People: How Public Opinion Has Influenced the Supreme Court and Shaped the Meaning of the Constitution*. New York: Farrar, Straus & Giroux.

Friedman, Thomas L. June 4, 2003. Because We Could. *New York Times*. www.cnn.com/2003/US/06/04/nyt.friedman/

———. June 15, 2005a. Let's Talk About Iraq. *New York Times*, p. A29.

———. November 11, 2005b. Thou Shalt Not Destroy the Center. *New York Times*. http://query.nytimes.com/gst/fullpage.html?res=9B02E6D9123EF932A25752C1A9639C8B63

———. January 6, 2006. The New Red, White and Blue. *New York Times*. http://www.nytimes.com/2006/01/06/opinion/06friedman.html

———. June 23, 2010. What's Second Prize? *New York Times*, p. A23.

Froomkin, Dan. June 6, 2008. The Propaganda Campaign Dissected. Washington Post.com. http://www.washingtonpost.com/wp-dyn/content/blog/2008/06/06/BL2008060602283.html

Gall, Carlotta. June 14, 2010a. Report Says Pakistan Intelligence Agency Exerts Great Sway on Afghan Taliban. *New York Times*, p. A8.

———. June 20, 2010b. U.S. Hopes Councils Will Help Undermine Taliban in Troubled Afghan Region. *New York Times*, p. 5.

———. September 14, 2010c. Floods Open a New Front for Troops in Pakistan. *New York Times*, p. A4.

———. February 5, 2011. In the Taliban's Heartland, U.S. and Afghan Forces Dig In. *New York Times*, p. A4.

Gelb, Leslie H. July 3, 1991. Why the Political Mess? *New York Times*, p. A13.

General McClellan's War. May 30, 2008. *Wall Street Journal*, p. A14.

George, Alexander L. 1980. *Decision-Making in Foreign Policy: The Effective Use of Information and Advice*. Boulder, CO: Westview.

Gerecht, Reuel Marc. January 8, 2010. The Meaning of Al Qaeda's Double Agent. *Wall Street Journal*. WSJ.com. http://online.wsj.com/article/SB10001424052748704130904574644132628157104.html

Geselbracht, Raymond and David C. Acheson. 2010. *Affection and Trust: The Personal Correspondence of Harry S. Truman and Dean Acheson, 1953–71*. New York: Knopf.

Goldsmith, Jack. 2007. *The Terror Presidency: Law and Judgment Inside the Bush Administration*. New York: Norton.

Goldsmith, W. M. 1980. *The Growth of Presidential Power: A Documentary History, Vol. I: The Formative Years; Vol. II: Decline and Resurgence; Vol. III: Triumph and Reappraisal*. New York: Confucian Press.

Goldstein, Gordon M. 2008. *Lessons in Disaster: McGeorge Bundy and the Path to War in Vietnam.* New York: Times Books.

Gorman, Siobhan. September 10, 2010. Terror Threat More Diverse, Study Says. *Wall Street Journal*, p. A3.

Graff, H. F. 1984. *The Presidents: A Reference History.* Library Binding. http://www.amazon.com/American-Presidents-Reference-History/dp/0684312263

Grant, Ruth W. and Robert O. Keohane. 2005. Accountability and Abuses of Power in World Politics. *American Political Science Review* 99: 29–43.

Greene, John Robert. 2000. *The Presidency of George Bush.* Lawrence, KS: University Press of Kansas.

Greenhouse, Linda. June 30, 2006. Guantanamo Case: Military Panels Found to Lack Authority—New Law Possible. *New York Times*, p. A1.

———. June 13, 2008. Detainees in Cuba Win Major Ruling in Supreme Court. *New York Times*, p. A1.

Greenstein, Fred I. 2000. *The Presidential Difference.* New York: Free Press.

Griffin, Stephen. 2010. *The Long War and the Constitution: From Truman to Obama.* Manuscript in process, Tulane University Law School.

Halberstam, David. 1993. *The Best and the Brightest.* New York: Ballentine.

———. 2007. *The Coldest Winter: America and the Korean War.* New York: Hyperion.

Hall, Kermit L. 2005. *The Oxford Companion to the Supreme Court of the United States*, 2nd ed. New York: Oxford University Press.

Hamby, Alonzo L. 1995. *Man of the People: A Life of Harry S. Truman.* New York: Oxford University Press.

———. November 20, 2010. Enthusiasts for Hard Power. Review of R. Geselbracht and David C. Acheson, *Affection and Trust: The Personal Correspondence of Harry S. Truman and Dean Acheson.* New York: Knopf. *Wall Street Journal*, p. C8.

Harnsberger, Caroline Thomas, ed. 1964. *Treasury of Presidential Quotations.* Chicago, IL: Follett Publishing Company.

Harwood, John. March 23, 1993. CBO's Budget Reviews Win Few Friends. *Wall Street Journal*, p. A2.

———. December 13, 2006. War-Weary Public Wants Congress to Lead. *Wall Street Journal*, p. A4.

Hastings, Max. 2010. *Winston's War.* New York: Knopf.

Heims, Ludger. 2004. Five Ways of Institutionalizing Political Opposition: Lessons from the Advanced Democracies. *Government and Opposition* 39: 22–54.

Henninger, Daniel. March 24, 2006. Whatever Laura's Feeding George, Pour It On. *Wall Street Journal*, p. A10.

———. January 14, 2010. An Obama-GOP Entente on Terror. *Wall Street Journal*, p. A17.

Herring, George C. 2001. Vietnam. In Paul S. Boyer, ed. *The Oxford Companion to United States History.* New York: Oxford University Press, pp. 806–9.

Herszenhorn, David. December 2, 2007. How the Filibuster Became the Rule. *New York Times*, wk 5.

Hiatt, Fred. May 24, 2010. In the Absence of Debate, Iraq and Afghanistan Go Unnoticed. *Washington Post*, p. A19.

Hickey, Patrick. 2011. Constituency, Electoral Vulnerability, and Presidential Support in Congress. Working Paper, Department of Government, University of Texas at Austin.

Hill, David. 2006. *American Voter Turnout.* Cambridge, MA: Westview-Perseus.

Hodgson, Godfrey. 2009. *The Myth of American Exceptionalism.* New Haven, CT: Yale University Press.

Hoffman, Bruce. January 16, 2010. Al Qaeda Has a Plan—When Do We Draft Ours? *Austin American-Statesman*, p. A17.

Hofstadter, Richard. 1948. *The American Political Tradition and the Men Who Made It.* New York: Knopf.

Horner, William. 1997. *Media Coverage of Presidential Performance*. Ph.D. dissertation, University of Texas at Austin.

How to Combat al Qaeda's New Focus. March 1, 2010. *Austin American-Statesman*, p. A9.

Howell, William G. and Pevehouse, Jon C. 2007. *While Dangers Gather: Congressional Checks on Presidential War Powers*. Princeton, NJ: Princeton University Press.

Hulse, Carl. December 23, 2005. Messy Congressional Finale. *New York Times*, p. A20.

Hulse, Carl. May 10, 2007. G.O.P. Moderates Warn Bush Iraq Must Show Gains. *New York Times*, p. A1.

——. September 26, 2007. In Conference: Process Undone by Partisanship. *New York Times*, p. A1.

Hulse, Carl and Robert Pear. December 21, 2007. Republican Unity Trumps Democratic Momentum. *New York Times*, p. A22.

Hulse, Carl, and Jim Rutenberg. May 11, 2007. President Open to Benchmarks in Iraq Measure. *New York Times*, p. A1.

Hulse, Carl and Jeff Zeleny. March 30, 2007. Defying Bush, Senate Passes Iraq Spending Measure Calling for Pullout of U.S. Troops. *New York Times*, p. A10.

Iraq Intelligence Findings Provide Crucial Lessons. June 6, 2008. *USA Today*, p. 14A.

Iraq: Will Congress Force Withdrawal? March 17–18, 2007. *Wall Street Journal*, p. A7.

Jacobs, Lawrence R. and Robert Y. Shapiro. 2000. *Politicians Don't Pander: Political Manipulation and the Loss of Democratic Responsiveness*. Chicago, IL: University of Chicago Press.

Jacobson, Gary C. 2007. *A Divider, Not A Uniter*. New York: Pearson Longman.

Janis, Irving. 1972. *Victims of Groupthink*. Boston: Houghton-Mifflin.

Jervis, Robert T. 1980. The Impact of the Korean War on the Cold War. *Journal of Conflict Resolution* 24: 563–92.

Johnson, David. December 18, 2006. Powell Doubts Need to Raise Troop Levels. *New York Times,* p. A10.

Jones, Seth. 2008. *Counterinsurgency in Afghanistan*. Santa Monica, CA: Rand Corporation, p. 10.

——. 2009. *In the Graveyard of Empires: America's War in Afghanistan*. New York: W.W. Norton.

Kakutani, Michiko. July 14, 2009. The Choices that Closed a Window into Afghanistan (Review of Jones, 2009). *New York Times*, p. C1.

Kaminski, Matthew. April 11–12, 2009. Holbrooke of South Asia. *Wall Street Journal*, p A7.

Kammen, Michael. 1993. *A Machine That Would Go of Itself: The Constitution in American Culture*. New York: Bedford/St. Martins.

Kann, Peter R. December 11, 2006. The Media is in Need of Some Mending. *Wall Street Journal,* p. A18.

Katz, Daniel and Robert L. Kahn. 1978. *The Social Psychology of Organizations*, 2nd ed. New York: Wiley.

Kaufman, Burton I. 1986. *The Korean War*. Philadelphia, PA: Temple University Press.

——. 1993. *The Presidency of James Earl Carter*. Lawrence, KS: University Press of Kansas.

Kaufman, Herbert. 2000 (1960). *The Forest Ranger*. New York: RFP Press Reprint.

Kearns, Doris. 1976. *Lyndon Johnson and the American Dream*. New York: Harper & Row.

Kernell, Samuel. 2007. *Going Public: New Strategies of Presidential Leadership*. Washington, DC: CQ Press.

Kernell, Samuel and Gary C. Jacobson. 2006. *The Logic of American Politics*, 3rd ed. Washington, DC: CQ Press.

Khurrum, Anis. August 16, 2010. Pakistan Warns of New Floods as Disease Fears Grow. http://noir.bloomberg.com/apps/news?pid=newsarchive&sid=aZq5emCyYOy4

Kinder, Donald R. and Susan T. Fiske. 1986. Presidents in the Public Mind. In Margaret G. Hermann, ed. *Political Psychology*. San Francisco: Jossey-Bass.

Kinzer, Stephen. 2006. *Overthrow: America's Century of Regime Change from Hawaii to Iraq*. New York: Times/Henry Holt.

Kirkpatrick, David D. and Adam Nagourney. March 27, 2006. In an Election Year, a Shift in Public Opinion on the War. *New York Times*, p. A12.

Kissinger, Henry A. June 24, 2010. America Needs an Afghan Strategy, Not an Alibi. *Washington Post*, p. A21.

Klein, Ezra. January 4, 2011. The History of Filibuster Reform. *Washington Post*. http:// voices.washingtonpost.com/ezra-klein/2011/01/the_history_of_filibuster_refo.html

Klein, Joseph. June 28, 2010. Obama's Afghan Dilemma. *Time*, p. 20.

Klein, Rick. April 11, 2005. Foes Cite Progress vs. Bush Agenda. *Boston Globe*, p. A1.

Kleinerman, Benjamin A. 2005. Lincoln's Example: Executive Power and the Survival of Constitutionalism. *Perspectives on Politics* 3: 801–16.

———. 2009. *The Discretionary President: The Promise and Peril of Executive Power*. Lawrence, KS: University Press of Kansas.

Koch, Adrienne and William Peden. 1972. *The Life and Selected Writings of Thomas Jefferson*. New York: Modern Library.

Krugman, Paul. July 31, 2006. If Bush Repeats It Often Enough, It Must Be So. *Austin American-Statesman,* p. A7.

———. December 21, 2009. A Dangerous Dysfunction. *New York Times*, p. A29.

Kuklinski, James H. and Paul J. Quirk. 2000. Reconsidering the Rational Public: Cognition, Heuristics, and Mass Opinion. In Arthur Lupia, Mathew D. McCubbins, and Samuel L. Popkin, eds., *Elements of Reason*. New York: Cambridge University Press, pp. 153–82.

———. 2001. Conceptual Foundations of Citizen Competence. *Political Behavior* 23, 285–311.

Landler, Mark and Elisabeth Bumiller. May 1, 2009. Now U.S. Sees Pakistan as a Cause Distinct From Afghanistan. *New York Times*, p. A9.

Ledbetter, James. 2010. *Unwarranted Influence: Dwight D. Eisenhower and the Military-Industrial Complex*. New Haven, CT: Yale University Press.

Levinson, Sanford. 2006. *Our Undemocratic Constitution*. New York: Oxford University Press.

Lewin, Leif. 2007. *Democratic Accountability*. Cambridge, MA: Harvard University Press.

Lewis, Anthony. October 28, 1994. The Public Citizen. *New York Times*, p. A19.

Lewis, Neil A. and Eric Lipton. April 26, 2007. Flexing Majority Muscles, Democrats Issue 3 Subpoenas. *New York Times*, p. A17.

Liptak, Adam. January 19, 2007a. The White House as a Moving Legal Target. *New York Times,* p. A1.

———. March 8, 2007b. After Libby Trial, New Era For Government and Press. *New York Times*, p. A14.

———. December 22, 2009. In Clerk's Careers, Signs of Polarization on the Supreme Court Bench. *New York Times*, p. A16.

———. February 6, 2011. Doing the Judicial Math on Health Care. *New York Times*, wk 3.

Lowi, Theodore J. 1985. *The Personal President*. Ithaca, NY: Cornell University Press.

Machiavelli, Niccolo. 1997. *The Prince*. New Haven, CT: Yale University Press.

Mahler, Jonathan. June 15, 2008. Why This Court Keeps Rebuking This President. *New York Times*, wk 3.

Maier, Pauline. 2010. *Ratification: The People Debate the Constitution*. New York: Simon & Schuster.

Malone, Dumas. 1970. *Jefferson the President: First Term 1801–1805*. Boston: Little, Brown.

Mann, Thomas E. and Norman J. Ornstein. 2006. *The Broken Branch: How Congress Is Failing America and How To Get It Back On Track*. New York: Oxford University Press.

Mann, Thomas E., Molly Reynolds, and Peter Hoey. April 28, 2007. Is Congress on the Mend? *New York Times*, p. A27.

Mann, Thomas E., Molly Reynolds, and Nigel Holmes. January 19, 2008. Could Congress Be Waking Up? *New York Times*, p. A31.

Mansfield, Jr. Harvey C. 1989. *Taming the Prince: The Ambivalence of Modern Executive Power*. New York: Free Press.

Marcus, Gregory B. 1982. Political Attitudes During an Election Year: A Report on the 1980 NES Panel Study. *American Political Science Review* 76: 538–60.

Matheson, Scott M. Jr. 2009. *Presidential Constitutionalism in Perilous Times.* Cambridge, MA: Harvard University Press.

Matlock, Jr. Hack F. October 20, 2002. Deterring the Undeterrrable. *New York Times,* Section 4, p. 11.

Matthews, Richard K. 1995. *If Men Were Angels: James Madison and the Heartless Empire of Reason.* Lawrence, KS: University Press of Kansas.

May, Earnest R. 1973. *Lessons of the Past: The Use and Misuse of History in American Foreign Policy.* New York: Oxford University Press.

Mayhew, David R. 1974. *Congress: The Electoral Connection.* New Haven, CT: Yale University Press.

Mazzetti, Mark and Scott Shane. June 6, 2008. Bush Overstated Evidence on Iraq, Senators Report. *New York Times,* p. A1.

McCarty, Nolan, Keith T. Poole, and Howard Rosenthal. 2006. *Polarized America: The Dance of Ideology and Unequal Riches.* Cambridge, MA: The MIT Press.

McClellan, Scott. 2008. *What Happened.* New York: PublicAffairs.

McConnell, Michael. January 10, 2012. Democrats and Executive Overreach. *Wall Street Journal,* p. A13.

McCullough, David. 1992. *Truman.* New York: Simon & Schuster.

——. 2001. *John Adams.* New York: Simon & Schuster.

McDonald, Forrest. 1994. *The American Presidency: An Intellectual History.* Lawrence, KS: University Press of Kansas.

Milkis, Sidney M. and Michael Nelson. 2008. *The American Presidency: Origins and Development, 1776–2007.* Washington, DC: CQ Press.

Miller, Greg. August 25, 2010. CIA Sees Increased Threat in Yemen. *Washington Post,* p. A1.

Miller, William Lee. 2008. *President Lincoln.* New York: Knopf.

Moncrief, Joy Marie. 1989. Reconceptualizing Political Accountability. *International Political Science Review,* 19: 387–406.

Morgan, Edmund S. 1988. *Inventing the People: The Rise of Popular Sovereignty in England and America.* New York: Norton.

Mosher, Frederick C. 1979. *The GAO: The Quest for Accountability in American Government.* Boulder, CO: Westview Press.

Mr. Obama's Task. November 19, 2009. *New York Times,* p. A26.

Mueller, John E. 1973. *War, Presidents and Public Opinion.* New York: Wiley.

Murray, Shailagh and Jonathan Weisman. May 10, 2007. Bush Told War is Harming the GOP. *Washington Post,* p. A1.

Nagourney, Adam. September 17, 2006. In Campaign Ads for Democrats, Bush is the Star. *New York Times,* p. 1.

——. February 15, 2009. In Gingrich Mold, a New Voice For Solid Resistance in G.O.P. *New York Times,* p. 1.

National War Powers Commission. July 8, 2008. *The Proposed Statute.* Charlottesville, VA: The Miller Center of the University of Virginia.

Nelson, Michael, ed. 2008. *The Evolving Presidency,* 3rd ed. Washington, DC: CQ Press.

Neustadt, Richard E. 1990. *Presidential Power and the Modern Presidents.* New York: Free Press.

Newsmax. 2012. NYT/CBS Poll: Almost Half Oppose Obamacare, Just 36% Back It. http://www.newsmax.com/US/obamacare-opposition-cbs-poll/2012/03/26/id/433914

Nickerson, Raymond S. 1998. Confirmation Bias: A Ubiquitous Phenomenon in Many Guises. *Review of General Psychology* 2: 175–220.

Noah, Timothy and Laurie McGinley. July 26, 1993. Advocate for the Poor, Respected on All Sides, Secures a Pivotal Role in Expanding Tax Credit. *Wall Street Journal,* p. A12.

Nordland, Rod and Jane Perez. May 28, 2010. Leading Member of Pakistan Taliban Said to Be Killed. *New York Times*, p. A8.

Obama, Barack. December 1, 2009. *Remarks by the President in Address to the Nation on the Way Forward in Afghanistan and Pakistan.* http://www.whitehouse.gov/the-press-office/remarks-president-address-nation-way-forward-afghanistan-and-pakistan

———. December 10, 2009. *Remarks by the President at the Acceptance of the Nobel Peace Prize.* http://www.whitehouse.gov/the-press-office/remarks-president-acceptance-nobel-peace-prize

———. May 22, 2010. *Commencement Speech to 2010 West Point Cadets.* http://www.cbsnews.com/2100-201_162-6509577.html

Offner, Arnold A. 2002. *Another Such Victory: President Truman and the Cold War 1945–1953.* Stanford, CA: Stanford University Press.

O'Hanlon, Michael. June 22, 2010. A Negotiated Solution for Afghanistan? *Wall Street Journal*, p. A17.

On Afghanistan: A Negative Shift. May 25, 2010. http://voices.washingtonpost.com/behind

Oshinsky, David M. 2001. Army-McCarthy Hearings. In Paul S. Boyer, ed. *The Oxford Companion to United States History.* New York: Oxford University Press, p. 50.

———. July 10, 2003. The Gaps of Watergate: Beyond the 18½ Minutes. *New York Times*, p. B9.

Pach, Jr., Chester J. and Elmo Richardson. 1991. *The Presidency of Dwight D. Eisenhower.* Lawrence, KS: University Press of Kansas.

Page, Jeremy. September 21, 2010. China, Pakistan Seek Nuclear Deal. *Wall Street Journal*, p. A15.

Pangle, Lorraine S. and Thomas L. Pangle. 1993. *The Learning of Liberty: The Educational Ideas of the Founders.* Lawrence, KS: University Press of Kansas.

Patch, Chester J. and Elmo Richardson. 1991. *The Presidency of Dwight D. Eisenhower*, rev. ed. Lawrence, KS: University Press of Kansas.

Patterson, James T. 1996. *Grand Expectations: The United States 1945–1974.* New York: Oxford.

Patterson, Thomas E. 2002. *The Vanishing Voter.* New York: Knopf.

Penguin 60's. 1995. *Franklin D. Roosevelt Fireside Chats.* New York: Penguin Group USA.

Perez, Marty. January 10, 2010. Clutching at Straws: The So-Called "Weakness" of Al Qaeda. *The New Republic.* http://www.tnr.com/blog/the-spine/clutching-straws-the-so-called-weakness-al-qaeda

Perlez, Jane. February 10, 2010a. Pakistan is Said to Pursue Role in Afghan Talks. *New York Times,* p. A1.

———. May 9, 2010b. U.S. Urges Swift Action in Pakistan After Failed Times Square Bombing. *New York Times,* p. A6.

———. June 3, 2010c. Official Admits Militancy Has Deep Roots in Pakistan. *New York Times*, p. A6.

Perlez, Jane and Eric Schmitt. July 5, 2010. Pakistan Army finds Taliban Tough to Root Out. *New York Times*, p. 1.

Perlez, Jane, Eric Schmitt, and Carlotta Gall. June 25, 2010. Pakistan is Said to Pursue an Afghanistan Foothold. *New York Times*, p. A1.

Perret, Geoffrey. 2007. *Commander in Chief.* New York: Farrar, Straus and Giroux.

Perry, William J. and George P. Shultz. April 11, 2010. How to Build on the Start Treaty. *New York Times*, wk 11.

Pfiffner, James P. 2009. *Power Play: The Bush Presidency and the Constitution.* Washington, DC: Brookings.

———. 2010. *The Federalist and Executive Power.* Paper presented at the annual meeting of the American Political Science Association, Washington, DC.

Pious, Richard M. 2003. Impeachment and the Post-Monica Presidency. In Jeffrey Cohen and David Nice, eds. *The Presidency: Classic and Contemporary Readings.* New York: McGraw Hill.

Pitkin, Hanna F. 1967. *The Concept of Representation*. Berkeley, CA: University of California Press.

PollingReport.com. 2010. PollingReport.com: Afghanistan. http://www.pollingreport.com/afghan.htm (accessed March 11 2010).

Pollack, Kenneth M. 2002. *The Threatening Storm: The Case for Invading Iraq*. New York: Random House.

———. June 20, 2003. Saddam's Bombs? We'll Find Them. *New York Times*, p. A25.

Pollock, David. November 8, 2010. Our Indian Problem in Afghanistan. *Washington Post*. http://www.washingtonpost.com/wp-dyn/content/article/2010/11/07/AR201011070 3840.html

Polsby, Nelson W. 1997. Political Opposition in the United States. *Government and Opposition* 32: 511–21.

Poole, J. R. 1987. *The American Constitution For and Against: The Federalist and Anti-Federalist Papers*. New York: Hill and Wang.

Powe, Lucas A. Jr. 2009. *The Supreme Court and the American Elite, 1789–2008*. Cambridge, MA: Harvard University Press.

President Taylor. August 18, 2006. *Wall Street Journal*, p. A14.

Presidential Elections 1789–2004. 2005. *Presidential Elections 1789–2004*. Washington, DC. CQ Press.

Purdum, Todd S. and Patrick E. Tyler. August 16, 2002. Top Republicans Break with Bush on Iraq Strategy. *New York Times*, p. A1.

Ragsdale, Lynn. 2009. *Vital Statistics on the Presidency*, 3rd ed. Washington, DC: CQ Press.

Rasiel, Ethan M. and Paul N. Friga. 2001. *The McKinsey Mind*. New York: McGraw Hill.

Reeves, Richard. 2001. *President Nixon: Alone in the White House*. New York: Simon & Schuster.

Riccards, Michael P. 1995. *The Ferocious Engine of Democracy: A History of the American Presidency*. In two volumes. Lanham, MD: Madison Books.

Rich, Frank. 2006a. *The Greatest Story Ever Sold: The Decline and Fall of Truth From 9/11 to Katrina*. New York: Penguin.

———. May 28, 2006b. The Cannes Landslide for Al Gore. *New York Times*, Section 4, p. 10.

———. October 22, 2006c. Obama is Not a Miracle Elixir. *New York Times*, Section 4, p. 4.

Richey, Warren. October 17, 2006. Will the Supreme Court Shackle New Tribunal Law? *Christian Science Monitor*, p. 1.

Riker, William H. and Peter C. Ordeshook. 1968. A Theory of the Calculus of Voting. *American Political Science Review*, 63: 25–43.

Risen, James. June 18, 2010. World's Mining Companies Covet Afghan Riches. *New York Times*, p. A4.

Roberts, Charles, ed. 1974. *Has The President Too Much Power?* New York: Harper's Magazine Press, p. 27.

Robinson, Greg. 2001. *By Order of the President: FDR and the Internment of Japanese Americans*. Cambridge, MA: Harvard University Press.

Rogers, David. December 13, 2007. Intraparty Feuds Dog Democrats, Stall Congress. *Wall Street Journal*, p. A1.

Rose, Gideon. 2010. *How Wars End*. New York: Simon & Schuster.

Roseboom, Eugene H. 1959. *A History of Presidential Elections*. New York: Macmillan.

Rosen, Gary. July 16, 2006. The Time of the Presidents. *New York Times Magazine*, Section 8, p. 21.

Rosenberg, Matthew. August 12, 2010. Afghanistan Money Probe Hits Close to the President. *Wall Street Journal*, p. A1.

Rossiter, Clinton. 1960. *The American Presidency*, 2nd ed. New York: Harcourt Brace.

———. 2009 [1948]. *Constitutional Dictatorship: Crisis Government in the Modern Democracies*. New Brunswick, NJ: Transaction Publishers.

Rubin, Alissa J. and Dexter Filkins. July 1, 2010. 8 Militants Killed After Attack on NATO Base in Afghanistan. *New York Times*, p. A12.

Rubin, James P. February 1, 2010. Indispensability. *The New Republic*. www.nr.com/book/review/indispensability.

Rudalevige, Andrew. 2006. *The New Imperial Presidency: Renewing Presidential Power after Watergate*. Ann Arbor, MI: University of Michigan Press.

Ruling for the Law. August 18, 2006. *New York Times*, p. A18.

Rutenberg, Jim. December 26, 2006. War Critics See New Resistance by Bush. *New York Times*, p. A21.

———. January 4, 2007. Bush Reaches Out but Keeps One Hand on the Wheel. *New York Times*, p. A16.

Sabato, Larry J. September 2, 2010a. Sixty Days to Go: Projections and Ratings. *Crystal Ball*, vol. 7, issue 35. www.centerforpolitics.org/crystallball

———. November 4, 2010b. Obama's Wake-Up Call. http://www.centerforpolitics.org/crystalball/articles/ljs2010110302/

Safire, William. November 30, 1998. King of Chutzpah. *New York Times*, p. A27.

Sanger, David E. May 4, 2009. Fighting May Put Nuclear Arsenal At Risk, U.S. Says. *New York Times*, p. A1.

———. November 7, 2010. Get Me Out of Here. Review of Gideon Rose, *How Wars End*. *New York Times*, p. br41.

Sanger, David E. and William J. Broad. November 18, 2007. U.S. Secretly Aids Pakistan in Guarding Nuclear Arms. *New York Times*, p. 1.

———. April 12, 2010. Agenda of Nuclear Talks Leaves Out a New Threat. *New York Times*, p. A1.

Sanger, David E. and Mark Mazzetti. July 1, 2010. New Estimate of Strength of Al Qaeda is Offered. *New York Times*, p. A12.

Sanger, David E. and Eric Schmitt. February 1, 2011. Pakistani Arms Pose Challenge to U.S. Policy. *New York Times*, p. A1.

Savage, Charlie. 2007. *Takeover: The Return of the Imperial Presidency and the Subversion of American Democracy*. New York: Little, Brown.

———. March 22, 2011a. Attack Renews Debate Over Congressional Consent. *New York Times*, p. A12.

———. December 30, 2011b. Mostly in Echo, Rivals Discuss Reach of Power. *New York Times*, p. A1.

Schattschneider, E. E. 1942. *Party Government*. New York: Rinehart.

———. 1960. *The Semisovereign People: A Realist's View of Democracy in America*. Hinsdale, IL: The Dryden Press.

Schedler, Andreas. 1999. Conceptualizing Accountability. In Andreas Schedler, Larry Diamond, and Marc F. Plattner, eds. *The Self-Restraining State: Power and Accountability in New Democracies*. Boulder, CO: Lynne Rienner, 14–17.

Schlesinger Jr., Arthur M. 1973. The *Imperial Presidency*. Boston: Houghton Mifflin.

———. 1997. Rating the Presidents: Washington to Clinton. *Political Science Quarterly* 112: 179–90.

———. 2004. *War and the American Presidency*. New York: Norton.

Schlesinger, James. March 18, 2005. Where Myth Trumped Truth. *Wall Street Journal*, p. W6.

Schmitt, Eric. January 26, 2010a. Envoy's Cables Show Concerns on War Plans. *New York Times*, p. A1.

———. August 15, 2010b. U.S. Extends a Hand to Rescue Pakistanis and Reclaim its Image. *New York Times*, p. 5.

Schmitt, Eric and Scott Shane. September 8, 2009. U.S. Buildup A Necessity? *New York Times*, p. A1.

Senate Intelligence Committee. June 5, 2008. *Senate Intelligence Committee Report*. Washington, DC: U.S. Government Printing Office.

Serwer, Daniel. June 25, 2010. How a Negotiated Peace Could Leave Afghanistan Looking Like Lebanon. washingtonpost.com/wp-dyn/content/article/2010/06/24/AR.201006240 5070.html?wpisrc=nl_opinions

Shane, Peter M. and Harold H. Bruff. 1988. *The Law of Presidential Power: Cases and Materials.* Durham, NC: Carolina Academic Press.

Shane, Scott. October 31, 2005. Doubts Cast on Vietnam Incident, But Secret Study Stays Classified. *New York Times,* p. A1.

——. December 28, 2006. Latest Blue-Ribbon Panel Awaits Its Own Ultimate Fate. *New York Times,* p. A24.

——. April 1, 2007. The Complicated Power of the Vote to Nowhere. *New York Times,* Section 4, p. 4.

——. January 13, 2010a. A Year of Terror Plots Through a Second Prism. *New York Times,* p. A1.

——. June 27, 2010b. Wars Fought and Wars Googled. *New York Times,* wk 1.

——. February 28, 2011. Al Qaeda Sees History Fly By. *New York Times,* p. A1.

Shane, Scott, Mark Mazzetti, and Robert F. Worth. August 15, 2010. A Secret Assault on Terror Widens on Two Continents. *New York Times,* p. 1.

Shane, Scott and Souad Mekhennet. May 9, 2010. From Condemning Terror to Preaching Jihad. *New York Times,* p. 1.

Shane, Scott and Eric Schmitt. January 23, 2010. C.I.A. Deaths Prompt Surge In Drone War. *New York Times,* p. A1.

Shanker, Thom and Elizabeth Bumiller. June 17, 2010. Military and Pentagon Leaders Urge Patience for Afghan Mission. *New York Times,* p. A10.

Sharp, James Roger. 1993. *American Politics in the Early Republic.* New Haven, CT: Yale University Press.

Shenon, Philip. December 18, 2007. White House Visitor Logs Are Public, Judge Rules. *New York Times,* p. A27.

Shepard, Scott. December 10, 2006. As Congress Limps to a Finish, It Earns a "Do Nothing" Label. *Austin American-Statesman,* p. A1.

Shklar, Judith. 1991. *American Citizenship: The Quest for Inclusion.* Cambridge, MA: Harvard University Press.

Sinopoli, Richard C. 1992. *The Foundations of American Citizenship.* New York: Oxford University Press.

Skowronek, Stephen. 1993. *The Politics Presidents Make: Leadership from John Adams to George Bush.* Cambridge, MA: Harvard University Press.

Skyttner, Lars. 2005. *General Systems Theory: Problems, Perspectives, Practice,* 2nd ed. New Jersey: World Scientific.

Slater, Wayne and G. Robert Hillman. January 8, 2007. Bush's Legacy Likely to Change Over Time. *Dallas Morning News,* p. A1.

Small, N. J. 1932. Some Presidential Interpretations of the Presidential Role. In *Johns Hopkins University Studies in Historical and Political Science.* 50: 93–300.

Snyder, Jr. James M. and Michael M. Ting. 2002. An Informational Rationale for Political Parties. *American Journal of Political Science.* 46: 193–211.

Sorley, Lewis, ed. 2005. *Vietnam Chronicles: The Abrams Tapes.* Lubbock, TX: Texas Tech University Press.

Sourcewatch. December 28, 2011. Think Tanks. http://www.sourcewatch.org/index. php?title=Think_tanks (accessed February 4 2012).

Spanta, Rangin Dadfar. August 23, 2010. Pakistan is the Afghan War's Real Aggressor. *Washington Post,* p. A13.

Spiegel, Peter. June 23, 2010. Sharp Words Expose Rift Over War Policy. *Wall Street Journal,* p. A12.

Stewart, Scott. February 10, 2010. *The Jihadist CBRN Threat.* http://www.stratfor.com/ weekly/20100210_jihadist_cbrn_threat

Stolberg, Sheryl Gay. January 29, 2006a. Return of Congress: New Tests for Bush. *New York Times,* p. 18.

——. June 11, 2006b. As Agenda Falters, Bush Tries a More Personal Approach in Dealing With Congress. *New York Times,* http://www.nytimes.com/2006/06/11/washington/11bushhtml?emc=etal

——. February 20, 2007a. Defending Nation's Latest War, Bush Recalls Its First. *New York Times,* p. A16.

——. May 19, 2007b. A Tentative New Reality. *New York Times,* p. A1.

——. December 14, 2007c. A Dealmaker He's Not, but Bush is Getting His Way. *New York Times,* p. A23.

——. February 21, 2009. Cutting the President Slack is So Old School. *New York Times.* http://www.nytimes.com/2009/02/22/weekinreview/22stolberg.html

Stolberg, Sheryl Gay and Robert Pear. February 26, 2010. Health Meeting Fails to Bridge Partisan Rift. *New York Times,* p. 1.

Suskind, Ron. 2004. *The Price of Loyalty.* New York: Simon & Schuster.

——. 2006. *The One Percent Doctrine.* New York: Simon & Schuster.

Taranto, James. January 28–29, 2006. A Strong Executive: The Weekend Interview with Dick Cheney. *Wall Street Journal,* p. A11.

Thach, C. C. 2007 [1923]. *The Creation of the Presidency, 1775–1789: A Study in Constitutional History.* New York: Liberty Fund.

The First Year. January 28, 2010. *New York Times,* p. A24.

The Truth About the War. June 6, 2008. *New York Times,* p. A22.

Toner, Robin. November 3, 1992. Political Metamorphoses: Voters Impose Discipline on the Candidates as Perot Finds a New Way of Campaigning. *New York Times,* p. A1.

Transcript. December 20, 2006. President Bush's News Conference. *New York Times.com,* p. 4.

Trofimov, Yaroslav. August 4, 2010. Karzai and U.S. Clash Over Corruption. *Wall Street Journal,* p. A8.

Trofimov, Yarolsav and Alan Cullison. September 21, 2010. Islamists Hit Central Asia in New Strikes. *Wall Street Journal,* p. A10.

Tucker, Cynthia. October 26, 2010. McConnell: Defeating Obama "Single Most Important Job." *AJC.* http://blogs.ajc.com/cynthia-tucker/2010/10/26/mcconnell-defeating-obama-single-most-important-job/?cxntfid=blogs_cynthia_tucker

Tugwell, Rexford G. 1960. *The Enlargement of the Presidency.* Garden City, NY: Doubleday.

Tulis, Jeffrey K. 1987. *The Rhetorical Presidency.* Princeton, NJ: Princeton University Press.

——. 2003. The Two Constitutional Presidencies. In Michael Nelson, ed. *The Presidency and the Political System.* Washington, DC: CQ Press, pp. 79–110.

Vanden Heuvel, Katrina. September 7, 2010. Finding a Way Out of Afghanistan. *Washington Post.* http://www.washingtonpost.com/wp-dyn/content/article/2010/09/07/AR2010090702980.html

Weiner, Tim. October 31, 1997. Transcripts of Nixon Tapes Show the Path to Watergate. *New York Times,* p. A1.

Weisman, Jonathan and Paul Kane. December 20, 2007. Key Setbacks Dim Luster of Democrats' Year. *Washington Post,* p. A2.

West, Bing. 2011. *The Wrong War: Grit, Strategy, and the Way Out of Afghanistan.* New York: Random House.

Wikipedia. February 4, 2012. McKinsey & Company: #8-Knowledge Management System. http://en.wikipedia.org/wiki/McKinsey_%26_Company#cite_note-10 (accessed February 4 2012).

Wilentz, Sean. 2005. *The Rise of American Democracy: Jefferson to Lincoln.* New York: W.W. Norton.

Will, George F. May 5, 2008. Remembering Truman. *Austin American-Statesman,* p. A9.

——. September 1, 2009. Time to Get Out of Afghanistan. *Washington Post*. http://www. washingtonpost.com/wpdyn/content/article/2009/08/31/AR2009083102912.html? hpid=opinionsbox1

Willbanks, James H. March 5, 2008. Winning the Battle, Losing the War. *New York Times*, p. 23.

Wills, Garry, ed. 1982. *The Federalist Papers by Alexander Hamilton, James Madison and John Jay*. New York: Bantam Books.

——. 2010. *Bomb Power: The Modern Presidency and the National Security State*. New York: Penguin.

Wilson, Scott. January 19, 2010. One Year Later: How Obama Has Learned to Become a Wartime Commander in Chief. *Washington Post*, p. A01.

Wittes, Benjamin. 2008. *Law and the Long War*. New York: Penguin.

Wolfe, Alan. 1998. *One Nation After All*. New York: Viking.

Wood, David. February 12, 2010a. Obama's Drone War: Does the Killing Pay Off? *Politics Daily*. http://www.politicsdaily.com/2010/02/12/obama-s-drone-war-does-the-killing-pay-off/

——. August 25, 2010b. The Long War: Afghanistan After July 2011. *Politics Daily*. http://www.politicsdaily.com/2010/08/25/the-long-war-afghanistan-after-2011/

Woods, Randall B. 2006. *LBJ: Architect of American Ambition*. New York: Free Press.

Woodward, Bob. 1999. *Shadow: Five Presidents and the Legacy of Watergate*. New York: Simon & Schuster.

——. 2004. *Plan of Attack*. New York: Simon & Schuster.

——. 2005. *The Secret Man*. New York: Simon & Schuster.

——. 2006. *State of Denial*. New York: Simon & Schuster.

Woodward, Bob and Gordon M. Goldstein. October 25, 2009. Roadmap to a Quagmire. *Austin American-Statesman*, p. F1.

Wright, Tom and Siobhan Gorman. August 17, 2010. Pakistan Says Militants Surpass India as Threat. *Wall Street Journal*, p. A9.

Yoo, John. 2005. *The Powers of War and Peace: The Constitution and Foreign Affairs after 9/11*. Chicago, IL: University of Chicago Press.

——. 2009. *Crisis and Command: A History of Executive Power from George Washington to George W. Bush*. New York: Kaplan.

Yost, Pete. January 6, 2007. White House Made Deal with Secret Service about Logs. *Austin American-Statesman*, p. A15.

Zakaria, Fareed. April 12, 2010a. Learning to Work with Our Man in Afghanistan. *Washington Post*, p. A17.

——. September 13, 2010b. Post 9–11, We're Safer Than We Think. *Washington Post,* p. A15.

Zardari, Asif Ali. December 10, 2009. How To Mend Fences with Pakistan. *New York Times*, p. A35.

Zeleny, Jeff and Megan Thee. November 8, 2006. Exit Polling Shows Independents, Citing War, Favored Democrats. *New York Times*, p. A8.

Zeleny, Jeff and Robin Toner. March 17, 2007. G.O.P. Savors Edge on Iraq Vote, but Uneasy Lies the Crown. *New York Times*, p. A7.

INDEX